Materials and Methods in ELT

Second Edition

A Teacher's Guide

Applied Language Studies
Series editors: David Crystal and Keith Johnson

This series aims to deal with key topics within the main branches of applied language studies – initially in the fields of foreign language teaching and learning, child language acquisition and clinical or remedial language studies. The series will provide students with a research perspective in a particular topic, at the same time containing an original slant that will make each volume a genuine contribution to the development of ideas in the subject.

Materials and Methods in ELT

Second Edition

A Teacher's Guide

JO McDONOUGH
and
CHRISTOPHER SHAW

Blackwell
Publishing

350 Main Street, Malden, MA 02148–5018, USA
108 Cowley Road, Oxford OX4 1JF, UK
550 Swanston Street, Carlton South, Melbourne, Victoria 3053, Australia
Kurfürstendamm 57, 10707 Berlin, Germany

First edition published 1993
Second edition published 2003 by Blackwell Publishing Ltd

Library of Congress Cataloging-in-Publication Data

McDonough, Jo.
    Materials and methods in ELT : a teacher's guide / Jo McDonough and Christopher Shaw.—2nd ed.
        p.cm. — (Applied language studies)
    Includes bibliographical references and index.
        ISBN 0-631-22736-9 (hardcover : alk. paper) — ISBN 0-631-22737-7 (pbk. : alk. paper)
        1. English language—Study and teaching—Foreign speakers. I. Shaw, Christopher. II. Title. III. Series.
        PE1128.A2 M383 2003
        428′.0071—dc21

                                                            2002007764

A catalogue record for this title is available from the British Library.

Set in 10.5/12.5pt Sabon
by Graphicraft Limited, Hong Kong
Printed and bound in the United Kingdom
by MPG Books, Bodmin, Cornwall

For further information on
Blackwell Publishing, visit our website:
http://www.blackwellpublishing.com

Contents

List of Figures

Preface to the Second Edition

Materials and Methods in ELT: A Teacher's Guide has been extensively up-dated to provide teachers of English as a foreign language with a contemporary account of major trends in ELT materials and methodology. This new edition of the book has the same rationale as the first edition in that we hope it will be equally useful to teachers who are following a scheme of study in language teaching methodology or applied linguistics as well as to classroom teachers of EFL around the world who may wish to keep abreast of current developments in the field.

The overall aim of the book is to provide a synthesis between 'principle' and 'practice' by making links between background issues in applied linguistics (views of language, psychological bases of language learning and so on) where appro-priate, and at the same time looking at the practical design of materials and methods.

The first edition of *Materials and Methods in ELT* appeared in 1993. Since that time we have been pleased to have received feedback and comments from teachers around the world who have told us that they would appreciate a new edition of the book. In this new edition we have attempted to update the discus-sion of the 'background' principles as well as providing recent examples from EFL materials.

We have decided to retain the general format of the existing chapters, as feedback that we received indicated that this seemed to work well. All modifica-tions to the text are thus within the chapters themselves. The main changes in this new edition are as follows:

- a discussion of task-based learning in chapter 3
- a new section on vocabulary learning and teaching in chapter 6
- a new section on teaching pronunciation in chapter 8
- a discussion of the uses of the Internet and learning technologies in chap-ter 12

- a discussion in each chapter of extensively updated secondary sources pertinent to the topic
- more examples of recent material from coursebooks

Each chapter has been written with the overall aim of providing a synthesis of background principle and classroom practice. By the end of the book we hope that readers will have the necessary skills to understand the most common design principles for teaching materials, to evaluate critically the principles upon which they are based and to assess their relevance to, and possibilities for, their own teaching context. It is our hope that readers will also gain some appreciation of materials and methods within educational frameworks that may differ from their own.

We have divided the book into three parts. The five chapters in the first part relate to the area of materials and syllabus design by looking at the *principles* on which materials and methods are based. Chapter 1 looks at the educational framework of materials and methods that are relevant to all ELT practitioners. Chapter 2 provides an analysis of the growth of the communicative approach to language teaching and the implications for materials that this approach entails. In chapter 3 we examine some critiques of the communicative approach and try to analyse some of the different 'post-communicative' trends in design principle over the last decade, notably the multi-syllabus, the process syllabus and the task-based syllabus, and show how these relate to teaching materials.

Chapters 4 and 5 on evaluating and adapting materials respectively should be considered as a 'pair' in that the issues discussed require much cross-referencing. Chapter 4 offers a working model for teachers to evaluate materials for adoption/ selection purposes. Chapter 5 follows on from this and is based on the premise that evaluating involves understanding the principles of textbook construction, and is therefore concerned with how teachers, from this understanding of their learners and the materials they are working with, can adapt textbooks to meet the demands of learners in a given teaching situation.

In part II of the book we attempt to relate to each individual language skill in turn the principles raised and discussed in part I. Each chapter, 6–9, is organized in such a way as to show how the 'theory' related to each individual skill of reading, speaking, listening and writing has affected approaches to the design and use of teaching materials in the respective skill areas. The last chapter in this part, chapter 10, is to be seen as a final 'unifying' chapter that looks at different ways of achieving effective skills integration in teaching materials.

The third and final part of the book focuses largely on different methods of organizing the resources and management of the classroom in relation to materials. In narrowing down the different topics for this section we decided to include only those topics that would relate directly to this theme. Consequently we have not included topics such as testing, partly because it does not fit neatly into this framework and partly because it enjoys extensive coverage elsewhere. The first two chapters in this section, 11 and 12, are linked in that they focus on classroom structures and interaction patterns pertaining to groups and pairs in chapter 11 and to the concept of the individual learner in chapter 12. This latter chapter also examines recent developments in self-access and learner training in relation to individualization, including the rapid growth in information technology. An appendix with a selected list of some key Websites for teachers and learners is also provided. Chapter 13 is concerned with discovering what further insights we can gain into the nature of the teaching/learning process by looking closely at language classrooms to see the kinds of interactions that take place between teachers and learners as well as between learners themselves. The final chapter, 14, discusses the diverse nature of the teacher's role in the contemporary ELT context by examining issues such as the 'good' language teacher, in-service education courses and suggestions for teacher development.

Our final goal in writing this book is still that of enabling readers to become better informed about contemporary ELT methods and materials by providing a relatively compact reference package that incorporates practical 'operational' tasks into the text with the desired outcome that readers will have the skills to make informed judgements about their present and future classroom practice.

Jo McDonough, Christopher Shaw
Colchester, October 2002

Acknowledgements

The authors and publisher gratefully acknowledge the permission granted to reproduce the copyright material in this book:

Chapter 2:
R. O'Neill, R. Kingsbury and A. Yeadon, Table of Contents from *Kernel Lessons Intermediate, Students' Book*. London: Longman, 1971. © Longman, 1971.
L. Jones, Table of Contents from *Functions of English*. Cambridge: Cambridge University Press, 1981. © Cambridge University Press, 1981.
P. Watcyn-Jones, Unit 4, pp. 49–57 from *Impact*. Harmondsworth: Penguin, 1979. © Peter Watcyn Jones, 1979; line drawings © David Lock, 1979.

Chapter 3:
M. Swan and C. Walter, Map of Book 1, pp. iv and v from *New Cambridge English Course*. Cambridge: Cambridge University Press, 1990. © Cambridge University Press, 1990.
S. Cunningham and P. Moor, pp. 64–5 from *Cutting Edge: Intermediate, Students' Book*. Harlow: Longman, 1999. © Longman, 1999. Used by permission of Pearson Education Ltd.

Chapter 4:
S. Cunningham and P. Moor, pp. 2–3 from *Cutting Edge: Intermediate, Students' Book*. Harlow: Longman, 1999. © Longman, 1999. Used by permission of Pearson Education Ltd.

Chapter 6:
L. and J. Soars, pp. 20–1 from *New Headway English Course: Intermediate Students' Book*. Oxford: Oxford University Press, 1996. © Oxford University Press, 1996. Reproduced by permission of Oxford University Press.
B. Milne, Unit 10, p. 60 from *Integrated Skills: Intermediate*. Oxford: Heinemann, 1991. © Heinemann, 1991.

H. Dellar and D. Hocking, p. 98 from *Innovations*. Hove: Language Teaching Publications, 2000. © Language Teaching Publications, 2000.

M. Geddes and G. Sturtridge, Unit 2 from *Reading Links*. London: Heinemann, 1982. © Heinemann, 1982.

E. H. Glendinning and B. Holmström, pp. 105–6 from *Study Reading: A Course in Reading Skills for Academic Purposes*. Cambridge: Cambridge University Press, 1992. © Cambridge University Press, 1992.

H. Dellar and D. Hocking, p. 113 from *Innovations*. Hove: Language Teaching Publications, 2000. © Language Teaching Publications, 2000.

Chapter 7:
A. Doff and C. Becket, Unit 18, pp. 44–5 from *Listening 2*. Cambridge: Cambridge University Press, 1991. © Cambridge University Press, 1991.

Chapter 8:
E. Keller and S. Warner, pp. 16–17 from *Conversation Gambits*. Hove: Language Teaching Publications, 1988. © Language Teaching Publications, 1988.

R. Gairns and S. Redman, p. 59 from *True to Life*. Cambridge: Cambridge University Press, 1998. © Cambridge University Press, 1998.

H. Dellar and D. Hocking, p. 82 from *Innovations*. Hove: Language Teaching Publications, 2000. © Language Teaching Publications, 2000.

G. Porter-Ladousse, Unit 5.1 from *Speaking Personally*. Cambridge: Cambridge University Press. © Cambridge University Press, 1983.

Chapter 9:
T. Hedge, p. 96 from *Resource Books for Teachers: Writing*. Oxford: Oxford University Press, 1988. © Oxford University Press, 1988.

M. Stephens, Unit 10, pp. 48–51 from *Practise Writing*. Harlow: Eurocentres/Longman, 1996 © Addison Wesley Longman Ltd, 1986, 1996. Reprinted by permission of Pearson Education Ltd.

Chapter 10:
B. Milne, Map of the Book and Unit 3 from *Integrated skills: Intermediate*. Oxford: Heinemann, 1991. © Heinemann, 1991.

R. O'Neill with P. Mugglestone, p. 64 from *The Third Dimension*. Harlow: Longman, 1989. © Longman, 1989.

Chapter 12:
S. Sheerin, pp. 59–60 from *Resource Books for Teachers: Self-Access*. Oxford: Oxford University Press, 1989. © Oxford: Oxford University Press, 1989.

B. Ellis and G. Sinclair, *Learning to Learn English*. Cambridge: Cambridge University Press, 1989. © Cambridge University Press, 1989.

Chapter 13:
D. Lubeleska and M. Matthews, pp. 48, 50–1, 126–8 from *Looking at Language Classrooms*. Cambridge: Cambridge University Press, 1997. © Cambridge University Press, 1997.

Every effort has been made to trace copyright holders and to obtain their permission for the use of copyright material. The publisher apologizes for any errors or omissions in the above list and would be grateful if notified of any corrections that should be incorporated in future reprints or editions of this book.

Part I

*Topics in the Design
of Materials and Methods*

1

The Framework of Materials and Methods

1.1   Introduction: setting the scene

As teachers of English as a foreign or second language (EFL/ESL), we are members of an established worldwide profession. As Richards (1985: 1) reminds us, 'the current status of English has turned a significant percentage of the world's population into part-time users or learners of English'. Wherever we work, we share many assumptions about what we do; we prepare and use teaching materials and classroom methods and techniques based on similar, or at least comparable, principles. Yet, despite this commonality, it is not unusual for teachers to report a sense of isolation from colleagues in other countries, and even in different areas of their own country. Another attitude that is sometimes expressed is that the teaching situation in our country, or school, is unique, with its own special problems and difficulties. There is some justification for these feelings, of course: many teachers work in geographical isolation, and may not have access to channels of professional communication (journals, conferences, in-service training courses); different countries have widely differing educational systems and philosophies, resulting in teachers being subject to different expectations and pressures.

   In this chapter we shall take some time to look beyond our individual teaching circumstances to what can be thought of as a professional 'common core'. This has relevance to all teachers, whether we work in a Japanese high school, a Mexican university, a private language school in Spain, a Chinese polytechnic, a Turkish secondary school, a Zairean college – this list could go on indefinitely. We shall argue that the idea of a 'common core' is also useful whether our materials and methods are selected by us or specified by the educational authorities. It is, then, broadly made up of two kinds of factors: firstly, of the various wide-ranging criteria on which decisions about language teaching programmes are based, and secondly, on the *pedagogic* principles according to which materials and methods are actually designed. We shall take these two kinds of factors together and refer to them as the shared *framework*.

In what follows, this notion of a 'framework' is set out in a little more detail. We then subdivide it under the two headings of 'context' and 'syllabus', both exploring their general implications and trying to relate them as we do so to our own familiar and specific teaching situation.

1.2   The framework: context and syllabus

In simple terms, the overall goals of a language teaching programme usually derive from an analysis of the reasons why a group of learners in a particular environment needs to learn English: these goals may be stated in general, educational, or very specific terms. They may, on the one hand, be set out in the large-scale categories of a national language policy with many associated implications for the development of the curriculum. For instance, the aim of English Language Teaching in Malaysia was earlier stated to be 'to create a society that is able to utilize the language for effective communication as the need arises, and as a key to wider experiences. For those furthering their studies, the skills learned should become an instrument with which they may cope with the necessities of using the language'. The new guidelines for language teaching in Japanese schools include such statements as 'to develop understanding of language and culture through a foreign language . . . to develop a positive attitude towards communication in a foreign language, and a basic practical communication ability in hearing and speaking'. Alternatively, at the other end of the scale, a course may be organized to address a particular learning need for, say, the identifiable purposes of a small group. For instance, a course may be designed 'to meet the needs of learners who need to improve their ability to communicate when socialising, telephoning, making business presentations and taking part in meetings', or 'to help international postgraduate students in English-medium universities develop the writing skills necessary for writing dissertations'.

There is, then, a whole spectrum of possibilities for defining the goals of language teaching, for a country, an age group, a whole school, a class, or an individual; and whether for general educational purposes, business, scientific development, cultural appreciation or many other reasons.

> 1   Is there an explicit statement of the goals of the language programme on which you work? If so, what are its primary aims?
> 2   If there is not such a statement, try to draft one that represents your own understanding of the goals.

To define what is meant here by 'framework' we start from the view that materials and methods cannot be seen in isolation, but are embedded within a broader professional context. This is represented in figure 1.1, which shows in a very simplified form the typical stages of planning an English language programme.

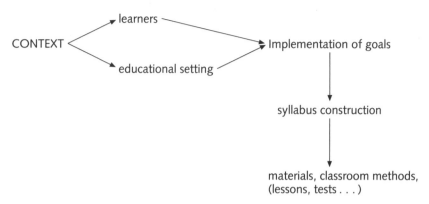

Figure 1.1 The framework of language teaching.

Whether goals are stated in terms of a national language policy, or in the more restricted environment of, say, a particular school or college, the possibilities for actually implementing them will be directly related both to the learners themselves – their needs, characteristics and so on – and to the whole educational setting in which the teaching is to take place. Obviously, as we shall see in our subsequent discussion, goals need to be realistic for specific circumstances. There is little use, for example, in planning for a multimedia course if appropriate equipment is unavailable or unreliable, or in making too many general assumptions about classroom methodology. The statement of goals, then, related to the learners and conditioned by the setting, leads to the selection of an appropriate type of syllabus content and specification. The broad syllabus outline will in turn have direct implications for the more detailed design and selection of materials and tests, the planning of individual lessons, and the management of the classroom itself. Clearly this logical planning sequence is an idealization of what is often a less well-defined procedure, where 'set' materials may linger behind aims that have been reformulated and updated, or conversely where new syllabus types may be ill-matched to existing educational objectives. The logical sequence will nevertheless be used as a reference point for discussion, and as a starting point for the exploration of individual teaching circumstances.

This whole topic is dealt with in considerable depth by Stern who, in his *Fundamental Concepts of Language Teaching* (1983: ch. 3), proposes a very detailed 'conceptual framework', designed as a model that is intended to capture what he sees as the complexity of language teaching. After surveying a number of earlier models, he then sets out his own scheme. Its main components are (a) views of the nature of language, (b) views of the learner and of language learning, (c) views of teaching and the language teacher, and (d) the whole context, which includes the educational setting, the language context, and the language teaching background. The chief characteristics of the model are that it should be *comprehensive*, covering any type of language teaching operation; that all factors under each heading are *interdependent*, so that 'no single factor, for example the teacher, the method, the materials, a new concept . . . or a technological device, can by itself offer a general solution to most language learning problems' (1983: 47); and that it should see language teaching as *multidisciplinary*. Stern's perspective will be evident both in this and most sub-sequent chapters.

The rest of this book will be concerned with the third stage of figure 1.1, the design of materials and methods. Let us now look at the most important contextual factors involved in planning, and then at the key types of syllabus from which actual courses are derived.

Contextual factors

In the preceding section, we took a broad view of 'context' and included both learners and setting under this heading. Let us examine each of these in turn in a little more detail.

Learners It is possible to identify a number of important learner character-istics or 'variables' which, as we have suggested, influence planning decisions and the specification of goals. The relative importance of these variables, and their effect on programme design, obviously depend to a certain extent on some of the situational factors to be discussed in the next section. For example, a pupil's mother tongue may be more, or less, significant depending on whether more than one native language is represented in the classroom, or perhaps on the educational philosophy of that particular environment.

For the moment we can list here the key characteristics of 'the learner', indic-ating how they might affect planning and noting that they form part of our common frame of reference as language teachers, wherever we work. Some of these are characteristics of whole groups or subgroups of learners; others are individual and less open to generalization. Again, some can be known in advance and incorporated at the initial planning stage, in principle at least. Others are more appropriately assessed in the classroom environment itself, and as such are more obviously susceptible to teacher reaction and influence.

We consider the learner's

- *Age:* this will particularly affect topics chosen and types of learning activity, such as the suitability of games or role play.
- *Interests:* as with age, this may help in the specification of topics and learn-ing activities.
- *Level of proficiency in English:* teachers will wish to know this even where their classes are based on a 'mixed proficiency' principle rather than streamed according to level.
- *Aptitude:* this can most usefully be thought of as a specific talent, in this case for language learning, as something that learners might show them-selves to be 'good at', perhaps in contrast to other subjects in a school curriculum. (It can be measured by formal aptitude tests, although they are

not very frequently used.) The relationship between aptitude and intelligence is not clear, and is certainly not direct.

- *Mother tongue:* this may affect, for instance, the treatment of errors or the selection of syllabus items – areas of grammar or vocabulary and so on.
- *Academic and educational level:* which help to determine intellectual content, breadth of topic choice, or depth to which material may be studied.
- *Attitudes to learning,* to teachers, to the institution, to the target language itself and to its speakers. This is directly related to the following point.
- *Motivation,* at least in so far as it can be anticipated. Obviously a whole range of factors will affect this.
- *Reasons for learning,* if it is possible to state them. With school age pupils this may be less significant than with many adult learners, where it is often possible to carry out quite a detailed analysis of needs.
- *Preferred learning styles:* which will help in the evaluation of the suitability of different methods, for instance whether problem-solving activities could be used, or whether pupils are more used to 'rote learning', where material is learned by heart.
- *Personality:* which can affect methodological choices such as a willing acceptance of role play and an interactive classroom environment, or a preference for studying alone, for example.

Many of these factors will recur in the relevant sections of subsequent chapters.

Setting   That aspect of the context that we refer to as *setting* is to be understood here as the whole teaching and learning environment, in a wide sense: it is the factors falling under this heading that will determine whether the aims of a language programme, defined with reference to the learners' needs and characteristics, are actually feasible and realistic. In certain situations, the setting itself may be so significant that it provides the foundation for the specification of aims. This might be the case, for instance, in a country with a single political or religious ideological base, where the education system is primarily an expression of that ideology. In the majority of circumstances, however, the setting is more likely to condition the way in which goals are carried out, and indeed the extent to which they can be.

For most EFL/ESL teachers, therefore, the following factors, in some combination and with varying degrees of significance, will influence course planning, syllabus design, the selection of materials and resources, and the appropriateness of methods:

- *The role of English in the country:* whether it is a regular means of communication or primarily a subject taught in the school curriculum, where, in turn, it may or may not be the first foreign language. This relates to the linguistic environment, and to whether English is spoken outside class in the community or alternatively never heard.
- *The role of English in the school,* and its place in the curriculum.

- *The teachers:* their status, both at national and institutional levels, their training, mother tongue, attitudes to their job, experience, expectations. This topic will be discussed in detail in the final chapter of this book.
- *Management and administration:* who is responsible for what level of decision, particularly which are the control points for employment of staff, budgets, resource allocation and so on. Additionally, the position of teachers in the overall system needs to be understood, as does the nature of the hierarchy in any particular institution.
- *Resources available:* books and paper, audio-visual material (hardware and software for cassette and video), laboratories, computers, reprographic facilities and so on. Design and choice of teaching materials will be particularly affected by resource availability, as will the capacity to teach effectively across a range of language skills.
- *Support personnel:* administrators, secretaries and technicians, and their specific roles in relation to the teaching staff.
- *The number of pupils* to be taught and the size of classes. Overall numbers may affect the total number of teaching hours available, and the large class problem is a very familiar one in many settings worldwide.
- *Time* available for the programme, both over a working year (longitudinally), and in any one week or term (intensive or extensive). Many teachers would also consider that time of day is a significant factor.
- *Physical environment:* the nature of the building, noise factors, flexibility of tables and chairs, size of room in relation to size of class, heat and cold, and so on.
- *The socio-cultural environment:* this can often determine the suitability of both materials and methods. For example, some textbooks contain topics inappropriate to the setting, and some classroom methods require an unacceptable set of teacher and learner roles.
- *The types of tests used,* and ways in which students are evaluated: assessment procedures may, for example, be formal or informal and subjective. They may also be external, in the form of a public or national examination, or internal to the institution and the course.
- *Procedures (if any) for monitoring and evaluating* the language teaching programme itself. This kind of evaluation may be imposed by 'senior management', or alternatively agreed between teachers as colleagues.

Hedge (2000) covers similar points, classifying them into social, educational, pupil and teacher variables. Malamah-Thomas (1987: 97) describes setting in terms of three levels in an education system – the country, the school, and the classroom. She then divides the various factors into (a) physical, (b) temporal, (c) psycho-social, and (d) educational, showing how the three different levels may be affected by each of these. Thus, for example, psycho-social factors are related at national level to culture, politics and religion; at institutional level to school atmosphere and staff attitudes; and in the classroom to student-teacher rapport. Holliday (1994) is particularly concerned with the need for methodology to be *appropriate* to its socio-cultural context, not inappropriately transplanted from a different – and often more privileged – system.

Teachers are affected, directly and indirectly, by all these variables. Some they may be able to influence or even control: for example, the deployment of resources and materials, or the pacing of work within an overall time-scale. Others, of course, arise from decisions taken far removed from a teacher's day-to-day professional life, perhaps at Ministry level, or at an earlier point in the country's educational history. Whatever their source, it is the teacher who is in the 'front line' – attempting to promote learning and fulfil the stated goals against the background of a complex network of interrelated factors. Not every-one will work in a situation as gloomy as that described by Gaies and Bowers (1990: 176), with large classes, low motivation, inadequate coursebooks, poorly trained teachers, lack of resources, heavy workload and the like, but we may all share their conclusion that 'by coming to grips not only with new ideas but with the evidence of what happens when they are introduced into the local con-text, [teachers] equip themselves with the tools for establishing an appropriate methodology that can set realistic national objectives for teacher training and education' (181).

Consider the following short case study of a fairly typical teaching environ-ment. Note how the factors associated with the learner and the teaching situ-ation can affect the organization of the language programme, the materials, the teachers and the methodology. For instance, most aspects are determined by decisions taken at some distance from the teacher, although teachers' views may have some effect. Again, the classes are on the whole conditioned by the exam-ination system, but a minority of pupils are able to select classes in line with their own interests, which in turn means that teachers may be less bound by coursebooks and able themselves to be more autonomous in choice of materials and methods. In other words, there is a complex set of factors in operation, and the teacher in the classroom is the focus of a variety of pressures and influences, both direct and indirect.

Teacher X works in a secondary school, with pupils ranging in age from 12 to 16. She teaches thirty periods a week, two of which are options selected by older pupils according to their interests. Course materials consist in the main of set textbooks graded according to age and proficiency level and focused heavily but not exclusively on accuracy. Materials are written by a Ministry of Education team according to Ministry guidelines, and teachers' opinions are solicited annually by an Area Language Teaching Adviser. It is Government policy to revise materials every 8 years.

Average class size is forty pupils. The pressure of the examination system ensures satisfactory attention, though – since there is little opportunity for travel – learners do not readily perceive the relevance of learning materials to their own lives.

The school has a language laboratory, and a very small collection of books (mainly stories) written in English. Classrooms are basic but adequate. Very few supplementary English language teaching materials are available, though teachers are encouraged to make their own small-scale resource materials, and to share ideas at local teachers' centres. The school has one computer, so far without internet access.

This teacher has been to Britain once, on a three-week summer school. She corresponds regularly with an English school teacher.

---

1   Now examine your own teaching environment in a similar way. First list the characteristics of your learners and of the teaching situation.
2   Then decide which are the more significant of these, and try to plot the patterns of cause and effect that they set in motion. For example, how are your classroom materials selected? To whom are you responsible? What possibilities do you have for innovation, or for professional development?
3   Finally, you might like to consider what kinds of changes in your teaching situation would have the strongest effect on your role as a teacher – a change in your status? Smaller groups? More time? The possibilities are many.
4   Discuss your analysis with colleagues, both with those working in the same environment and, if possible, with others from different backgrounds. Keep a note of your analysis: it will be helpful to refer to it again in subsequent chapters.

The syllabus

We can now assume that the goals of an English language programme have been set out and that the contextual factors affecting its implementation have been established and understood. The next step in the task of planning is to select a type of syllabus relevant to the learners for whom it is intended, appropriate to the situation, and which fulfils the aims as closely as possible.

The 'syllabus' can be seen for our purposes as the overall organizing principle for what is to be taught and learned. In other words, it is a general statement as to the pedagogical arrangement of learning content. Richards and Rodgers (2001) have proposed a useful framework for the comparison of language teaching methods that illustrates the place of the syllabus in programme planning. Their model has three distinct levels, which they term *approach*, *design* and *procedure*, and is intended to show the relationship between the theory and practice of language teaching as an 'interdependent system'. Briefly, 'approach' is the most general level, and refers to the views and beliefs – or theories – of language and language learning on which planning is based. The most obvious example here is a view of language described as a set of grammatical structures. The next level, 'design', is where the principles of the first level are converted into the more practical aspects of syllabuses and instructional materials. It is here that decisions are taken about the arrangement of content to be taught and learnt, the choice of topics, language items to be included in the programme, and so on. Finally, 'procedure' refers to techniques and the management of the classroom itself.

The English Language Teaching profession nowadays has available a range of different types of syllabus from which a choice will be made for a specific situation. So however diverse our teaching contexts, our courses will be based on one, or a combination of, these principles of organization. Although syllabuses typically are written and published documents, their circulation is often restricted to the particular situation for which they have been drawn up. Therefore, one of the simplest ways of surveying the types of syllabus available is to examine the contents pages of published English language teaching textbooks, because they reveal the underlying principles and assumptions on which the writers have based their material. At one and the same time, they tell us something both about the approach and the design adopted, thus bringing together principle and practice in a directly observable way.

This is not a book about syllabus design as such, and it will not be necessary or appropriate to analyse each syllabus type in depth here. References to more detailed discussion are given at the end of the chapter, and the next chapters will examine the major areas of current debate. Let us simply try to identify the key principles of syllabus organization by examining the types of contents page most often found in the materials we use, because these distinctions will be the foundation for our discussion of 'design and procedure' in the remainder of the book.

> Look at the coursebook(s) that you use most frequently. With which of our samples in figure 1.2 does the table of contents in your own material compare most closely?

The first of these obviously is organized according to a list of grammatical structures, and is one that will readily be recognized by most English language teachers. The second is based on the communicative and interpersonal uses to which language is put and, in contrast to the formal structural system of the first type, highlights what people do through language. It is normally referred to as a 'functional' syllabus. This design principle is often found together with the other list of items in the same box: they are technically called 'notions', a term used to describe the rather general and abstract categories a language is able to express, such as concepts of time and place. For convenience – and in line with common practice – they will be placed together here, and the syllabus as a whole designated 'functional-notional'. The most important distinctions between this on the one hand and the so-called structural syllabus on the other will be taken up in the next chapter. The third sample presents a set of everyday situations or 'settings'. The fourth focuses on language skills, and is concerned with what learners do as speakers, listeners, readers, writers. The fifth uses topics or themes as its starting point. The sixth invokes the concept of task, discussed in chapter 3.

We can now identify six broad types of syllabus:

1 grammatical or structural
2 functional-notional
3 situational

(1) Simple past; irregular verbs The passive Formation of adverbs Type 3 conditionals Gerunds and infinitives	(2a) Making suggestions Asking for directions Giving advice Introducing yourself - (2b) Location Duration Ability
(3) In the restaurant At a hotel In the post office At a garage	(4) Making notes from a talk Reading for information Using a dictionary Writing an exam answer
(5) Space travel Intelligence tests Smoking The weather	(6) Language focus: question forms Vocabulary: meeting people Skills: speaking, reading, listening Task preparation: listen to people meeting Task: Interviews Task follow-up

Figure 1.2 Principles of syllabus organization. (Adapted from *Cutting Edge* (Cunningham and Moor, 1998).)

4   skills based
5   topic-based
6   task-based

We comment on 'process' and 'procedural' syllabuses in chapter 3. (See also Ur's list (1996: 178–9), which gives a useful overview.)

It is, of course, unusual to find just one of these as the only organizing principle, in isolation from others, and before leaving this discussion of syllabus types two final explanatory points must briefly be made.

First, most syllabuses are based on a combination of two or more of the types we have illustrated. Some, like this one, for example, may have a 'primary' and a 'secondary' organizing principle:

At the bank: question forms
At a garage: imperatives
At a hotel: present perfect

Indeed, many situational and topic-based syllabuses are part of a broader pattern of this kind, where a grammatical point to be taught is linked to an interesting theme or practised in a 'real-world' setting rather than learnt mechanically and outside any context. Other syllabuses are multilayered, using several different principles (ideally) interwoven in a systematic way:

Talking about holidays
Requesting information
Question forms
At the travel agent
Listening and role play
Intonation practice

This deliberately is a somewhat extreme example, but it does show how topics, functions, structures, skills, situations (and pronunciation practice) can be brought together.

The second point to bear in mind here is the need to distinguish between the syllabus itself, and what we might call a 'syllabus inventory'. The inventory is simply a list of the contents to be covered in the language programme, whether that is a list of functional or grammatical items, or of skills, or of topics and situations. The 'syllabus' is the way in which that content is organized and broken down into a set of teachable and learnable units, and will include consideration of pacing, sequencing and grading of items, methods of presentation and practice, and so on. Harmer (2001b: 296) also refers to the criteria of learnability, frequency, coverage and usefulness.

> Examine the list below, which shows a number of different types of learners and teaching situations. Work with a colleague if possible, and select two or three of them to look at in a little more detail.

Where?	*Who?*	*Why?*
China: university of technology	Undergraduates	Reading purposes: English is a library language
Turkey: secondary school	School pupils	Part of general school curriculum
Britain: university	Postgraduates in various subjects	To follow postgraduate studies after one year English
An English town: secondary school withdrawal class	Refugees, newly arrived	Language survival
France: evening class	Mixed group: retired people, housewives	Tourism and general purposes
London: private language school	Young adults from the Middle East (male)	To do engineering in further education
Japan: university	Undergraduates	To be tourist guides for foreign visitors
Malaysia: technical institute	Post-'O'-level student	To enter higher education in Australia

1   Try to decide what you think might be the most important factors to do
    with the *learners* and the *setting* for the situations you have chosen. For
    example, you may think that learners' proficiency levels, or attitudes to
    English, are significant, and that class size and resources are the key
    elements affecting the teaching situation.
2   Consider the kind of syllabus that might be selected as the most appropri-
    ate in each case, bearing in mind the stated learning purpose. It does not
    matter if you are not personally familiar with these kinds of teaching
    context. They are quite representative, and the task here is to practise
    applying and integrating some of the principles that we have been dis-
    cussing in this chapter.

1.3   Conclusion

This chapter has discussed the background against which teaching materials
and classroom methods evolve. Our professional activities as language teachers
are not carried out in a vacuum and, in Richards' (1985: 11) words, 'Planning a
successful language program involves consideration of factors that go beyond
mere content and presentation of teaching materials.' Although we work in
specific situations with specific groups of learners, according to a specified set of
aims, our work can be described along a number of shared and generalizable
dimensions. These dimensions are the characteristics of learners, the range of
factors in the teaching situation itself, and the syllabus types available to us as a
profession. The differences lie in the relative importance of these factors, and
the choices that are made.

1.4   Further reading

1   Chapters 1 and 2 of Richards, J. C. (1985): *The Context of Language Teaching*.
    Chapter 1 is entitled 'The context of language teaching'. Chapter 2, which was
    written with Rodgers, is entitled 'Method: approach, design and procedure', and is a
    summary of the arguments set out in Richards and Rodgers (2001).
2   Harmer (2001b, ch 21) has a useful overview of the main types of syllabus.

2

The Impact of the Communicative Approach

2.1 Introduction

In the previous chapter we examined in very general terms the most common types of syllabus organization for English language teaching. We also noted that these syllabus types form an essential component of the framework within which objectives are specified and the details of language teaching programmes are set out. This happens, as we have seen, according to certain principles and with various possibilities for combination. It is the purpose of the present chapter to take a closer look at the approach to syllabus and materials design that has had the greatest significance worldwide for the current practice of English language teaching. This approach is most usually called 'communicative', and although other labels, particularly 'functional–notional', are sometimes taken as synonyms, 'communicative' will be used here as the cover term.

It is important for the aims of this book to understand that communicative design criteria permeate both general coursebooks and materials covering specific language skills, as well as the methodology of the classroom. In other words, a number of assumptions are now an explicit or implicit part of the everyday professional lives of teachers in many parts of the world.

We shall first very briefly survey the recent history of English language teaching, emphasizing the period when dissatisfaction began to be voiced with what was then the dominant approach to syllabus and materials design. We shall then see how the gradual adoption of a communicative approach expressed itself in the claims made for the appropriacy of language teaching materials. The main section of this chapter will pick out the key implications of the concept for teaching purposes, and we shall end with an attempt to evaluate its potential advantages and disadvantages. The following chapter will contain a selective discussion of developments in syllabus and materials design in the 'post-communicative era'.

2.2 *Some background*

It is neither appropriate nor possible within the scope of this book to set out all the many ramifications of 'the communicative approach': inappropriate, because our main intention is to look at its impact on teaching and learning rather than at the theory and background in themselves; not possible, because the concept covers a potentially vast area touching on many disciplines (philosophy, linguistics, sociology, psychology, even anthropology), and a full treatment would require at least one book in its own right. The 'further reading' section at the end of this chapter lists several readily available works for teachers interested in following the discussion further. For present purposes, we shall simply outline the reasons that led to the growth of a concern for 'communication' in language teaching and learning, indicating a few of the background sources from which practice has evolved.

The communicative approach is essentially a manifestation of the 1970s, in the sense that this was the decade when the most explicit debate took place, especially in the UK. By the end of the seventies it was clear that many features of the approach were here to stay. As we shall see in chapter 3, the subsequent period has been characterized by explorations of other, related possibilities for the design of materials and methods. The original 'communicative revolution' has subsided, and it has inevitably been the subject of critical comment: never-theless, its central tenets have not been rejected, and we shall find them incorpor-ated in a great deal of current thinking. More importantly, perhaps, teachers in many parts of the world are finding that they need to come to terms with changes in their role, as communicative principles in language teaching become central goals of their educational systems.

Towards the end of the 1960s we can discern amongst language teaching practitioners and applied linguists a growing dissatisfaction with the prevailing methodology of the time, the main emphasis of which was on the mastery of language structure. This is a generalization, but it is true to say that language learners were required, above all, to manipulate grammatical forms accurately, and that this procedure was the main measure of competence in a foreign lan-guage. All English language teachers will be familiar with the type of exercise instruction that asks (or more usually tells!) students to convert active sentences into their passive voice equivalent, or to supply the correct verb form for a given tense, or to distinguish adjectives from adverbs. A glance at many of the tables of contents of teaching materials published in the 1950s and 1960s will confirm this focus. It was argued that this kind of teaching produced 'structurally com-petent' students who were often 'communicatively incompetent' (Johnson, 1981), able perhaps to form correct sentences to describe the daily habits of the fictitious textbook 'Jones family', but unable to transfer this knowledge to talk about themselves in a real-life setting. In a much quoted phrase, this kind of gram-matical competence has been described as 'necessary but not sufficient' (Newmark and Reibel, 1968, quoted in Johnson, 1981).

One of the indirect reasons for this dissatisfaction was undoubtedly the fact that, by the late 1960s, the world had started to shrink, in the positive sense that there were increasing possibilities for international professional cooperation and travel, whether for business, further study, or other purposes. Particularly in Western Europe, interdependence grew with the development of the European Common Market, and with it a parallel educational need for changes in the way in which the various European languages were taught (Richards and Rodgers, 2001). These changes were addressed within the Council of Europe when a number of experts worked on far-reaching proposals for the establishment of a scheme to teach the languages of Europe, particularly with the needs of adult learners in mind. Wilkins (1976) was instrumental in setting out the fundamental considerations for a 'functional–notional' approach to syllabus design based on communicative criteria. More detailed specifications for courses for different languages were then developed (for English see, for example, van Ek, Alexander and Fitzpatrick, 1980). Work within Europe has had an impact far beyond its original context, as we shall see in the next sections.

These educational perspectives evolved alongside, and to some extent were derived from, significant theoretical developments in linguistics and sociolinguistics. There are a number of quite well-known arguments that are clearly explained in the references given at the end of this chapter, and they will not be repeated here. We should just note – should readers wish to seek more detail – that they centre particularly on the sociolinguist Hymes's (1972) concept of 'communicative competence', and his criticism of Chomsky's view of language on the grounds that Chomsky paid exclusive attention to 'correctness' at the expense of 'appropriacy' of use in specific contexts. This perspective was further developed by Canale (1983), who put forward four components of communicative competence: grammatical, sociolinguistic, discourse, and strategic competence. (These are usefully summarized and explained in Johnson, 2001: ch. 1.) Hedge (2000: 56) illustrates how each of these components has implications for teaching and learning.

We conclude this section with the observation that, although the 1970s were the years in which 'structural' design criteria started to receive widespread critical attention, the gradual shift to a more communicative methodology obviously did not take place simultaneously throughout the world. In many countries the debate is still current, reflecting the differing and changing perceptions of the international roles and needs of education systems.

Try to characterize the approaches to materials design that the two tables of contents represent. Compare them with the textbook(s) you most frequently use: are your materials close to either of these approaches?

18

Contents

Foreword
Students' Introduction

Source: R. O'Neill, R. Kingsbury and A. Yeadon, Table of Contents from *Kernel Lessons Intermediate, Students' Book*. London: Longman, 1971. © Longman, 1971.

Contents

Source: L. Jones, Table of Contents from *Functions of English*. Cambridge: Cambridge University Press, 1981. © Cambridge University Press, 1981.

2.3　The claims for communicative materials

During the 1970s there was, not surprisingly, a great boom in the publication of teaching materials designed according to 'communicative' principles. It is instructive to look at the kinds of claims that were being made for this 'new direction', and the following statements, taken from a number of standard published materials, are typical (italics are ours):

1　'for students interested in *using* language rather than learning more about structure ... students learn to use the *appropriate* language they need for *communicating in real life*'
2　'... is a dynamic, *functionally-based* coursebook. It is an intensely practical book, giving the students opportunity for thorough and *meaningful* rehearsal of the English they will need for effective *communication*'
3　'... to use the language to *communicate in real life*'
4　'... teaches students to *communicate* effectively by understanding and controlling the relationship between language forms and *functions*'
5　'... places emphasis on developing skills of *discourse* within a wide range of *communicative settings*. It actively trains the learner in important discourse functions ... All the language practice is presented in *real-life contexts* and related to the learner's own experience.'

　It is clear even from this short selection that certain terms recur: communication, real-life, use, functions, appropriate, meaningful, context, setting and discourse. It should also be noted that in a few cases there is an either/or type of statement – 'using language *rather than* learning more about structure'. Particularly in the early days of enthusiasm for the new communicative movement, there was sometimes a tendency to regard the design of communicative materials as the only way forward, and to polarize 'functions versus grammar' as if they were somehow in opposition. A moment's thought will show that this is a very unbalanced perspective, indeed one that is entirely incorrect: it is clearly not possible to engage in purposeful communication in a language without being able to formulate the structures of that language as well. Seedhouse (1997) uses lesson transcripts to show how meaning and form are most effective when combined in teaching. We might further recall Newmark and Reibel's position, quoted earlier in this chapter, that an ability to control grammatical structure is 'necessary but not sufficient'. In other words, for most learners this ability will be part, but not the whole, of language learning. As Dubin and Olshtain (1986: 88) put it:

> There are ... prevailing misconceptions regarding the communicative approach to language learning. One such frequently expressed misunderstanding is the belief ... that it is a new methodology which has come to *replace* the structural approach ... The most significant contribution of the communicative approach is that it has brought about a more comprehensive view of teaching and learning (Italics added.)

In one sense, then, the italicized terms in the numbered extracts above are labels, intended to make the materials more attractive to a potential purchaser/user. They are also much more than labels, however: they are like doors behind which is to be found a rich ground for the discussion of both the 'theory' and 'practice' of communicative language teaching. We shall pick out the key implications of these terms in the next section.

> You might like to look at the claims made for the materials that you most frequently work with. In what terms are those claims expressed (if they are explicitly stated)?

2.4   Implications of the communicative approach for teaching purposes

We stated in the introduction to this chapter that the literature on the communicative approach is very large, and draws on several theoretical areas of debate. We shall restrict ourselves here to trying to show those implications that have most helped to form the kinds of teaching materials we work with and our attitudes to managing our classrooms. As we go through this section, we suggest from time to time some points for you to consider in relation to your own experience, both of language and of teaching. The seven implications discussed are

1   'Communicative' implies 'semantic', a concern with the meaning potential of language.
2   There is a complex relationship between language form and language function.
3   Form and function operate as part of a wider network of factors.
4   Appropriacy of language use has to be considered alongside accuracy. This has implications for attitudes to error.
5   'Communicative' is relevant to all four language skills.
6   The concept of communication takes us beyond the level of the sentence.
7   'Communicative' can refer both to the properties of language and to behaviour.

The relative importance of these implications depends, for example, on the skill(s) being practised and on the nature and purpose of particular classrooms: this will be explored in the relevant chapters of parts 2 and 3.

Implication 1

In its broadest sense, the concept of 'being communicative' has to do with what a language has the potential to mean, as well as with its formal grammatical properties. The research of the 1970s laid the foundations for this view, which is particularly associated with the work of Wilkins (1976) originally carried out for the Council of Europe. Wilkins proposed two categories of communicative meaning: 'notional' (or 'semantico-grammatical') and 'functional'. The distinction between these two terms is clearly set out by Johnson (1981). 'Notions' are rather abstract concepts – frequency, duration, dimension, location, quantity and so on – which in English are closely related to grammatical categories. So, for instance, expressing 'frequency' involves tense selection and certain adverbial constructions. ('They often used to visit friends'; 'I talk to my students regularly,' for example.) 'Functions', on the other hand, refer to the practical uses to which we put language, most usually in interaction with other people. Johnson suggests that, to find out the function of any particular utterance, we can simply ask, 'what was the speaker's intention in saying it?' (1981: 5). For example, a short statement like 'I'll do that!' could be an offer of help, but it could also be a warning, if the speaker believes that the other person is likely to be in danger when trying to carry out some activity; while 'Do you smoke?' could be a straightforward enquiry, perhaps asked during a medical examination, or it could be an indirect request for a cigarette. Other functional categories often found in teaching materials include making requests, greeting, making suggestions, asking for directions, giving advice.

For our purposes, we can note that the majority of published coursebooks for English give more emphasis to functional rather than notional categories, presumably because real-life interaction expresses itself most obviously in this way. However, it must also be pointed out that the syllabus specifications carried out within the Council of Europe and following on from Wilkins's original work go into considerable details of both notions and functions (van Ek, 1977).

The semantic criteria outlined here have obvious implications for the design and organization of teaching materials. If our coursebook is primarily aimed at mastery of the formal grammatical system, then a sentence such as 'When does the next train leave for London?' will probably occur in a unit on 'interrogatives' or 'auxiliary "do"'. In a functional–communicative coursebook, such a sentence is more likely to be found under a heading like 'requests for information'. Similarly 'You ought to see the doctor' can be taken either as part of an exercise on modal verbs, or as one way of giving advice.

Implication 2

This is closely linked to the first, and concerns the relationship between the grammatical forms of a language and their communicative function. Let us consider a simple conversational statement like 'Give me your telephone number.' This could, of course, be an order, if spoken by a policeman to a motorist who has committed a traffic offence. However, if said, with suitable intonation, to an acquaintance, it could be a suggestion about a way of getting in touch. Or 'If you don't sit down, there'll be a problem' could be interpreted as either threatening or helpful. In other words, a grammatical structure can in principle perform a number of different communicative functions – an imperative might, for example, be a command or a suggestion, a conditional might be selected to threaten, to warn, or alternatively to give advice.

Figure 2.1 Form and function.

The converse relationship also holds, where a single function can be expressed in a number of different ways. To make a suggestion, for instance, we can choose to say, 'You should . . .' 'You ought to . . .' 'Why don't you . . . ?' 'You'd better . . .' 'I think you should . . .' 'Have you thought of . . . ?' and undoubtedly there are several other possibilities. (In the Council of Europe's terms (van Ek, 1977), these structural items are referred to as 'exponents' of a particular function.) Figure 2.1 summarizes the relationships. For a longer list of examples, readers are directed to Wilkins (1976: 147), who shows how the imperative form can be used for suggestion, threat, instruction, direction, warning or invitation, and how the functional category 'command' can be expressed by conditional, active declarative, 'you' + verb, present continuous negative, or the future tense.

In more traditional teaching materials, this complex form–function relationship tends to be simplified, often implying a one-to-one correspondence, so that 'interrogatives' are used for 'asking questions', 'imperatives' for 'giving commands', 'conditionals' for 'making hypothetical statements' and so on. In a communicative perspective, this relationship is explored more carefully, and as a result our views on the properties of language have been expanded and enriched. However, there are a number of pedagogic problems associated with this approach to materials design, particularly to do with the sequencing of the language to be practised. We shall leave comment on this until later in the chapter.

1 Think of some more examples of functions in English, and the grammatical structures related to them. You could also think about comparable patterns in your own language.
2 How do your teaching materials handle the relationship between grammar and communicative function? For instance, is a 'function' taught together with several grammatical forms, or just one? Alternatively, is a 'function' just used as an example where the main focus is on teaching grammar?

Implication 3

It is possible for most teachers to think of classroom situations where grammar practice takes place with very little reference to everyday reality, where learners rehearse patterns simply in order to get them right rather than to express meaning. Equally, it unfortunately is just as possible for a list of language functions to be practised as ritualistically as grammar with, say, a few structural items for 'giving advice' applied in turn to imaginary people and situations. We need, then, to be a little cautious here, because there is no reason in principle why grammar practice should not be placed in a communicative context, and functional practice take place only as a list of separate and decontextualized items.

However, real-world language in use does not operate in a vacuum, and this is the third implication of the communicative approach. When we give advice, we do so to someone, about something, for a particular reason. If we are invited, it is by someone to do something, or to attend something. So in addition to talking about

1　*Language function* and
2　*Language form*, as we did in the previous two sections, there are other dimensions of communication to be considered if we are to be offered a more complete picture. These are, at least:
3　*Topics*, for example health, transport, work, leisure activities, politics and so on.
4　*Context or setting*, which may, as Yalden (1983) points out, refer to both physical and social settings, and may therefore include personal conversation and business discussion as well as the more traditional 'situations' such as travel or medical or leisure-time settings.
5　*Roles* of people involved: whether, for example, stranger/stranger, friend/friend, employee/boss, colleague/colleague, customer/person supplying a service.

Two short and simple examples will serve to illustrate this:

A.　Can I have a kilo of those red apples, and three lemons please?
B.　Anything else?
C.　That's all, thanks.
D.　£1.50 please.

A.　This is really good, but a bit expensive.
B.　Manchester restaurants are much cheaper.
C.　Who's paying?

Language function and language form, then, do not operate in isolation but as part of a network of interconnected factors, all of which need to be taken into account in materials that use a communicative concept as their design principle.

Implication 4

Once we move away from the idea that mastery of grammar = mastery of a language, we are obliged at the same time to move away from evaluating our learners' proficiency on the basis of accuracy alone. It is undoubtedly desirable that their language production should be as 'correct' as possible, but we have seen that grammaticality also takes place in a wider social and communicative context. The implication here is that we should concern ourselves not only with accuracy of form, but also with appropriacy in relation to the context. This derives in part from Hymes's view of language as including 'what a speaker needs to know in order to be communicatively competent in a speech community' (Richards and Rodgers, 2001: 70). The communicative approach has therefore led to a broadening of the criteria by which language proficiency is defined. We now have the concepts of appropriacy as well as accuracy, communicative as well as grammatical competence, use as well as usage (Widdowson, 1978).

For teaching purposes, these considerations clearly lead to a rethinking of attitudes to, and the treatment of, learners' grammatical errors. For example, if a learner tries to buy a train ticket by saying 'Give me a ticket to London (please),' or writes to a college for information with the phrase 'Send me your prospectus,' he may show satisfactory mastery of language form, but he is offending certain forms of sociolinguistic behaviour. We may say, 'What?' to a friend we have not understood, but we would be advised to say, 'Pardon?' to the boss; 'Shut the door, will you?' may be appropriate within the family, but 'Excuse me, would you mind closing the door?' for a stranger on the train (example from Littlewood, 1981: 4). We can also look at 'error' from another perspective, and ask whether to prefer *'Please could you to send me your prospectus?' or *'Can I have six air letters, please?' to the choice of an imperative form. (* is a symbol used to denote grammatical inaccuracy.)

We can see from this that the notion of error is no longer restricted only to incorrect grammar or perhaps choice of vocabulary. If 'being communicative' includes also paying attention to context, roles and topics, then it is logically possible to make an error at any of these levels. It is even possible – though this can only be mentioned in passing – to make 'cultural' errors: an English person's way of thanking someone for a present is to say, 'You really shouldn't have done that,' readily interpretable as a reprimand by a giver who is not familiar with the normal response. (See also Cook, 1989: 123–5, for other examples and Bartram and Walton (1991).)

The extent to which error types are significant depends very much on particular teaching situations, and on the objectives of specific programmes. It is certainly not possible to make generalizations, and what may be tolerated in one case may be unacceptable in another. But even a partial acceptance of communicative criteria will allow for a certain amount of creativity and exploration in language learning, and this will inevitably extend the framework in which errors are evaluated.

Implication 5

Particularly in the early phase of the 'communicative revolution', it was sometimes assumed – mistakenly – that the approach was only really valid for teaching the spoken language, when learners needed to make conversation in English. The assumption is an understandable one, since face-to-face interaction is the most obvious kind of communication with other people, and learners were and are increasingly felt to need oral skills, given the greater opportunities for travel and for communication with English speakers visiting their countries.

It is important to realize that 'communicative' can in fact refer to all four language skills. We can look at this in two different ways. Firstly, we can divide the 'four skills' into 'productive' (speaking and writing) and 'receptive' (listening and reading) and practise them separately. It is possible to do this successfully from a communicative perspective, as we shall see in part II of this book. However, treating the skills discretely can also lead to a concern for accuracy in production and an emphasis, in comprehension, on the grammatical characteristics of written and spoken material. More usefully, we can group together the oral/aural skills of speaking and listening, and the 'paper skills' of reading and writing. In both cases, we have a giver and a receiver of a message, and the ways in which the information in the message is understood by the receiver is an integral part of the communication. This is true whether we think of a brief exchange, a letter, a book, or an extended discussion. Possibilities of this kind for exploring the four skills, and integrating them with each other, will be examined in more detail in part II.

> How do you interpret the idea of 'communicating in English' for your own learners? What, in other words, are their particular 'communicative needs', and to what extent are each of the 'four skills' important?

Implication 6

Materials based on an approach to teaching that takes mastery of the formal system of a language as its major objective are likely to use the grammatical concept of the sentence as the basis for exercises. We may find, for example, the instruction 'Put the verb in infinitive form into the present perfect' or 'Join each pair of sentences with a relative pronoun,' followed perhaps by ten numbered sentences. Not much real-life communication proceeds strictly according to such fixed patterning. A letter to a friend, for instance, is unlikely to be only a string of sentences:

> I went to the USA.
> I went to New York.
> I saw the Statue of Liberty.
> I flew by Concorde.

Nor does this conversation sound natural, although, like the letter, it practises some useful verb structures, and the questions and answers are at least related:

> Where did you go for your holidays? I went to New York.
> What did you do? I saw the Statue of Liberty.
> How did you travel? I flew by Concorde.

A concept of communication does not have to be based on sentence-level criteria, and it can allow language to be described, and language learning to take place, over longer stretches. In principle it can handle whole conversations, or paragraphs, or even longer texts. In recent years, a number of categories for describing language have been developed that are not based on sentence-level criteria, but on the broader notion of 'discourse'. There is a large and growing background literature on 'discourse analysis', and a detailed explanation of these categories is outside the scope and intention of this book. Essentially, the notion gives us the possibility of showing how different parts of a text or a conversation or any stretch of language are interlinked. This may be, for example, by cross-referencing with pronoun use or definite articles; by semantic links across items of vocabulary; by markers of logical development ('however', 'therefore', 'so', 'because' and the like); by ellipsis in conversation (the 'short answers' of coursebook practice); and by substitution ('this is my book, yours is the other one'). This is usually referred to as the concept of 'cohesion', whereby relationships between different elements in a text (written or spoken) are made explicit. Alternatively, a 'text' in this sense may be described in terms of its intention and its thematic coherence, in simple terms whether it 'makes sense' or not. It is important to note that a stretch of language may be 'coherent' even if it contains no explicit markers of cohesion; and conversely may be 'cohesive' but make no sense. Readers who wish to follow these ideas further are referred to the work of Halliday and Hasan (1976) and Brown and Yule (1983b). A useful summary is also provided in Nunan (1999: ch. 4). Celce-Murcia and Olshtain (2000) have devoted a whole book to showing how notions of discourse have practical applications in teaching.

Implication 7

Finally, the term 'communicative' itself has been used in relation to teaching in two distinct though related ways, and this apparent ambiguity has sometimes been a source of confusion. Firstly, as we have seen from a number of the implications outlined in this section, the concept can refer to a view of the nature of language, leading to the procedures that have been detailed for a 'functional' analysis of language. In other words, language is seen to have inherent communicative as well as grammatical properties.

Secondly, a communicative approach also implies a concern with behaviour, with patterns of interaction as well as linguistic content. Morrow (1981) makes a simple and useful distinction between the 'what' – the contents of a language programme – and the 'how' – the ways in which that content might be learned and taught. This behavioural 'how' would cover the kinds of activities we carry out and the tasks we perform, such as writing a letter, or an essay, or talking to a friend, at a meeting, to a stranger and so on. We shall see in the next two parts of the book how such activities can be implemented in the classroom (a) in terms of the framework of skills and activities that we use for language practice, and (b) in the various possibilities available for structuring and managing the classroom itself.

Thompson (1996) looks at some of these implications from a different angle, arguing that considerable confusion still surrounds clear definitions of CLT, leading to four fundamental misconceptions, namely that (a) CLT means not teaching grammar, (b) CLT means teaching only speaking, (c) CLT means pairwork, which means role play, and (d) CLT means expecting too much from the teacher.

2.5   Conclusion: possibilities and problems

There are a number of reasons why a communicative approach is an attractive one, providing a richer teaching and learning environment. It can

- include wider considerations of what is appropriate as well as what is accurate
- handle a wider range of language, covering texts and conversations as well as sentences
- provide realistic and motivating language practice
- use what learners 'know' about the functions of language from their experience with their own mother tongues

At the same time, other questions are still not fully resolved, answers to some of which depend on the nature of the particular situation in which we teach. Some of the more important of these issues are as follows:

- Having selected appropriate language functions, and having 'filtered out' the most useful grammatical exponents, on what basis should we take decisions about sequencing and grading? It is unlikely that all grammatical items can be taught at the same time, so there is a problem of systematicity. We might refer back here to the structurally different ways of making a suggestion noted in the second implication, above.
- Is the approach a useful one for all proficiency levels, particularly for beginners? Do beginners perhaps require an initial one-to-one correspondence between a function and a form?
- Is is equally appropriate in all teaching contexts, regardless of objectives, location, ages of learners, length of course, mother tongue of teachers and so on? For example, it has been argued that a more grammatically oriented syllabus is to be preferred in a context where English is a foreign language and where learners are unlikely to be exposed to it. Again, some teachers whose mother tongue is not English claim to have little confidence when working with communicative materials. G. Ellis (1996) develops this point further by asking about the *cultural* appropriacy of the approach. He argues that CLT has a number of elements of cultural

specificity in the sense that the 'social principles' underlying the approach are concerned with behaviours set against a background of different value systems.

- Does it always matter if the 'real world' is not being practised in the classroom?

There is much in the approach, then, that is still open to debate and, as the next chapter will show, more recent materials have reacted in various ways to and against the communicative movement of the 1970s. However, the main principles, with varying degrees of change and modification, have had a lasting impact on materials and methods that should not be underestimated. As Thompson (1996: 14–15) puts it: 'CLT is by no means the final answer... But whatever innovations emerge, they will do so against the background of the changes brought about by CLT... Certain of them are too important to lose: the concern with the world beyond the classroom, the concern with the learner as an individual, the view of language as structured to carry out the functions we want it to perform.'

1 Look at the syllabus guidelines for your own situation, if they are available. Are claims made there for 'communicative' objectives? Since it is the teacher who has to interpret them, how are the general objectives translated into your everyday classroom reality? (If you are working in a group of teachers from different backgrounds, you might like to compare your observations with those of others.)

2 The unit on pp. 31–9 is taken from a popular and representative coursebook written during the 1970s. Look at the unit carefully and consider the following points (some of which will be taken up again in the chapters on the evaluation and adaptation of teaching materials):

- What is the role of grammar in the unit?
- What language skills are practised?
- To what extent does the unit deal with (a) communicative functions as properties of language, (b) communicative behaviour and activities?
- How large are the stretches of language that learners are asked to deal with? How much of the language practice is concerned with the manipulation of sentence structure?
- Do learners have any freedom to 'create' meanings and language for themselves? Can they in any sense 'be themselves', and talk about their own interests, wishes, needs?
- Would these materials be suitable for your learners? It not, how would you wish to change them? (With this question we are anticipating chapter 5.)

2.6   Further reading

1   Johnson, K. and K. Morrow (eds) (1981): *Communication in the Classroom*. This is a useful collection of articles that relates communicative principles to teaching materials and to classroom techniques.
2   Littlewood, W. T. (1981): *Communicative Language Teaching*. A standard introductory text on the communicative approach, illustrated with many examples.
3   Johnson and Johnson (1998) have very useful encyclopedic-style entries on CLT, and on many of the other topics covered in the remainder of this book.

Unit 4:
Suggestions

Sally is at home watching television with Peter. It is Friday evening.

SALLY: Do you feel like doing anything tomorrow evening, Peter?

PETER: Yes, all right. What do you suggest?

SALLY: How about going to see *Star Wars*? It's on locally and they say it's very good.

PETER: Well, we could, I suppose, but I don't really like science-fiction films all that much. Of course, if you'd like to see it ...

SALLY: No, no ... I don't mind. It was just a suggestion, that's all.

> *[A slight pause. They continue watching television.]*

PETER: We could always go to Dave's party, I suppose.

SALLY: Dave?

PETER: Yes, Dave Wilkins. You know – that chap who works for the B.B.C. He's having a sort of house-warming party. Everyone's invited. So if you fancy going, then we ...

SALLY: No, I don't think so somehow! You know what Dave's parties are like. I still haven't recovered from the last one we went to.

PETER: Well, it was only an idea.

SALLY: No, I'd prefer to go somewhere else, if you don't mind. Just the two of us.

PETER: Would you like to go for a meal, then? We could go to that super restaurant in Chelsea. Brian told me the food was really great.

SALLY: Yes, that would be nice. Let's do that. And why don't we call in on Bob and Sue on the way home? We've been promising to go and see them for ages.

PETER: Yes, good idea. We could even go on to Dave's party afterwards.

SALLY: Peter! If you think I'm going ...

PETER: *[laughing]* It's all right. I'm only joking!

a) How to ask for a suggestion

When you ask someone to suggest something, here are some phrases you can use:

What	shall we do you suggest we would you like to do you want to can we	do tonight?
Where	do you fancy	going at the week-end?

b) How to make a suggestion

When you make a suggestion, here are some phrases you can use:

What about How about Do you fancy Do you feel like	going to the pictures?
Shall we Let's Why don't we Why not I suggest we Would you like to	spend the week-end in Brighton(?)

PRACTICE 1

Match up the requests from A with an appropriate suggestion from B.

A	What do you fancy eating tonight? Where do you want to go tonight? Who do you suggest we invite to the party? What can we do at the week-end? Where shall we go for our holidays? When would you like to visit your cousin in Wales?

B	Let's go and stay with my sister in Brighton. How about a nice curry? Why don't we ask our English teacher? I suggest we go and see her at Easter. Why not go to the pub? What about going to Spain?

PRACTICE 2

Work in pairs. A makes up a question using the following words. B answers with an appropriate suggestion.

A asks:

1. where they should go tonight.
2. what they should do at the week-end.
3. how much they should pay.
4. what they should eat tonight.
5. when they should go and see that film.
6. how many people they should invite to the party.

c) How to accept a suggestion

Yes,	good idea. that's a marvellous idea. that would be nice. that seems all right.

d) How to half-accept a suggestion

Well,	we could, that's a good idea, it's not a bad idea,	I suppose,	but (there aren't any good films on at the moment).
Yes, I suppose we could,			

e) How to reject a suggestion

No,	I can't. I don't think so. I don't think I can. I don't really feel like (going to the pictures).
Well,	I'm not sure. I don't really like (curry) very much. I'd rather not, if you don't mind.

f) How to make a counter-suggestion

Well,	I'd rather I think I'd prefer to	(go to the pub),	if you don't mind. if that's all right with you.
Mmm, but wouldn't you	prefer to rather	(go dancing)?	

PRACTICE 3

Match up the suggestions from A with the most appropriate response from B.

A
> What about going for a walk?
> Shall we watch *Coronation Street* tonight?
> Let's get married next week-end.
> How about having a party on Friday?
> Why not go to Majorca in the summer?
> Do you fancy going to a Chinese restaurant tonight?

B
> I'm not sure. I don't really like Chinese food very much.
> Mmm, but wouldn't you prefer to go to Scotland again?
> Well, I'd rather not, if you don't mind.
> I can't. I'm already married.
> Well, I think I'd prefer to watch the serial, if that's all right with you.
> Well, we could, I suppose, but remember we've got to get up early on
>   Saturday morning.

PRACTICE 4

Work in pairs. A looks at the pictures and makes a suggestion. B answers by accepting, half-accepting, rejecting or making a counter-suggestion.

1. on Saturday

2. tonight

3. in the summer

4. at the week-end

5. tomorrow night

6. tonight

Written Practice

Complete the following dialogues:

1. A: Where shall we go tonight?
   B: What about . . . .
   A: Yes, ...

2. A: What do you suggest I wear to the party?
   B: How about . . . .
   A: No, ...

3. A: . . . . at the week-end?
   B: Why don't we . . . .?
   A: Well, ..., but . . . .

4. A: When . . . . visit Tom and Alice?
   B: Let's . . . .
   A: Well, I'd rather . . . .

5. A: Where . . . .?
   B: . . . . Spain?
   A: . . . .

6. A: . . . .?
   B: . . . .
   A: Yes, I suppose we could, but it's always so crowded on Saturdays.

Dialogue

Practise reading the following dialogue in pairs. Read the dialogue again, replacing the phrases in **bold** with phrases of similar meaning. Then write out the new dialogue.

A: What **shall we** do tonight?

B: **Why don't we** go to the cinema?

A: **Well, we could, I suppose,** but there aren't really any good films on at the moment.

B: Well, what **do you suggest,** then?

A: **How about** going out for a meal?

B: **No, I don't really fancy** eating anything.

A: All right. **Do you feel like** going to the pub, then?

B: **Well, I'd prefer to** go dancing, **if you don't mind.**

A: That's O.K. by me. And **why not** go on to a restaurant afterwards?

B: Yes, **that's a marvellous idea.**

Role Play

SITUATION 1: AN EVENING'S VIEWING

Work in pairs or groups of three.

You want to watch television tonight.
Look through the following Programme Guide and try to decide which programme to watch.
One person starts: '*What shall we watch tonight?*'

TV/RADIO Programme guide by Celia Brayfield

BBC 1

12.35.—On the Move. 12.45.—Midday News. 1.0.—Pebble Mill. 1.45.—Trumpton. 2.0.— You and Me. 2.35.—For Schools, Colleges. 3.0. —Children's Wardrobe. 3.55.—Play School. 4.20.—Winsome Witch. 4.25.—Jackanory. 4.40.—Scooby Doo. 5.0.—John Craven's Newsround. 5.5.—Blue Peter. 5.35.—Paddington. 5.40.—Evening News. 5.55.—Nationwide. 6.45.—Tomorrow's World.

7.10 TOP OF THE POPS with Earth, Wind and Fire, ELO, Blondie, Real Thing, The Stranglers, Manhattan Transfer and Abba.

7.40 THE GOOD LIFE : Just My Bill. The rates bill sends farmer Briers off to market to sell his compost-grown wholefood. Also starring Felicity Kendal and Penelope Keith.

8.10 WINGS: Officer and Gentlemen. Young Farmer (Tim Woodward), with promotion on his mind, accidentally shoots down a peaceful German. More of the World War I flying aces.

9.0 NEWS with Angela Rippon, Weather.

9.25 CANNON : Bloodlines. Grieving father hires overweight detective to investigate doubtful suicide of brilliant son. Starring William Conrad.

10.15 OMNIBUS : Warsaw Autumn. A film by Dennis Marks, whose work can be expected to be confident, intelligent and in keeping with the sombre beauties of Northern Europe's artistic capitals, about last year's modern music festival in Warsaw. The film reports on the reflowing of the arts in Poland, and the meeting of the country's two leading resident composers, Lutoslawski and Penderecki, with her most notable musical exile, Andrzej Panufnik.

11.0 TONIGHT investigates top people's crime wave — highly organised trade in stolen Rolls-Royces. 11.40.—Weather.

BBC 2

7.0 NEWS, Weather. 7.5.—Your Move with Brian Redhead, Terence Alexander, Fenella Fielding and Julian Holloway. (Repeat.)

7.30 NEWSDAY with Michael Charlton and Richard Kershaw.

8.10 LIVING IN THE PAST : March. The start of an intriguing report on an experiment in Iron Age living. Six young couples and three children have been living in secret in the West Country using the farming methods and the survival secrets of Iron Age tribesmen. They have planted prehistoric strains of wheat, herded ancient breeds of sheep and goats, cut what needed to be cut with stone axes and lived in primitive shelters. This opening programme shows how the group was chosen, trained and installed in an ancient British settlement.

9.0 GARDENERS' WORLD. Back in the days of bio-humus and Gro-bags, blind gardener Bob Roberts joins Peter Seabrook and Arthur Billitt on the modern farm.

9.25 JEREMIAH JOHNSON. (1972) (A). Robert Redford, Will Geer. *Scenic if slightly worthy story of an idealistic ex-soldier taking to the hills of Utah to live at one with nature. Nature is less hospitable than expected, and the advice of a veteran trapper is all that saves our hero from the mountain winter.*

11.10 NEWS, Weather. 11.20.—Men of Ideas: Logical Positivism and its Legacy. Sir Alfred Ayer joins Bryan Magee in this heavyweight series on leading Western philosophers. 12.0.—Music At Night

ITV ANGLIA, as London except :

1.25.—Anglia News. 2.0.—Women Only. 4.20. —The Secret Lives of Waldo Kitty. 4.45.— Solo One. 5.15.—Emmerdale Farm. 6.0.— About Anglia. 6.20.—Arena. 7.0.—Bygones. 7.30.—Now Who Do You Do? 10.30.—Folk in the East. 11.0.—Film: The Mystery of the Wax Museum. 12.30.—The Living Word.

ITV

12.0.—Charlie's Climbing Tree. 12.10.— Stepping Stones. 12.30.—Make It Count. 1.0. —News. 1.20.—Help! 1.30.—Crown Court. 2.0.—After Noon. 2.25.—Shades of Greene. 3.20.—Quick on the Draw. 3.50.—The Sullivans. 4.20.—Little House on the Prairie. 5.15.—Mr and Mrs 5.45.—News. 6.0.— Thames at 6. 6.35.—Crossroads.

7.0 THE BIONIC WOMAN : The Night Demon. Return of the slow motion Amazon (Lindsay Wagner) who unwisely visits the teepee of an Indian mythology buff.

8.0 ROBIN'S NEST : As Long As He Needs Me. Return of this amiable comedy series set in a bistro run by Richard O'Sullivan.

8.30 ARMCHAIR THRILLER : Rachel In Danger. Second instalment of this new thriller series, in which 11-year-old swot Rachel discovers the body in the cupboard, and the plotting terrorists fall out.

9.0 GEORGE AND MILDRED : Your Money or Your Life. Battling marrieds squabble over insurance. With Yootha Joyce and Brian Murphy. (Repeat.)

9.30 THIS WEEK: Jonathan Dimbleby reports from Ethiopia, now fighting three wars.

10.0 NEWS.

10.30 TIME FOR BUSINESS brought New York women's rights campaigner Gloria Greenberg over to discuss the Equal Pay Act with Barbara Castle. 11.15. — Kitchen Garden: Buyez British! Keith Fordyce and Claire Rayner on planting your own vineyard. 11.45. —What the Papers Say with Peter Paterson. 12.0.—Close.

ITV SOUTHERN, as London except :

1.20.—Southern News. 2.0.—Women Only. 4.20.—Betty Boop. 4.25.—Little House on the Prairie. 5.20.—Crossroads. 6.0.—Day by Day. 6.30.—University Challenge. 7.0.—Emmerdale Farm. 7.30.—Hawaii Five-O. 10.30.—Westside Medical. 11.30.—Southern News Extra. 11.40. —What the Papers Say. 12.0. — Weather; Children, Books and God.

SITUATION 2: CHOOSING A DAY TOUR

Work in pairs or groups of three.

You are staying in Eastbourne and want to go somewhere for the day.
Look through the following Tour Guide and try to find somewhere to go.
One person starts: *'What do you fancy doing today?'*

Hampton Court Palace

This magnificent Palace on the banks of the River Thames was built by Wolsey and presented to King Henry VIII in 1526. At the rear, large additions were made by Wren for King William III, including the attractive Fountain Court. Of particular interest are also the Great Kitchen, the Great Vine and the Wine Cellars, the Maze and the Flower Gardens.

Depart 1000   *Return* 2000   *Fare* **£2·25**

Canterbury

This ancient city whose history can be traced to Roman and Medieval times is dominated by the Cathedral, the building of which was started in the 12th century and continued until the early 15th century. Thomas à Becket was murdered in the Cathedral in 1170 and from that date until King Henry VIII destroyed the Martyr's Shrine it was a place of pilgrimage from all over Europe. The Norman Crypt is the largest in the world.

Depart 0930   *Return* 1730   *Fare* **£1·65**

COACHDAY  Eastbourne Area

Stratford-Upon-Avon

Established as a market in 1196 by King John it has continued as such until modern times. The buildings are predominantly Elizabethan and Jacobean and the whole town forms a natural backcloth to Shakespeare, his times and work.

Depart 0800   *Return* 2200   *Fare* **£3.60**

Windsor and Maidenhead

A delightful way of spending a day is to travel by coach to Windsor and then by river to Boulter's Lock. Tea may be obtained on board during the river trip.

Depart 0900   *Return* 2100   *Fare* **£3·35**

Stonehenge

Situated on Salisbury Plain, Stonehenge is the most famous prehistoric megalithic monument in Britain.

Depart 0715   *Return* 2215   *Fare* **£3·45**

Windsor Safari Park

The Royal Windsor Safari Park is one of the finest wild-life parks in Europe, where young and old may enjoy seeing the many species of animals.

Depart 0900   *Return* 2030   *Fare* **£2·90**

Source: P. Watcyn-Jones, Unit 4, pp. 49–57 from *Impact*. Harmondsworth: Penguin, 1979.
© Peter Watcyn Jones, 1979; line drawings © David Lock, 1979.

3

Current Approaches to Materials Design

3.1 Introduction

The previous chapter identified the most significant factors within the broad concept of the 'communicative approach'. We noted in particular the shift in focus towards the 'real-world' use of language along the dimensions of context, topic, and roles of the people involved. Alongside this there is often a stated requirement for 'authenticity' – a term that loosely implies as close an approximation as possible to the world outside the classroom, in the selection both of language material and of the activities and methods used for practice in the classroom. The issue of 'authenticity' has been somewhat controversial, and there is no space here to go into the complexities of the argument: for readers who wish to do so, Clarke (1989) offers an interesting discussion on the relationship between communicative theory, teaching materials, and the concept of authenticity. We also looked at the redefinition of the place of grammar in language learning, at different attitudes to error and error correction, and by implication at the possible perspectives on teaching and learning, teachers and learners, suggested by the approach. These themes will all reappear in different ways throughout this book.

The present chapter uses a selection of courses produced over the last 10 to 15 years – in other words, as the main communicative debate began to die down – in order to examine the design perspectives that they demonstrate. We shall take some fairly popular courses available on the general market, partly on the argument that if a course is used frequently, then its users probably find it relevant and appropriate. It is not the intention to carry out an evaluation of their inherent quality, but rather to follow through developments and identify trends, in particular the so-called multi-syllabus and the current interest in task-based course design. Readers will again be invited to contextualize the discussion by commenting on materials familiar to them. We shall concentrate particularly on organization and coverage, and on views of learners and learning underpinning current materials, including the growing interest in learner strategies. Towards the end of the chapter we shall look briefly at how some recent ideas in syllabus design have led to rather novel views on the nature of materials.

3.2 New beginnings?

An obvious question, when discussing developments in materials design over the last ten to fifteen years or so, is whether a new 'movement' can be detected – at least in the sense in which proponents of communicative methodology took up a strong position on (even against) the status of grammar as the basis for teaching. Nunan's view (1999: 2) is explicit: 'contemporary practice represents an evolution, and . . . the best practice incorporates the best of "traditional" practice rather than rejecting it.' We need, then, to ask to what extent current materials represent a radical departure from the kinds of criteria set out in chapter 2.

One writer who has taken an explicitly critical view of some of the more extreme forms of the communicative approach is Swan. Much of his argument is directed against the ideas that syllabuses and materials can be based on *either* function *or* form, that meaning can be accounted for *only* on two levels, and that learners do not know how to use the functions of language unless they are taught to do so – as if they had no 'experience and common-sense'. 'Normal students', he claims, 'know what they want to say more often than they know how to say it', since 'unfortunately, grammar has not become any easier to learn since the communicative revolution' (1985: 11, 78). He makes several other specific criticisms. His general view is expressed in the following terms: 'What has happened . . . might be called the "new toy" effect. A limited but valuable insight has been over-generalized, and is presented as if it applied to the whole of language and all of language teaching . . . The "new toy" effect is leading us to look at everything in functional terms . . .' (1985: 7, 81). And finally, 'the Communicative Approach, whatever its virtues, is not really . . . a revolution. In retrospect, it is likely to be seen as little more than an interesting ripple on the surface of twentieth century language teaching' (1985: 87).

Swan is of course right to remind us of the need for teachers to take a critical, or at least a questioning, view of any new movement or set of beliefs claiming to revolutionize our profession. However, much of his criticism is levelled against the more simplistic interpretations of the term 'communicative', and he deliberately overstates his case in order to reinforce his points. In fact the 'retrospect' that Swan invites, taken from the 1990s and into the next millennium, shows that current materials do not constitute a rejection of the 'communicative approach', and no major new movement can be identified, although there have been some very significant developments. Certainly the bases outlined in chapter 2 have not yet been matched by a new set of theories. Some of the rejection has stemmed from criticism of the false polarization of language form and language function, and the 'phrase-book' approach to materials, where a certain use of language (perhaps 'Requesting a service') is offered along with a fixed set of grammatical expressions.

Many of the key principles of the approach have been incorporated into materials, although not necessarily directly. We shall see, for example, how certain aspects have come into more central focus, how others have been re-interpreted depending on teaching objectives, and how more recent insights into the nature of language and language learning have come to join them.

3.3 Some claims for current materials

In the last chapter, we saw that the kinds of statements made in relation to materials by their writers and publishers can serve as a helpful indicator of the principles on which those materials are based.

> Look back at those claims, and compare them with the following, taken from some standard coursebooks of the last few years. Note particularly the terminology used to describe the materials, and compare it with our list in chapter 2.

1 'carefully structured multi-syllabus approach . . . systematic development of all 4 skills . . . emphasis on pronunciation, study skills and vocabulary learning . . . authentic and semi-authentic reading and listening practice . . . language for immediate communication'
2 'thorough, communicative practice of grammatical structures . . . coverage of all the 4 skills . . . comprehensive coverage of the English tense system'
3 'plenty of practice in "core" grammatical structures and deals with language at a deeper level . . . covers all the 4 skills . . . makes students think about the language they are using'
4 'proven multi-syllabus approach . . . careful pacing . . . allowance for different learning styles and teaching situations . . . authentic reading and listening material . . . motivating range of up-to-date topics'
5 'focuses on the real English students will encounter and need to use in today's world . . . regular Grammar sections focus on important grammatical areas at sentence level and above . . . wide cross-section of real texts promotes reading for pleasure, as well as developing functional reading skills . . . word study . . . encourages students to be selective in their vocabulary building'
6 'combines thorough language work with real life skills to give students the confidence and ability to communicate successfully in English'
7 'builds on and expands students' existing knowledge, encourages learner independence and develops fluency, accuracy and confidence'
8 'gives learners a new set of skills and strategies for mastering the language'

It is not difficult to identify some mainstream communicative themes in this selection – real English, authenticity, the sentence *and above*, communication. At the same time there clearly are a number of further elements here. We find more explicit statements about the place of grammar practice; much reference to language skills, including 'study skills'; specific comment on vocabulary learning and pronunciation; and mention of 'styles' and strategies in learning as well as learner independence. For convenience we shall now divide these claims into two broad and related areas: content and learning. Several of them come together in the phrase 'the multi-syllabus approach', which we shall explore in the first of the next two sections.

3.4   Organization and coverage

Multi-syllabus

Teaching materials following a traditional structural approach typically appear as an ordered list of grammatical items – perhaps

1   Simple present active
2   Present continous
3   Simple past

and so on. There is here a single organizing principle that provides the material to be taught and learned in each unit or section of the course. However, it is likely that learners will not only be expected to formulate rules and manipulate structures in a vacuum; they will probably be given a situation or a topic as a context for practice. In other words, even traditional materials may have a *primary* organizing principle (structures) and a *secondary* one (topics, or situations) – see the discussion of syllabus in chapter 1. We might, say, teach the present perfect by asking our students about things they have done or places they have visited; regular activities and habits are often used to teach the simple present. In chapter 2 we saw how the development of the communicative approach not only consolidated a two-tier arrangement (functions and structures), but also opened up the possibility of the principled inclusion of other 'layers' of organization (functions, structures, roles, skills, topics, situations), although, with some exceptions, this was not fully explored in the materials of the time. It is in the last twenty years or so that the idea of a multilayered syllabus has begun to be more explicitly and systematically addressed.

The table of contents on pp. 44–5 – referred to as a 'Map' – is a good illustration of a typical multi-syllabus approach. Look back at the 'communicative' contents page reproduced in chapter 2 on p. 19, and note down some of the similarities and differences you find between the two approaches illustrated.

Map of Book 1

Grammar

Students will learn these grammar points

Phonology

Students will work on these aspects of pronunciation

	Grammar	Phonology
1 to 4	Present tense of *be*; *have got*; *a* and *an*; noun plurals; subject personal pronouns; possessives; possessive *'s* and *s'*; predicative use of adjectives; questions (question word and yes/no); *be* with ages; prepositions of place; *this*; *any* in questions.	Word and sentence stress; rhythm; linking; intonation; consonant clusters; /θ/ and /ð/; /ə/; pronunciation of *'s*; weak form of *from*.
5 to 8	Simple Present tense; *there is/are*; imperatives; *was* and *were* (introduction); countable and uncountable; *some/any*, *much/many* and other quantifiers; *the*; omission of article in generalisations; object personal pronouns; attributive use of adjectives; frequency adverbs; adverbs of degree; prepositions of time, place and distance; omission of article in *at home* etc.; *-ing* for activities; *be* with prices.	Word and sentence stress; rhythm; linking; intonation; weak forms; /ɪ/; /θ/ in ordinals; pronunciations of *the*.
9 to 12	*Have got*; Present Progressive tense (introduction); more Simple Present tense; Simple Past tense; past tense of *be*; *I'd like* + noun phrase / infinitive; *when*-clauses; demonstratives; *be* and *have*; *both* and *all*; *a . . . one*; prepositions of place; *say* and *tell*; *ago*; *What (a) . . . !*	Linking; sentence stress; weak forms; hearing unstressed syllables; rhythm and stress in questions; rising intonation for questions; high pitch for emphasis; stress in negative sentences; stress for contrast; spelling/pronunciation difficulties; /h/; voiced *s* in verb endings; Simple Past endings; strong form of *have*.
13 to 16	*Can*; Present Progressive tense (present and future meanings); *be* with ages and measures; difficult question structures; comparative and superlative adjectives; structures used for comparison; *a bit / much* before comparative adjectives; *good at* + noun/gerund; *look like* + noun phrase; *look* + adjective; *What is . . . like?*; prepositions in descriptions; prepositions of time.	Stress and rhythm recognition and production; decoding rapid speech; hearing unstressed syllables; pronunciations of the letter *a*; pronunciations of the letter *e*; pronunciations of the letter *i*; /ə/ and stress; weak and strong forms of *can* and *can't*; weak forms of *as, than* and *from*; /θ/ in ordinals.
17 to 20	Present Perfect tense; more Simple Past tense; verbs with two objects; *Could you, Why don't we, Let's* and *Shall we* + infinitive without *to*; question words as subjects; elementary reported speech; reply questions; *So . . . I*; *say* and *tell*; *for* and *since*; *How long . . . ?*; *no = not any*; *some* and *something* in offers and requests; article and prepositional usage; sequencing and linking words; *both . . . and*; *neither . . . nor*; *Do you mind if . . . ?*	Decoding rapid speech; linking with initial vowels; contrastive stress; pronunciations of the letter *u*; /ɪ:/ and /ɪ/; polite intonation for requests; rising intonation in reply questions; weak forms of *was* and *were*.
21 to 24	*Going to*; *will*-future; infinitive of purpose; imperatives; conditional structures; structures with *get*; adverbs vs. adjectives; adverbs of manner; paragraph-structuring adverbials; position of *always* and *never* in imperatives.	Spellings of /ɜ:/; 'long' pronunciation of vowel letters before (consonant +) *e*; pronunciations of the letter *o*; /w/; /i:/ and /ɪ/; 'dark' *l* in Future tense contractions; recognition and pronunciation of *going to*; pronunciation of *won't*.

Swan (1985: 79) justifies this approach in the following terms:

When deciding what to teach to a particular group of learners, we need to take into consideration several different meaning categories and several different formal categories. We must make sure that our students are taught to operate key

Functions	Topics and notions	Skills
Students will learn to	**Students will learn to talk about**	The Student's Book and Practice Book between them provide regular practice of the basic 'four skills'. Special skills taught or practised at Level 1 include decoding rapid colloquial speech, reading and listening for specific information, writing longer sentences, writing paragraphs, writing friendly letters, writing friendly letters and notes, and filling in forms.
Greet; introduce; begin conversations with strangers; participate in longer conversations; say goodbye; ask for and give information; identify themselves and others; describe people; ask for repetition; enquire about health; apologise; express regret; distinguish levels of formality; spell and count.	People's names; age; marital status; national origin; addresses; jobs; health; families; physical appearance; relationships; numbers and letters; approximation; place.	

Vocabulary

Students will learn 900 or more common words and expressions during Level 1 of the course.

Functions	Topics and notions
Ask for and give information, directions, personal data, and opinions; describe places; indicate position; express likes and dislikes; tell the time; complain; participate in longer conversations; express politeness.	Addresses; phone numbers; furniture; houses and flats; work; leisure occupations and interests; food and drink; prices; likes and dislikes; preferences; things in common and differences; days of the week; ordinal numbers; existence; time; place; relative position; generalisation; countability; quantification; degree; frequency; routines.
Ask for and give information; describe people and things, and ask for descriptions; talk about resemblances; greet; make arrangements to meet; ask for information about English; make and reply to offers and requests; narrate; shop; make travel enquiries and hotel bookings; change money.	People's appearances; clothing; families; colours; parts of the body; relationships; physical and emotional states; clothes; places; prices; sizes; people's pasts; history; poverty; happiness; racism; childhood; growing up; resemblance.
Compare; ask for and give information and opinions; describe and compare people; speculate; make and reply to requests; invite and reply; describe and speculate about activities; plan; count (ordinals); telephone.	Abilities; physical characteristics and qualities; weights and measures; numbers (cardinal and ordinal); ages; personalities; professions; names of months; future plans; the weather; holidays; places; travel; time; similarities and differences; temporary present and future actions and states.
Request and reply; borrow; suggest; agree, disagree and negotiate; invite and reply; narrate; report what people have said; ask for, give and refuse permission; show interest; compare; ask for and give information and opinions; distinguish levels of formality; ask for information about English; start conversations; make arrangements to meet; order food *etc.* in a restaurant.	Holidays; going out; food and drink; daily routines; historical personalities; people's careers; interests and habits; likes and dislikes; contrast; sequence; past time; frequency; duration up to the present; similarity.
Talk about plans; make predictions; guess; make suggestions; express sympathy; give instructions; give advice; predict; warn; announce intentions; raise and counter objections; narrate.	Houses; seasons; holidays; places; plans; health and illness; sports; machines; horoscopes; danger; purpose; intention; manner; the future.

Source: M. Swan and C. Walter, Map of Book 1, pp. iv and v from *New Cambridge English Course*. Cambridge: Cambridge University Press, 1990. © Cambridge University Press, 1990.

functions ... to talk about basic *notions* ... to communicate appropriately in specific *situations* ... to discuss the *topics* which correspond to their main interests and needs ... At the same time, we shall need to draw up a list of *phonological* problems ... of high priority *structures*, and of the *vocabulary* which our students will need to learn. In addition, we will need a syllabus of *skills* ...

At first sight this is a complex, if rich, view of materials design, because several (in this case, eight) syllabus possibilities are in play. Not only do the details have to be specified for each individual organizing principle, but the principles themselves then have to be linked in a systematic way that does not leave the learner faced with a number of separate lists of items. A more straight-forward way of looking at this kind of multi-syllabus is to see it in terms of a merging of two broad approaches. One of these is concerned with a view of language in use, and includes categories of function, context and language skill. The other is a version of a more formal linguistic syllabus, which comprises elements of grammar, pronunciation, and vocabulary. Obviously these two approaches are not mutually exclusive: pronunciation and vocabulary, for instance, can both be practised in a context of use, or alternatively can be rehearsed in isolation. What a multi-syllabus does is to build on a range of communicative criteria at the same time as acknowledging the need to provide systematic practice in the formal properties of language.

In passing we can recall the earlier argument that current approaches have grown out of those immediately preceding them, and have not on the whole developed from a complete break with the past. Elements of the multi-syllabus idea can be traced in some of the explicitly 'communicative' writing of the 1970s. Johnson, for example (1982, though written before this date), uses the terms 'uni-dimensional' and 'multi-dimensional' to denote types of syllabus, and discusses three possible dimensions of organization – functions, settings, and notions. The focus here was certainly on semantic criteria: nevertheless, the teaching materials derived from this perspective (Morrow and Johnson, 1980) have both communicative and formal elements, and include work on functions, settings, roles, and grammar.

The lexical syllabus

In the approach to materials design that has been discussed here, we have seen that the two general headings of 'semantic' (or 'language in use', or 'functional', or 'pragmatic') and 'formal' are broken down into a number of components, each of which can generate a set of syllabus items. Thus 'topics' might include talking about class members and their families, interests and hobbies, different countries, world news, weather and so on. Pronunciation (or 'phonology') can cover individual sounds, minimal pairs, sentence stress, weak forms, intonation, and several other features. While some coursebooks have taken the whole spread of organizing principles, others have chosen to give particular emphasis to specific areas. One area that has recently received considerable attention is that of vocabulary, or lexis.

The teaching of vocabulary is a very large topic, and we shall restrict ourselves here to commenting briefly on its role in some current coursebooks. (For more discussion, see chapter 6 for more details, and see D. Willis, 1990.) Most of us – whether as learners or teachers – have experience of classrooms where practising vocabulary means learning lists of words, not always in relation to a real-world context and sometimes in the form of two columns, with a mother tongue equivalent for the foreign language word. We have probably noticed that vocabulary approached in this way is not always efficiently remembered and reused. It is typical of many current coursebooks that they are concerned (a) to rationalize vocabulary as content, in other words, to establish a principled framework and a set of contexts within which vocabulary development can take place, and (b) to base teaching on an understanding of the psychological mechanisms whereby people learn and remember lexical items. We shall comment on the background to the second of these in the next section. As far as the first point is concerned, we can note that it is unusual to find merely a list of words to be learned by rote: the multi-syllabus concept means that vocabulary is selected according to the other dimensions on which the materials are built. For example, *Signature* (Phillips and Sheerin, 1990) takes three large-scale categories in sequence, and then subdivides each, linking the vocabulary practice directly to the subtopics, as follows (only a few examples are given under each heading):

1 *People:*
   nationalities
   languages
   personal information

2 *The world around us*:
   travel
   medicine
   house and home

3 *Past, present, future*:
   education
   the media
   the world of the future

As with a number of other courses, this is linked to work in grammar and pronunciation, and involves different language skills.

For most of us, of course, 'vocabulary' also means using a dictionary. A new dictionary for learners of English was published in 1987. The dictionary is called COBUILD, which stands, rather technically, for the 'Collins [Publisher] – Birmingham University International Language Database'. It is based on an extremely large corpus of language of many millions of words, stored on a computer database. Sources of data are both the spoken and written language, and include magazines, books, broadcasts, conversations and many more. The philosophy of the dictionary is to provide 'above all a guide to ordinary everyday English', and frequency of occurrence is a key criterion for inclusion. It focuses particularly on the most common 2,000 to 3,000 words, the 'powerhouse of the language', and the examples given in the dictionary entries are taken from the source material. Both the philosophy and the database of the dictionary have led to an approach to materials design that is usually termed the 'lexical syllabus'. One course based directly on the COBUILD work covers about 2,500 words over the three levels of the course (Collins, 1989). Its central claim is that the lexical database provides 'a rich input of *real* language', thus giving authenticity and context to the tasks and exercises. Each unit has a set of lexical objectives, so that by the end of unit 15 ('Newspapers') of the third level, for example, students should have learned 44 new words, making a cumulative total of 625 for this level so far. (In this particular unit, items include 'arrest', 'bomb', 'criticize', 'explode', 'explosion', 'headline', 'identity', 'target', 'violence' etc.) COBUILD has subsequently spawned a good deal of further practice material, in particular on grammar and usage.

The task-based approach

Approaches to task-based learning (TBL) can be seen as a significant further evolution of communicative language teaching, both in terms of views of language in use and the development of classroom methodology. Although teachers have been operating with the notion for some time, it is only in recent years that frameworks have become more explicit and formalized. J. Willis (1996: 23) offers a simple definition: 'tasks are always activities where the target language is used by the learner for a communicative purpose . . . *in order to achieve an outcome*' (italics added). In other words, TBL is goal-oriented, leading to a 'solution' or a 'product'. Nunan (1989, cited in 1999: 25) makes a further distinction between 'real-world' and 'pedagogical' tasks, the latter defined as 'a piece of classroom work that involves learners in comprehending, manipulating, producing, or interacting in the target language while their attention is focused on mobilizing their grammatical knowledge in order to express meaning, and in which the intention is to convey meaning rather than manipulate form.'

Despite this emphasis on communication and interaction, it is important to note that the TBL approach is concerned with accuracy as well as fluency. It achieves this most obviously through the TBL framework, which has three key phases:

1   the pre-task phase, which includes work on introducing the topic, finding relevant language and so on
2   the task cycle itself
3   language focus.

As Willis notes (ibid: 55), 'to avoid the risk of learners achieving fluency at the expense of accuracy and to spur on language development, another stage is needed after the task itself'. TBL, then, takes a holistic view of language in use. Willis also offers an extensive set of suggestions for task possibilities, from simple to complex, and also shows how mainstream textbooks can be adapted to introduce tasks. A simple task may require learners just to make lists (for example, 'the features of a famous place'); more complex tasks may incorporate simulation and problem-solving, such as how to plan a dinner menu on a limited budget (Willis's examples).

Before leaving this section, it is worth noting that TBL has also generated some critical comment. Seedhouse (1999), for instance, whilst not rejecting the approach outright, used TBL lesson transcripts, which, he claimed, showed that language use is not always particularly rich, with some tendency to 'minimalisation' and rather limited discourse. His conclusion is that TBL needs to be incorporated into language pedagogy but should not be the sole approach used.

> Examine the following task from a mainstream coursebook. Try to characterize the nature of the task, and comment on its design from the point of view of both 'fluency' and 'accuracy'.

Part B **Task**

Prepare a review or entertainment guide

Task link: 'extreme' adjectives

Personal vocabulary

Preparation for task

1 The words in the box are all things you might hear on the radio. Complete the gaps in the sentences below with one of the words.

| review | phone-in | entertainment guide | advert |

a   An .... tries to persuade people to buy goods or services.

b   In a .... a critic gives his / her opinion of a new film, book, play, etc.

c   In a .... people call the radio station to express their opinions or ask questions.

d   An .... tells you where and when you can see films, concerts, etc.

2 [6.5] You are going to hear four extracts from radio programmes. Listen and write what each extract is, using a word from the box in Exercise 1.

a ....   b ....   c ....   d ....

3 Listen again and answer the following questions.

a   What three types of music are mentioned in the entertainment guide?
b   What other form of entertainment does she talk about?
c   What kind of film is being advertised?
d   What is the phone-in about?
e   Is the reviewer talking about a book, a play or a film? Is she generally positive or negative about it?

Task

1 You are going to prepare an item for a radio programme. You can choose:

Either: a review of a television programme, film, video, play, concert or CD that you have seen or heard recently.

or: an entertainment guide to cinemas, theatres, concerts, etc. in your local area, or a guide to programmes on television over the next few days.

Make your choice and then read the appropriate instructions.

Entertainment guide

• Work in pairs. Try to choose programmes, films, plays, etc. that you think will interest the other students. If possible, choose things that you know something about. Include both factual information and reasons why you recommend it.

• Spend about fifteen minutes preparing your entertainment guide. Do *not* write it out word for word, but make notes about what you are going to say. Look at the phrases in the *Useful language* box. Ask your teacher about any words or phrases you need and write them in the *Personal vocabulary* box.

Useful language

"If you like ... you should try / go to / see ..."

"It's on at ..."

"It starts / finishes at ..."

"It's about ..."

"It stars ... "

"It's written / directed by ...".

"It looks good / interesting / exciting / unusual / fun ..."

"There are ... performances every day. Tickets are on sale at ..."

"You can get more information from ..."

Useful language

"It's about ..."

"It stars ..."

"It's set in ..."

"It was written / directed / produced by ..."

"The story / acting / photography is ... excellent / not very good ..."

"The thing I liked best about it was ..."

"Another thing I really liked was ..."

"The thing I didn't like was ..."

"I'd recommend it to people who like ..."

Review

• Work on your own. Try to choose a programme, film, etc. that you think will interest the other students. (Ideally it will be something recent.) Include both factual information (where you saw it / what it's about / who's in it, etc.) and your opinion of it.

• Spend about fifteen minutes preparing your review. Do *not* write it out word for word, but make notes about what you are going to say. Look at the phrases in the *Useful language* box. Ask your teacher about any words or phrases you need and write them in the *Personal vocabulary* box.

2 *Either:* present your review or entertainment guide to the class. The other students should listen and note down:

• which films, programmes, etc. they would like to see.
• any questions they would like to ask.

or: make a radio programme of your own called *News and Reviews*. Record your entertainment guides and reviews onto a cassette. Decide:

• what order to put the items in.
• who is going to be the radio announcer and what he / she will say.

Optional writing

Write a review of the film, play, etc. you have already described, or another one you are interested in.

Source: S. Cunningham and P. Moor, pp. 64–5 from *Cutting Edge: Intermediate, Students' Book*. Harlow: Longman, 1999. © Longman, 1999. Used by permission of Pearson Education Ltd.

In this section we have discussed the principle of the multi-syllabus, have shown how some coursebooks have highlighted vocabulary as one particular area of design, and have commented on the task-based approach as an important area of development. In the next section we shall turn our attention to ways in which current approaches view the learners themselves.

3.5   *Learners and learning*

There are a number of ways in which current coursebook design is concerned in general terms with a perspective on 'the learner', as well as with the language material itself. These ways can be grouped as follows:

1   Although the majority of learners study in the environment of a whole class, and often in a large one, an analysis of the characteristics of learners as individuals can offer a helpful view on the construction of materials and methods.
2   Learners will naturally need to engage in the process of both comprehending and producing language. In doing this they use a range of strategies, some of which are probably shared by all language users, whether learning a foreign language or using their mother tongue.

The first of these perspectives is normally characterized by the concept of 'individual differences'; the second is studied under the headings of both language acquisition and learning strategies. Skehan (1989) points out that the one is a view of *differences*, the other of *similarities* and *universals*. Both perspectives have come into some prominence as factors affecting materials design, and we shall briefly survey each of them in turn.

Learners

In the previous section on the organization and content of current materials, we did not discuss in any detail the selection of topics for language practice, whether for discussion, or comprehension, or writing. We have chosen to start this section with them because they are the most obvious way in which learners' needs and interests can be taken into account. The possibilities for topic choice are potentially so wide that a meaningful classification is difficult. Themes may or may not be drawn from a source of 'authentic' language data; they may come from the field of world affairs, or medicine, or sport, from social and family life, from everyday topics, and from other areas too many to enumerate. Here is a small selection of themes taken from some of the coursebooks used as examples in the preceding section. You might like to consider whether such topics would be relevant for your own learners, and whether learning context determines topic choice. For instance, materials appropriate for students in an English-speaking environment – social situations, travelling, everyday 'survival' – may not be applicable in other educational settings, and vice versa:

Travelling	Clothes	Historical people
Dangerous animals	Music and singing	Driving
Food and drink	Health and illness	The environment
Dreams and fears	Television	The role of computers
Money	Racism	Leisure time
Relationships	Education	Getting old

Topics in this form are listed as content, as material to be covered. Some coursebook writers, however, even if they themselves make the initial selection, prefer to help learners to develop their language proficiency by devising techniques for personalizing these topics. One set of materials (*Third Dimension* and *Fourth Dimension*) made this into a design principle. The authors defined the term 'dimension' rather differently from the way it was used in the previous section to designate a component of a multi-syllabus. Their 'dimension' was what they called 'expressivity'. It went beyond the other (important) dimensions of accuracy, fluency and intelligibility: 'expressivity means not only the ability to say and write things fairly clearly, accurately and fluently but also to express what you really want to express and to give some real depth to that expression. Depth comes from a knowledge of choices in language' (O'Neill, 1989). Expressivity, it was claimed, helps learners to 'take off', and to achieve independence and personal involvement in their use of language. The aim of personalization was linked directly to grammar practice and vocabulary building across all the language skills. Techniques included interpreting pictures introducing the theme of a unit, imagining one's own thoughts and actions in certain situations, commenting on one's own culture, advising others, finishing a story, and many more.

> What kinds of topics could you personalize in this way with your own students? The materials just discussed include loneliness, honesty, friendship, success and failure, love, sport and violence. Are these appropriate for your own classroom?

Topics, of course, are by no means the only way in which attention can be paid to the learners themselves. Although for most teachers, especially those faced with big classes, the goal of large-scale individualization of instruction is not a very realistic one, some differences between learners can be taken into account in a limited way. The third part of this book will explore the possibilities in more detail. Here we shall simply highlight the 'individual differences' that appear to be significant in current materials.

Researchers in the psychology of second language learning have investigated a number of learner characteristics that have implications for the language classroom. An understanding of such characteristics, or 'variables', can make it possible for teachers and materials designers to adjust and vary certain aspects of the classroom to allow for the different individuals in it. Skehan (1989) and S. H. McDonough (1986), for example, suggest the following key learner variables:

- *Personality:* learners may be quiet, or extrovert, for instance
- *Motivation:* learners may have chosen to learn; they may be obliged to take a course or an examination; they may or may not perceive the relevance of material
- *Attitude:* learners have attitudes to learning, to the target language, and to classrooms
- *Aptitude:* some people seem more readily able than others to learn another language
- *Preferred learning styles:* some learners are more comfortable in a spoken language situation, others prefer written material
- *Intelligence*

We are not concerned here with the relationships between these factors. This is an interesting and complex issue, which readers can follow up in the references provided.

Some of the dimensions along which individuals vary, particularly intelligence, do not have an obvious effect on language learning potential. Others are difficult to measure, and certainly to change: it is not normally considered part of a teacher's role to try to adjust students' personalities. Yet others, such as motivation, can more obviously be affected by the learning environment. What we should note, in other words, is that some individual differences can have an influence on language instruction, and others can be influenced by it. A distinction also needs to be made between the possible effects of the coursebook and those of the structure and management of the classroom itself.

Several of the English language teaching materials now available attempt to incorporate some consideration of learner characteristics into their methodology. As far as variables differentiating between learners are concerned, mention is made most frequently of differences in learning styles. The pedagogic response to this is to allow in a principled way for variety, especially in content and in language skills, and to build in suggestions for variability in pacing – the speed at which learners are able to work through the material. Pacing, in turn, implies a concern for aptitude, a factor that interests all teachers even if no formal measurement of aptitude is available. We also find reference to the importance of understanding learners' attitudes. As one coursebook puts it, 'Students have their own ideas about language learning. Up to a point, these must be respected . . . however, learners sometimes resist important and useful activities which do not fit in with their preconceptions, and this can hinder progress' (Swan and Walter, 1990: viii). In other words, students may have expectations, perhaps about the role of correction, or about pronunciation, and ignoring them will certainly have an adverse effect on motivation.

As mentioned earlier, most of the teaching we do is to learners in a class with others, so all materials necessarily have to be a compromise, as do teachers' interpretations of materials.

> Taking the individual differences discussed in this section, to what extent do you think they influence your own teaching, and how far can you, as a teacher, influence them? Compare your observations if possible with someone who works in a different educational environment.

Learning processes and strategies

Some readers will be familiar with the terms 'learning' and 'acquisition'. Except to note that, in the psychological literature, they conventionally distinguish more conscious and logical processes from the spontaneous nature of acquisition, particularly by children (S. H. McDonough, 1986: 95), we shall not make use of the distinction here and shall continue to refer to 'learning'. The purpose of this subsection is simply to introduce what have arguably been the most significant approaches to materials design and classroom practice in recent years. Details of learning skills and processes in particular are the subject of much of Part II of this book; and the strategies work is taken up again in Part III, in the discussion of learner autonomy and learner training.

This can be considered as typical of an earlier approach to reading comprehension where the text might, for example, be about the life of a famous person, and the questions are there to find out whether the text has been understood. ('Mr X was born in Edinburgh in 1835.' Question: 'When was Mr X born?') Such a format is more like a *test* of comprehension, and does not itself *teach* the learners any strategies for understanding the passage. Alternatively, learners were often required to *translate* the English text into their mother tongue. Despite new ways of analysing and describing language material, it took some time for our profession to turn its attention to the psychology of learning, particularly in relation to the comprehension skills of reading and, subsequently, listening. A 'test' or 'translation' method clearly tries to check that learners have understood a particular piece of language, but does little to develop techniques that can be transferred to other texts. Currently, then, there is a growing concern to ensure that practice is given in activating these generalizable skills that are believed to represent underlying (even universal) processes for all language users. Thus the reading skill, for instance, as we shall see in chapter 6, is seen in terms of a number of different 'subskills', such as reading for general information, scanning, skimming and so on. These subskills or strategies can then be used as the basis for specific tasks and exercises in a lesson. It is important to note that 'comprehension' is therefore no longer just a way of doing more grammar practice

Text

Questions

1.
2.
3.

Figure 3.1 Traditional approach to reading comprehension.

using a text, but opens up a perspective on psychological text-processing mechanisms.

Let us look at how some current materials make use of this perspective. The subskills of comprehension most frequently found are

1 Reading/listening for the general idea, or 'gist'. In relation to reading, this is sometimes referred to as 'skimming'.
2 Looking for specific items of information (or 'scanning' for details).
3 Predicting, or anticipating what is coming next.
4 Making inferences or deductions when a 'fact' cannot simply be identified.

These skills are practised through a number of exercises and techniques. For example, we find various activities to be carried out before reading; activities that require different groups in the class to share different information; questions in the middle of a text to help with anticipation; and true–false questions that require learners to combine two or more parts of a text before they can answer. Overall we can observe that different kinds of texts and different reasons for reading or listening can be allowed for in the methodology used. The aim is not primarily to ensure that every word and every grammatical structure are understood – there are more efficient ways of doing this – but to equip learners with useful and transferable skills.

Finally, we should comment on a further dimension of the concept of a 'skill'. The kinds of strategies discussed above have developed from general work in the psychology of language processing which need not necessarily be applied to questions of language *learning*. Most teachers are also concerned with the *conscious* skills their students need in order to learn as efficiently as possible. With this in mind, we find that increasing attention is being paid to two related areas. The first of these is usually referred to under the heading of 'study skills', the second of 'learning strategies'.

Study skills can be thought of as a range of learnable and practical techniques that help students to adopt more effective methods of study. In the area of

English language teaching known as English for Specific Purposes (ESP) the concept is very well developed, particularly for students studying their own specialism through the medium of English where a mastery of a large number of academic-related skills is very important. In terms of general English coursebooks, study skills have a more restricted scope. The most frequently practised skill is that of using a monolingual dictionary. Learners are taught, for example, to understand the different parts of a dictionary entry, to select relevant information from a longer entry, and to recognize the significance of word parts, especially prefixes. Other skills include keeping a vocabulary book containing definitions and examples in English as well as (or instead of) the mother tongue equivalent, and sometimes the wider reference skills involved in using the different sections – contents page, index and so on – of a textbook.

The second area – learning strategies – owes much to research that analyses the components of successful language learning and offers definitions of a 'good language learner'. 'Success' is thought to be based on such factors as checking one's performance in a language, being willing to guess and to 'take risks' with both comprehension and production, seeking out opportunities to practise, developing efficient memorizing strategies, and many others. Many current materials draw on this research, and incorporate practice in 'good learner' strategies across all language skills, often asking learners to be explicit about their own approach to learning so as to be able to evaluate its efficiency for them.

The available literature on learning strategies has grown enormously in recent years, covering strategies and skills, methods for researching strategy use, universality and individuality, strategy 'teachability' and so on. Cohen (1998: 12) cautions that 'the effectiveness of strategies may depend largely on the characteristics of the given learner, the given language structure(s), the given context, or the interaction of these'. Clear discussion of various aspects of strategy research of particular interest to the language teacher can be found in Wenden and Rubin (1987), Oxford (1990), who offers a comprehensive list of strategies under such headings as metacognitive, cognitive, social and affective, and S. H. McDonough's (1999) accessible 'state of the art' paper on current perspectives.

There has only been space here to look briefly at approaches to materials design drawn from various aspects of the literature on the psychology of language learning. We conclude the chapter by commenting on a rather different focus altogether.

3.6   The 'process' syllabus

This final short section is really concerned with an approach to syllabus rather than materials design, and much though not all of the work is as yet experimental. The most common labels attached to this kind of syllabus design proposal are 'process', 'task based', and 'procedural' (we shall not discuss the internal distinctions here). The essence of all of them is described by Breen: 'One of the major sources of impetus for the recent interest in alternative methodologies has been an intensified theoretical and research focus upon the language learning process and, in particular, the contributions of the learner to that process' (1987: 159). In other words, the focus is on 'how' rather than 'what'. This is obviously true (up to a point) of the discussion in the preceding section, but the 'process syllabus' concept takes the claim further. Most importantly, it contains the far-reaching implication that syllabuses cannot be fully worked out in advance but must evolve as learners' problems and developing competence gradually emerge. The idea of project work, for example, where only the outline of the task is specified, is based on this view. Course design is therefore more likely to start with a 'bank' of possible tasks rather than a tightly controlled set of contents, whether that content is based on linguistic or psychological criteria.

This approach to syllabus design has been worked out in detail by Prabhu (1987), whose 'procedural' syllabus was based on a classroom experiment in India (the so-called 'Bangalore Project'). He lists three categories of problem-solving tasks:

1 *Information-gap activities:* for example where each person in a pair has only part of the required information.
2 *Reasoning-gap activities:* for example making a decision or an inference based on given information.
3 *Opinion-gap activities:* for example taking part in a discussion of an issue, or completing a story.

'Materials' from this point of view, then, become sources for the development of tasks and are only loosely, not fully, preconstructed: Prabhu refers to this as a 'simple', not a 'sophisticated' syllabus. He regards tightly structured materials as restrictive, and is particularly critical of the 'multi-syllabus', and indeed of any syllabus approach that is 'materials-driven'. These are challenging ideas that potentially give teachers more responsibility in classroom decision-making and that arguably involve them more directly in the learning development of their students.

3.7 Conclusion

We said earlier in the chapter that it was not our purpose to evaluate particular teaching materials. However, it is worth noting the rather critical comments made by Tomlinson et al. (2001) concerning trends in current coursebooks. They express disappointment that learning styles are not much catered for, and comment that an increasing prominence given to grammar is paralleled by a decreasing attention to skills, functions, communication and learning strategies. Their conclusion is that 'there seems to be a reaction against the freer, open-ended, learner-centred days of the communicative approach', with a 'focus on teaching rather than learning' (87). Readers may wish to compare their own assessment with this rather negative view.

This chapter has discussed a number of important growth areas in materials since the 'communicative revolution' of the 1970s. We looked first at the concept of a multi-syllabus, where a number of components are interwoven, touched on the lexical syllabus, and examined the current focus on task-based learning. We then commented on the increasing interest in various areas of the psychology of language learning and language use, both in the characteristics of individuals and in underlying processes and strategies. Clearly not all coursebooks incorporate all the elements that have been covered here, and it would probably not be appropriate for them to do so. They are design principles, and cannot have equal and universal applicability: as we have seen, different teaching situations have different requirements and expectations. The final two chapters in this part of the book will discuss procedures for evaluating and adapting general design criteria for specific contexts.

1 Consider again Swan's eight headings for the divisions of a syllabus: Grammar, Functions, Notions, Situations, Pronunciation, Skills, Vocabulary, Topics. In your own teaching situation, are all of these equally relevant?
2 When you have decided which headings you would include/exclude, list a few items under each category, and sketch out some ideas for how you might relate them to each other. For example, you might decide to select Functions, Grammar, Skills, Vocabulary. You might then include

• Giving advice (functions)
• Modal verbs (grammar)
• Conversation (skill)
• Topic areas (education, health, i.e., vocabulary)

3.8 Further reading

1 Cook, V. J. (2001): *Second Language Learning and Language Teaching*. Relates various aspects of learning processes to the classroom context.
2 Johnson, K. (1982): 'Units of organization for a semantic syllabus'. Chapter 4 of *Communicative Syllabus Design and Methodology*. This is a useful analysis of some of the possibilities for constructing a 'multilayered' syllabus.
3 McDonough, S. H. (1999): 'Learner Strategies,' for an overview of strategy research and its applicability to teaching.
4 Willis, J. (1996): *A Framework for Task-Based Learning*. Contains definitions, discussion of principles and procedures, and many practical examples.

4

Evaluating ELT Materials

4.1 Introduction

The ability to evaluate teaching materials effectively is a very important profes-sional activity for all EFL teachers and in this chapter we shall examine the reasons why teachers need to evaluate materials in the first instance. We shall then move on to discuss the criteria that can be used to evaluate materials by suggesting a working model which we hope will be an effective one to use for teachers working in a variety of contexts. The model that we suggest is based on the view that it is useful for us as teachers to perform an external evaluation of materials first of all in order to gain an overview of the organizational principles involved. After this we move on to a detailed internal evaluation of the materials to see how far the materials in question match up to what the author claims as well as to the aims and objectives of a given teaching programme.

4.2 The context of evaluation

Let us look at why we need to evaluate materials in the first place. Cunningsworth (1984) suggests that there are very few teachers who do not use published course materials at some stage in their teaching career. Many of us find that it is something that we do very regularly in our professional lives. We may wish at this stage to make a distinction between teaching situations where 'open-market' materials are chosen on the one hand, and where a Ministry of Education (or some similar body) produces materials that are subsequently passed on to the teacher for classroom use on the other.

The nature of the evaluation process in each of these scenarios will prob-ably differ as well. In the first type of situation teachers may have quite a large amount of choice in the materials they select, perhaps being able to liaise freely with colleagues and a Director of Studies / Principal with respect to this material. However, there are many situations around the world where teachers in fact get a very limited choice or perhaps no choice at all, and this second scenario mentioned above may well obtain for teachers who are 'handed' materials by a Ministry or a Director and have to cope as best they can within this framework. This situation will more than likely involve teachers in an understanding of why the materials have been written in such a way and how they can make effective use of them in the classroom. For the vast majority of teachers working in the first situation, that of having a good deal of choice in the selection of appropriate materials, writing their own materials can be very time consuming and not necessarily cost-effective; hence the need to be able to discriminate effectively between all the coursebooks on the market. Today there is a wealth of EFL material available, with literally hundreds of new, commercially available titles appearing every year in the English-speaking countries. Brumfit (1980) writes about how there is no *Which?* (a British magazine that reviews consumer products) for textbooks, and that putting a book on the market implies that the book has been cleared of basic faults. However, this is not always the case.

Another fairly typical factor to consider is that teachers or course organizers are often under considerable professional and financial pressure to select a coursebook for an ELT programme that will then become *the* textbook for years to come. Added to this pressure is the fact that in many contexts materials are often seen as being the core of a particular programme and are often the most visible representation of what happens in the classroom. Even though some practitioners may take issue with O'Neill's comment that 'no other medium is as easy to use as a book' (1982: 107), the reality for many is that the book may be the only choice open to them. The evaluation of current materials therefore merits serious consideration as an inappropriate choice may waste funds and time, not to mention the demotivating effect that it would have on students and possibly other colleagues.

For some teachers the selection of a good textbook can be valuable, particularly in contexts where the assimilation of stimulating, authentic materials can be difficult to organize. Other teachers working with materials given to them by a Ministry or similar body will clearly have some different issues to contend with. They may, for example, have to work with materials they find very limiting, and will probably need to resort to adapting these materials as best they can to suit the needs of their particular context. (See the next chapter for a full discussion of materials adaptation.) Even though such teachers will not have to evaluate to adopt materials, they may well be interested in evaluation as a useful process in its own right, giving insight into the organizational principles of the materials and helping them to keep up with developments in the field. This in turn can help the teacher to focus on realistic ways of adapting the materials to a particular group of learners where pertinent. Chambers notes how many people may be involved in textbook selection and shows how it is not always an easy task to select materials. He suggests using management techniques (1997: 30) so that everyone involved in the process can contribute.

We have assumed that as teachers we all use published teaching materials. What do you feel are the reasons for this? What are teaching materials expected to achieve and how might they do it? Could we ever teach a foreign language without published materials? Is it ever possible for everything we need for a course to be contained in one textbook?

No textbook or set of materials is likely to be perfect and even though 'it is clear that coursebook assessment is fundamentally a subjective, rule-of-thumb activity, and that no neat formula, grid or system will ever provide a definite yardstick' (Sheldon, 1988: 245), we nonetheless need some model for hard-pressed teachers or course planners that will be brief, practical to use and yet comprehensive in its coverage of criteria, given that everyone in the field will need to evaluate materials at some time or other. We hope to do this by offering a model that distinguishes the purpose behind the evaluation – be it to 'keep up to date with current developments' or to adopt/select materials for a given course. As Cunningsworth (1995: 5) notes, 'it is important to limit the number of criteria used, the number of questions asked, to manageable proportions. Otherwise we risk being swamped in a sea of detail.' Tomlinson (1999: 11) also suggests that 'the obvious but important point is that there can be no one model framework for the evaluation of materials; the framework used must be deter-mined by the reasons, objectives and circumstances of the evaluation'.

In the first instance, teachers may be interested in the evaluation exercise for its own sake. For example, we may wish to review all the materials that have come out during a given period of time and require some criteria with which to assess these materials. In doing this, we may of course find materials suitable for adoption/selection at some future date. For teachers wishing to select, however, this distinction is clearly important since there is no point in doing a full evalu-ation for selection purposes if a preliminary evaluation can show that those materials will be of little use for a particular group.

We thus examine criteria in two stages; an external evaluation that offers a brief 'overview' of the materials from the outside (cover, introduction, table of contents), which is then followed by a closer and more detailed internal evalu-ation. We cannot be absolutely certain as to what criteria and constraints are actually operational in ELT contexts worldwide and some teachers might argue that textbook criteria often are very local. We may cite examples of teachers who are involved in the evaluation process. One teacher from a secondary school in Europe is able to 'trial' a coursebook with her students for two weeks before officially adopting it. Some secondary school teachers in Japan team-teach their classes with native speakers and are able to evaluate materials jointly with them. However, as we pointed out in chapter 1, we are attempting to look at areas where our professional framework shares similar interests and con-cerns, and with this in mind the criteria that we shall examine here will be as comprehensive as possible for the majority of ELT situations on a worldwide basis. Of course the evaluation process is never static; when materials are deemed appropriate for a particular course after a preliminary evaluation, their ultimate success or failure may only be determined after a certain amount of classroom use (summative evaluation).

> 1 In chapter 1 we looked at the educational framework in which we all work. With reference to this, you might like to think about who actually evaluates materials in your educational system; i.e., what is the role of published materials and therefore the role of evaluation? Do teachers do it (by themselves, jointly with other teachers/students?), or does the Ministry of Education choose or write the materials for you?
> 2 You might also like to think about the criteria you used to select the ELT materials you are using at the moment. Or, if you did not select the materials, think about the criteria you would use. Discuss your answers with a colleague if at all possible. Did you select the same criteria? Note down your answers because we shall refer to them again at the end of this chapter to see how far the criteria you mention overlap with ours.

4.3   The external evaluation

In this central stage of the model we have included criteria that will provide a comprehensive, external overview of how the materials have been organized. Our aim is basically that of examining the organization of the materials as stated explicitly by the author/publisher by looking at

- the 'blurb', or the claims made on the cover of the teacher's/students' book
- the introduction and table of contents

that should enable the evaluator to assess what Cunningsworth (1984: 2) has termed 'what the books say about themselves'. We also find it useful to scan the table of contents page in that it often represents a 'bridge' between the external claim made for the materials and what will actually be presented 'inside' the materials themselves. At this stage we need to consider why the materials have been produced. Presumably because the author/publisher feels that there is a gap in the existing market that these materials are intended to fill: so we shall have to investigate this further to see whether the objectives have been clearly spelt out. To illustrate what we mean, here is an example of one such 'blurb' taken from a well-known EFL textbook from the 1970s:

> for upper-intermediate and more advanced students interested in *using* language rather than learning more about structure. Students at these levels often have a very good knowledge of English structure and vocabulary but cannot apply their knowledge to communicate effectively . . . introduces the major communicative functions for which language is used and provides stimulating presentation and practice material.

It appears, therefore, that this textbook is aiming at the higher proficiency student who has a very good 'usage' background but needs a course that will activate language use. Later, when the evaluator investigates the organization of the materials he or she will have to ascertain whether or not this is really the case.

Let us see the types of claim that can be made for materials in the introduction. The following example is part of the introduction taken from a recent EFL series. We have italicized certain terms and key concepts that we feel need further investigation:

> This book is intended for *good intermediate level* students who have already got a *basic knowledge of grammar*. The *aims* of the book are to:
>
> - expose students to a variety of *authentic written and spoken language*, and to give them confidence in coping with it.
> - provide plenty of *opportunities for oral fluency*, from *discussion* activities to full-scale *role plays*.
> - expose the students to *language in use*, with *opportunities to revise areas of grammar* or *functional language* which may still be causing problems.
> ... these *themes* have been chosen as ones which are likely to *interest and motivate the average learner*, and which are *generative* in terms of *useful vocabulary areas*.

We can deduce from this that the claims made for the materials by the author/publisher can be quite strong and will need critical evaluation in order to see if their claims can be justified. From the 'blurb' and the introduction we can normally expect comments on some/all of the following:

- *The intended audience*. We need to ascertain who the materials are targeted at, be it teenagers aged 13 and upwards or adults, for example. The topics that will motivate one audience will probably not be suitable for another.
- *The proficiency level*. Most materials claim to aim at a particular level, such as false beginner or lower intermediate. This will obviously require investigation as it could vary widely depending on the educational context.
- *The context in which the materials are to be used*. We need to establish whether the materials are for teaching general learners or perhaps for teaching English for Specific Purposes (ESP). If the latter, what degree of specialist subject knowledge is assumed in the materials?
- *How the language has been presented and organized into teachable units/ lessons*. The materials will contain a number of units/lessons and their respective lengths need to be borne in mind when deciding how and if they will fit into a given educational programme. Some materials will provide guidelines here such as 'contains 15 units, providing material for 90–120 hours of teaching'. In other words, the author expects that between 6 and 8 hours will be required to cover the material.
- *The author's views on language and methodology* and the relationship between the language, the learning process and the learner.

In many cases the date of publication of the materials will be of importance here. For materials written over the last 20 years or so designed to fit into a multi-syllabus or process syllabus, we might expect the author to make claims about including quite a large amount of learner involvement in the learning process. This will require investigation. For example, the materials may claim to help the learner in an understanding of what is involved in language learning and contain various activities and tasks to develop this.

> Look at the 'blurb' and the introduction to the materials you typically use. Also look back at the 'blurbs' we examined in chapters 2 and 3. What kinds of information do they give you?

To give an overview of some typical 'blurbs', we have selected a range of examples taken from EFL coursebooks. We may notice how certain 'key' words and expressions come up time and time again.

> As you are reading them, note down some of the claims that are made for the materials that you would want to investigate further in the next (internal evaluation) stage.

1 'is a beginners course in English for complete or near beginners . . . has a careful structural progression with specific communicative aims'.
2 'is a new beginners course for students aged 14 and over. It presents a totally new approach to language learning as it takes account of basic communication needs as its first priority.'
3 'systematically covers the notional, functional and grammatical areas that are important to students at this (intermediate) level. In each unit, students are taught the relationship between structures and meaning and learn how to use structures in a communicative context.'
4 'focuses on the real English students will encounter and need to use in today's world. Book 1 is for false beginner adult learners. Fifteen units will provide about 100 hours of class work, at the end of which students will be able to cope confidently with a very wide range of straightforward situations.'

When evaluating materials it is useful to keep a note of these claims, which we can then refer back to later in the process. Other factors to take into account at this external stage are as follows:

• *Are the materials to be used as the main 'core' course or to be supplementary to it?* This will help to evaluate their effectiveness in a given context as well as the total cost. It may be that sheer economics will dissuade the evaluator from selecting these particular materials, especially if they are not going to be the core part of the course.

- *Is a teacher's book in print and locally available?* It is also worth considering whether it is sufficiently clear for non-native speaker teachers to use. Some teacher's books offer general teaching hints while others have very prescribed programmes of how to teach the material including lesson plans. Non-availability of the teacher's book may make the student edition difficult to work with.

- *Is a vocabulary list/index included?* Having these included in the materials may prove to be very useful for learners in some contexts, particularly where the learner might be doing a lot of individualized and/or out-of-class work. Some materials explicitly state that they are offering this: 'student's book with an introductory unit, forty double-page units, four self-check units, ... an interaction appendix, a vocabulary appendix with phonetic spelling, a list of irregular verbs, and a listening appendix', and the claims made are worthy of investigation. The table of contents may sometimes be seen as a 'bridge' between the external and internal stages of the evaluation and can often reveal useful information about the organization of the materials, giving information about vocabulary study, skills to be covered, functions and so on, possibly with some indication as to how much class time the author thinks should be devoted to a particular unit. Consequently, it is often useful to see how explicit it is.

- *What visual material does the book contain (photographs, charts, diagrams) and is it there for cosmetic value only or is it integrated into the text?* In recent years there has been a tendency to use glossy prints in some materials to make the book appear more attractive. It is worth examining if the visual material serves any learning purpose; i.e., in the case of a photograph or a diagram, is it incorporated into a task so that the learner has to comment on it/interpret it in some way?

- *Is the layout and presentation clear or cluttered?* Some textbooks are researched and written well, but are so cluttered with information on every page that teachers/learners find them practically unusable. Hence a judicious balance between the two needs to be found. Tomlinson (1999) suggests that we also include clarity of instructions and stipulate which activity goes with which instruction as part of the overall concept of the layout of the materials. The potential durability of the materials is another important factor in teaching contexts where materials may be selected for several groups over a period of years. Factors such as paper quality and binding need to be assessed.

- *Is the material too culturally biased or specific?*

- *Do the materials represent minority groups and/or women in a negative way? Do they present a 'balanced' picture of a particular country/society?* It is possible that the content of some materials will cause offence to some learners. The investigation by Littlejohn and Windeatt (1988) into teaching materials shows how textbooks may be 'biased' in subtle, and in some cases not so subtle, ways in their representation of class, ethnic background and reference to smoking and drinking.

- *The inclusion of audio/video material and resultant cost. Is it essential to possess this extra material in order to use the textbook successfully?*
- *The inclusion of tests in the teaching materials (diagnostic, progress, achievement); would they be useful for your particular learners?*

During this external evaluation stage we have examined the claims made for the materials by the author/publisher with respect to the intended audience, the proficiency level, the context and presentation of language items, whether the materials are to be core or supplementary, the role and availability of a teacher's book, the inclusion of a vocabulary list/index, the table of contents, the use of visuals and presentation, the cultural specificity of the materials, the provision of audio/video material and inclusion of tests.

Look at the example on pp. 68–9. What information does it give us about the materials?

After completing this external evaluation, and having funds and a potential group of learners in mind, we can arrive at a decision as to the materials' appropriacy for adoption/selection purposes. If our evaluation shows the materials to be potentially appropriate and worthy of a more detailed inspection then we can continue with our internal or more detailed evaluation. If not, then we can 'exit' at this stage and start to evaluate other materials if we so wish, as figure 4.1 illustrates.

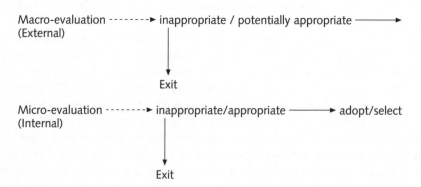

Figure 4.1   An overview of the materials evaluation process.

4.4   *The internal evaluation*

We now continue to the next stage of our evaluation procedure by performing an in-depth investigation into the materials. The essential issue at this stage is for us to analyse the extent to which the aforementioned factors in the external evaluation stage match up with the internal consistency and organization of the materials as stated by the author/publisher – for, as we saw in the previous section, strong claims are often made for these materials. In order to perform an effective internal inspection of the materials, we need to examine at least two units (preferably more) of a book or set of materials to investigate the following factors:

- *The presentation of the skills in the materials.* We may want to investigate if all the language skills are covered, in what proportion, and if this proportion is appropriate to the context in which we are working. Are the skills treated discretely or in an integrated way? The author's presentation and treatment of the skills may conflict with the way in which we wish to teach – if the skills are presented too much in isolation, for example. If they are integrated, is this integration natural? (See chapter 10 for a discussion of integrated skills.)
- *The grading and sequencing of the materials.* This criterion is an important one and merits some investigation as it is not always patently clear what the principle is. Some materials are quite 'steeply' graded while others claim to have no grading at all.

  In this example the materials are based on a lexical frequency count: 'The course is in three levels, each covering about 100 hours of classwork, and each level is complete in itself. Together they cover the most useful patterns of 2500 of the most frequently used words in English. Book 1 covers the first 700 of these . . .' Sometimes the grading of the materials will be within the unit, other materials will be graded across the unit allowing a progression of difficulty in a linear fashion. Other materials claim to be modular by grouping a set of units at approximately the same level. In cases where there is virtually no grading at all – 'Most of the units do not have to be taught in any particular order . . .' – we have to investigate the extent to which we think this is true, and how such a book would suit our learners.
- *Where reading/'discourse' skills are involved, is there much in the way of appropriate text beyond the sentence?* As teachers we sometimes find that materials provide too much emphasis on skills development and not enough opportunity for students to practise those skills on extended reading passages.
- *Where listening skills are involved, are recordings 'authentic' or artificial?* We need to ascertain whether or not dialogues have been specially written, thereby missing the essential features of spontaneous speech.
- *Do speaking materials incorporate what we know about the nature of real interaction or are artificial dialogues offered instead?*
- *The relationship of tests and exercises to (a) learner needs, and (b) what is taught by the course material.* Where these are included as part of the materials, we need to see if they are appropriate in context.
- *Do you feel that the material is suitable for different learning styles? Is a claim and provision made for self-study and is such a claim justified?* With the growth of interest in independent learning and learner autonomy, many

Part A **Language**

Module	Language focus	Vocabulary	Speaking
Module 1 About you **page 6**	1) Questions and answers (auxiliary verbs) *Pronunciation: stressed and weak forms in questions and answers* 2) **Present Simple and Continuous**	People around you *(best friend, acquaintance, classmate, etc.)* **Wordspot:** *have* (and *have got*)	**Mini-task:** find five things you have in common with a partner Talk about the changing state of the family
Module 2 Memories **page 17**	1) **Past Simple and Continuous** *Pronunciation: -ed forms / weak forms of was, were* 2) **Comparing past and present** *(used to, still, not ... any more / longer)*	Remembering and forgetting *(remember, learn, remind, forget, recognise, lose)* **Wordspot:** *time*	Talk about ways of remembering **Mini-task:** describe an important meeting in your life
Module 3 Around the world **page 26**	1) **Comparatives and superlative** *(slightly higher than, one of the biggest ... in the world, etc.)* 2) **Comparing things in different ways** *(not as ... as, fewer / less than, similar to, etc.)* *Pronunciation: /ə/ in comparative phrases*	**Wordspot:** *place* Describing towns and cities	Do a geography quiz **Mini-task:** describe similarities and differences between two countries
Module 4 Life stories **page 36**	1) **Present Perfect Simple (and Past Simple)** *Pronunciation: strong and weak forms of have* 2) **for, since and ago (and Present Perfect Continuous)** *Pronunciation: weak form of been /bɪn/*	Life experiences *(leave home, start work, move house, etc.)* **Wordspot:** *get*	**Mini-task:** find three things that you and a partner have both done
Consolidation Modules 1–4 (pages 46–47)			
Module 5 Making plans **page 48**	1) **Future plans and intentions** *(Present Continuous, will, going to, intend to, due to, etc.)* *Pronunciation: future forms and phrases* 2) **Future clauses with if, when, etc.**	**Wordspot:** *work* Training and work *(well-paid, challenging, stressful, etc.)*	Discuss how organised you / people you know are **Mini-task:** talk about the plans and ambitions of friends / family
Module 6 News and media **page 59**	1) **-ing / -ed adjectives** 2) **Passive forms** *Pronunciation: was /wəz/ and were /wə/ in passive sentences*	Television *(advertisements, sports coverage, thrillers, etc.)* **Wordspot:** *by*	**Mini-task:** talk about stories in the news

Part B **Task**

Reading / Listening	Task	After the task
Reading: *A quiet revolution?* (the changing state of the family)	**Preparation for task**: listen to people meeting for the first time **Task**: interview another student using a pie-chart (extended speaking)	**Task link**: how you spend your time (*I absolutely love ..., I'm not very good at ...,* etc.) **Real life**: writing an informal letter Do you remember?
Reading: *All in the memory*	**Preparation for task**: listen to two descriptions of childhood memories **Task**: describe a childhood memory (extended speaking and writing)	**Task link**: short questions *Pronunciation:* using intonation to show interest Do you remember?
Listening: geography quiz Reading: *Amazing cities!*	**Preparation for task**: listen to recommendations for a tour of Ireland **Task**: plan a tour of your country or region (extended speaking and writing)	**Task link**: recommending and advising *Pronunciation:* intonation for giving recommendations Do you remember?
Reading: *Twin lives*	**Preparation for task**: discuss / read about famous people **Task**: design a set of stamps of famous people (extended speaking and writing)	**Task link**: describing people (*He's the sort of person who ..., She's always ...,* etc.) **Real life**: filling in an application form
Reading: *Quiz – how organised are you?* Listening: working in something different (people talking about their jobs)	**Preparation for task**: listen to a conversation describing a job vacancy **Task**: select the best candidate for a job (extended speaking)	**Real life 1**: writing a covering letter **Real life 2**: making a formal telephone call *Pronunciation:* connected speech Do you remember?
Listening: television (people talking about types of television programmes) Reading: newspaper articles	**Preparation for task**: listen to radio extracts **Task**: prepare a review or entertainment guide (extended speaking and writing)	**Task link**: 'extreme' adjectives (*brilliant, tragic, furious,* etc.) Do you remember?

Source: S. Cunningham and P. Moor, pp. 2–3 from *Cutting Edge: Intermediate, Students' Book*. Harlow: Longman, 1999. © Longman, 1999. Used by permission of Pearson Education Ltd.

materials will claim that 'self-study modes' are also possible. From the knowledge that we have of our learners, we will need to assess this particular claim.

• *Are the materials sufficiently 'transparent' to motivate both students and
  teachers alike, or would you foresee a student/teacher mismatch?* Some materials may seem attractive for the teacher but would not be very motivating for
  the learners. A balance therefore has to be sought. At this stage it is also useful
  to consider how the materials may guide and 'frame' teacher–learner interaction and the teacher–learner relationship. Does the coursebook 'take account
  of the students' needs as learners and . . . facilitate their learning processes
  without dogmatically imposing a rigid method' (Cunningsworth 1995: 16).

In the internal evaluation stage we have suggested that as evaluators we need
to examine the following criteria: the treatment and presentation of the skills, the
sequencing and grading of the materials, the *type* of reading, listening, speaking
and writing materials contained in the materials, appropriacy of tests and exercises, self-study provision and teacher–learner 'balance' in use of the materials.

4.5   *The overall evaluation*

At this stage we hope that we may now make an overall assessment as to the
suitability of the materials by considering the following parameters:

1 *The usability factor.* How far the materials could be integrated into a particular syllabus as 'core' or supplementary. For example, we may need to
   select materials that suit a particular syllabus or set of objectives that we
   have to work to. The materials may or may not be able to do this.
2 *The generalizability factor.* Is there a restricted use of 'core' features that
   make the materials more generally useful? Perhaps not all the material will
   be useful for a given individual or group but some parts might be. This
   factor can in turn lead us to consider the next point.
3 *The adaptability factor.* Can parts be added/extracted/used in another
   context/modified for local circumstances? There may be some very good
   qualities in the materials but, for example, we may judge the listening material or the reading passages to be unsuitable and in need of modification. If
   we think that adaptation is feasible we may choose to do this. (Again, refer
   to chapter 5 for a full discussion of materials adaptation.)
4 *The flexibility factor.* How rigid is the sequencing and grading? Can the
   materials be entered at different points or used in different ways? In some
   cases materials that are not so steeply graded offer a measure of flexibility
   that permits them to be integrated easily into various types of syllabus.

The following remarks illustrate the types of comments that teachers have
made to us regarding the suitability of certain published ELT materials for their
teaching situations:

'There is a wide variety of reading and listening material available but the speaking material is not very good and is too accuracy based. I would therefore have to add something in terms of fluency. The book is usable and could be adapted, but given the cost factor I would prefer to look for something else.'

'The materials are very good. I was looking for something that would present the skills in an integrated way and would make a connection with the real lives of my students. I checked the "blurb", the table of contents and made a detailed inspection of several units. On the whole the author's claims are realized in the materials. Consequently I could use this as a core course with very few adaptations.'

Thus, when all the criteria that we have discussed have been analysed, we can then reach our own conclusions regarding the suitability of the materials for specified groups or individuals, as the aim of this final stage is intended to enable the evaluator to decide the extent to which the materials have realized their stated objectives. Even after the internal evaluation we still have the option of not selecting the materials if we so wish. (Refer back to figure 4.1.) This is usually avoided, however, if we undertake a thorough internal inspection of the material outlined above. But once materials have been deemed appropriate for use on a particular course we must bear in mind that their ultimate success or failure can only be determined after trying them in the classroom with real learners. Indeed, R. Ellis (1997) devotes a lot of attention to this very important point. He outlines a scheme for what he calls 'retrospective' evaluation. In other words, most evaluation models are based on predictive evaluation, that is, what we think will happen if we use these materials. A more pertinent method might be to set up a retrospective evaluation by conducting a micro-evaluation of teaching tasks relating to the materials. This would also have the advantage of enabling teachers to reflect on their practice, which links very closely with the small-scale action research notion that has gained wide currency in the last decade. (Refer to chapter 14 for a full discussion of the teacher.)

1 At the beginning of the chapter we asked you to note down some criteria you would use to evaluate materials. Now refer back to those criteria. How far do they match the ones we have mentioned? Are any different?
2 Now take a coursebook or set of ELT materials unfamiliar to you and put into operation the criteria we have examined in this chapter.

4.6 Conclusion

In this chapter we have suggested that materials evaluation can be carried out in two complementary stages, which we have called the external and internal stages. We then outlined and commented upon the essential criteria necessary to make pertinent judgements with reference to ELT materials in order to make a preliminary selection. We suggested that this particular model should be flexible enough to be used in ELT contexts worldwide, as it avoids long checklists of data and can operate according to the purpose the evaluator has in evaluating the materials in the first place. We also suggested that materials evaluation is one part of a complex process and that materials once selected can only be judged successful after classroom implementation and feedback.

4.7   Further reading

The following contain useful information on materials evaluation:
1   Chambers, F. (1997): Seeking consensus in coursebook evaluation.
2   Cunningsworth, A. (1995): *Choosing Your Coursebook* (especially the overview of analysing and evaluating coursebooks in ch. 2).
3   Ellis, R. (1997): The empirical evaluation of language teaching materials.

5

Adapting Materials

5.1   Introduction

The main concern of all the chapters in this part of the book has been to examine the principles on which current teaching materials and classroom methodology are built. This final chapter in part I looks at some of the factors to be considered in the process of adapting teaching materials within particular classroom environments where there is a perceived need for change and manipulation of certain design features. There is clearly a direct relationship between evaluating and adapting materials, both in terms of the reasons for doing so and the criteria used: this chapter can therefore usefully be seen as forming a pair with chapter 4. We shall first set the scene for a discussion of adaptation by looking at ways in which the concept can be understood. We shall then try to enumerate some of the reasons why teachers might need to adapt their teaching material. Finally, in the main part of the chapter, these reasons will be examined in terms of the procedures typically used in adaptation.

5.2   The context of adaptation

A straightforward starting point for considering the relationship between evaluation and adaptation is to think of the terms 'adopting' and 'adapting'. We saw in the previous chapter that a decision about whether a particular coursebook should be used in a specific teaching situation can be taken on the basis of a number of evaluative criteria. These criteria, formulated as a set of questions to ask about the materials, provide answers that will lead to acceptance or perhaps rejection. For instance, typical questions concerned aspects of 'skills', different ways in which language content is handled, and the authenticity of both language and tasks. However, a decision in favour of adoption is an initial step, and is unlikely to mean that no further action needs to be taken beyond that of presenting the material directly to the learners. It is more realistic to assume that, however careful the design of the materials and the evaluation process, some changes will have to be made at some level in most teaching contexts. As G. White (1998: 73) points out, 'published materials of any kind have to cater for a very wide range of possible users, which means that they cannot address any individual student or group of students directly'. Adaptation, then, is a process subsequent to, and dependent on, adoption. Furthermore, whereas adoption is concerned with whole coursebooks, adaptation concerns the parts that make up that whole.

An important perspective on evaluation – though of course not the only one – is to see it as a management issue whereby educational decision-makers formulate policy and work out strategies for budgeting and for the purchasing and allocation of resources. In this sense, teachers do not always have direct involvement: they may well influence decisions about whole textbooks only if they are part of a Ministry of Education team concerned with trialling or writing materials, for example. Others, perhaps, may be invited to make suggestions and comments as part of a corporate process of materials selection, but even then the final decision will be taken at a managerial point in the school hierarchy. A far more widespread, and necessary, activity among teachers is therefore that of adaptation, because the smaller-scale process of changing or adjusting the various parts of a coursebook is, as we shall see, more closely related to the reality of dealing with learners in the dynamic environment of the classroom.

This said, let us remind ourselves of another major and persuasive reason for evaluating textbooks even in a context where teachers have little direct say in decision-making. Evaluation as an exercise can help us develop insights into different views of language and learning and into the principles of materials design, and is something we do against the background of a knowledge of our learners and of the demands and potential of our teaching situation. It is difficult to see how the dependent activity of adaptation can take place without this kind of understanding – how can we change something unless we are clear about what it is we are changing?

With this wider perspective in mind, and as a starting point for thinking about the process of adaptation, it will be useful to extend a little the criteria put forward in chapter 4 under the headings of 'external' and 'internal'. External factors comprise both the overt claims made about materials and, more significantly for the present chapter, the characteristics of particular teaching situations. Internal factors are concerned with content, organization and consistency. Thus:

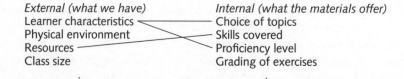

Figure 5.1   Matching external and internal criteria.

To adapt materials is to try to bring together these individual elements under each heading, or combinations of them, so that they match each other as closely as possible. The horizontal lines indicate only a very small number of the possibilities for cross-referencing. For instance, we may be unable to use the full range of listening skills practised in a coursebook because of resource limitations; and the link between a stated proficiency level and that of our own learners is an obvious one. Madsen and Bowen refer to this matching as the principle of 'congruence': 'Effective adaptation is a matter of achieving "congruence" ... The good teacher is ... constantly striving for congruence among several related variables: teaching materials, methodology, students, course objectives, the target language and its context, and the teacher's own personality and teaching style' (1978: ix). With an emphasis on materials, Stevick talks of bridging a gap: 'the teacher must satisfy the demands of the textbook, but in ways that will be satisfying to those who learn from it' (1972). (Even if we agree with Prabhu's (1987) critique of 'materials-driven' classes referred to at the end of chapter 3, we must recognize that most teachers work with coursebooks, so Stevick's comment is entirely realistic.) In general, then, teaching materials may be internally coherent but not totally applicable in context; alternatively, they may be largely appropriate at the same time as they show signs of an inconsistent organization.

The final point in this section is frequently overlooked, perhaps because it is so much a part of our everyday professional practice that we are unaware of its implications. Adaptation tends to be thought of as a rather formal process in which the teacher makes a decision about, say, an exercise that needs changing, and then writes out a revised version for the class. In fact, although the concept of adaptation clearly includes this kind of procedure, it is also broader than this. Adapted material does not necessarily need to be written down or made permanent. It can be quite transitory: we might think of the response to an individual's learning behaviour at a particular moment, for instance when the teacher rewords – and by doing so adapts – a textbook explanation of a language point that has not been understood. The recognition of the short-term needs of a group may similarly require teachers to 'think on their feet' by introducing extra material, such as a grammatical example or some idiomatic language, from their own repertoire in the real-time framework of a class. Madsen and Bowen make the point clearly:

> the good teacher is constantly adapting. He adapts when he adds an example not found in the book or when he telescopes an assignment by having students prepare 'only the even-numbered items'. He adapts even when he refers to an exercise covered earlier, or when he introduces a supplementary picture ... While a conscientious author tries to anticipate questions that may be raised by his readers, the teacher can respond not merely to verbal questions ... but even to the raised eyebrows of his students. (1978: vii)

To focus only on these kinds of activities would obviously not give us a complete picture of the concept of adaptation, because it would be necessary at some stage to extend and systematize its possibilities. Nevertheless, it is worth noting that the task of adapting is not an entirely new skill that teachers must learn.

1 Before you read on, consider the materials you use most frequently: to what extent do you feel they need, in principle, to be adapted? Try to note down the main aspects of change or modification you think are necessary or at least desirable.
2 It will also be useful to think about adaptation from the point of view of the *source* of your materials. Are they commercially produced and widely used internationally; are they designed at national level by your Ministry of Education; or are they perhaps more localized, produced by a team of teachers for a particular area or school?
3 If possible, share your comments with other teachers. You could also discuss the scope you have for adapting materials – do you have time? Is it acceptable to do so in your teaching situation? Are you required to adapt?

In this part of the chapter, we have tried to show that adaptation is essentially a process of 'matching'. Its purpose is to maximize the appropriacy of teaching materials in context, by changing some of the internal characteristics of a coursebook to suit our particular circumstances better. We shall now look in more detail at possible reasons for adaptation, and at some of the procedures commonly used.

5.3   Reasons for adapting

We have just asked you to consider your reasons for needing to make modifications to your own materials, and some of the changes you would wish to make. These reasons will depend, of course, on the whole range of variables operating in your own teaching situation, and one teacher's priorities may well differ considerably from those of another. It is certainly possible that there are some general trends common to a large number of teaching contexts: most obviously there appears to be a widespread perception that materials should aim to be in some sense 'communicative' and 'authentic'. Nevertheless, it is worth bearing in mind that priorities are relative, and there is no absolute notion of right or wrong, or even just one way of interpreting such terms as 'communicative' and 'authentic'. It is also the case that priorities change over time even within the same context. For instance, decontextualized grammar study is not intrinsically 'wrong' in a communicatively oriented class, just as role-play is not automatically 'right'. Nor does a need to adapt necessarily imply that a coursebook is defective.

It will be useful to compare your own reasons with those in the following list. The list is not intended to be comprehensive, but simply to show some of the possible areas of mismatch ('non-congruence') that teachers identify and that can be dealt with by adaptation:

- Not enough grammar coverage in general.
- Not enough practice of grammar points of particular difficulty to these learners.
- The communicative focus means that grammar is presented unsystematically.
- Reading passages contain too much unknown vocabulary.
- Comprehension questions are too easy, because the answers can be lifted directly from the text with no real understanding.
- Listening passages are inauthentic, because they sound too much like written material being read out.
- Not enough guidance on pronunciation.
- Subject matter inappropriate for learners of this age and intellectual level.
- Photographs and other illustrative material not culturally acceptable.
- Amount of material too much or too little to cover in the time allocated to lessons.
- No guidance for teachers on handling group work and role play activities with a large class.
- Dialogues too formal and not representative of everyday speech.
- Audio material difficult to use because of problems to do with room size and technical equipment.
- Too much or too little variety in the activities.
- Vocabulary list and a key to the exercises would be helpful.
- Accompanying tests needed.

Undoubtedly much more could be added to this list, but it serves as an illustration of some of the possibilities. All aspects of the language classroom can be covered: the few examples above include (a) aspects of language use, (b) skills, (c) classroom organization, and (d) supplementary material. Some useful examples of adaptation with a particular focus on task-based learning can be found in J. Willis (1996: 145), with some simple suggestions for changing such variables as the class management or the sequence of activities; in Nunan (1999, ch. 11), with procedures for making materials more interactive; and in G. White (1998, ch. 4), with a very useful extended set of examples for dealing with listening materials to help learners to participate more.

5.4 Principles and procedures

The reasons for adapting that we have just looked at can be thought of as dealing with the modification of content, whether that content is expressed in the form of exercises and activities, texts, instructions, tests and so on. In other words, the focus is on what the materials contain, measured against the requirements of a particular teaching environment. That environment may necessitate a number of changes that will lead to greater appropriacy. This is most likely to be expressed in terms of a need to personalize, individualize or localize the content. We take 'personalizing' here to refer to increasing the relevance of content in relation to learners' interests and their academic, educational or professional needs. 'Individualizing' will address the learning styles both of individuals and of the members of a class working closely together. 'Localizing' takes into account the international geography of English language teaching and recognizes that what may work well in Mexico City may not do so in Edinburgh or in Kuala Lumpur. Madsen and Bowen (1978) include a further category of 'modernizing', and comment that not all materials show familiarity with aspects of current English usage, sometimes to the point of being not only out of date or misleading but even incorrect.

In this section we shall now look at questions of procedure – at the main techniques that can be applied to content in order to bring about change. There are a number of points to bear in mind. Firstly, this can be seen as another kind of matching process or 'congruence', where techniques are selected according to the aspect of the materials that needs alteration. Secondly, content can be adapted using a range of techniques; or, conversely, a single technique can be applied to different content areas. For example, a reading passage might be grammatically simplified or its subject matter modified, or it can be made shorter or broken down into smaller parts. The technique of simplification can be applied to texts, to explanations and so on. Thirdly, adaptation can have both quantitative and qualitative effects. In other words, we can simply change the amount of material, or we can change its methodological nature. Finally, techniques can be used individually or in combination with others, so the scale of possibilities clearly ranges from straightforward to rather complex. All these points will be raised again in the discussion of individual techniques.

The techniques that we shall cover are as follows:

Adding, including expanding and extending
Deleting, including subtracting and abridging
Modifying, including rewriting and restructuring
Simplifying
Reordering

Each will be briefly introduced, and a few examples given. There are implications for all of them in parts II and III of this book where we consider language skills and classroom methodology. Readers interested at this stage in more detailed examples of procedures for adaptation are referred to the 'Further reading' at the end of this chapter. The first references have broadly similar lists of techniques, and offer a large number of worked examples.

1 When you have finished reading through the discussion of techniques, select one or two of them and consider their application to any materials with which you are familiar.
2 It will be useful at this stage to work on a small scale, taking single-content areas, such as an exercise, a text, or a set of comprehension questions.

Adding

The notion of addition is, on the face of it, straightforward, implying that materials are supplemented by putting more into them, while taking into account the practical effect on time allocation. We can add in this simple, quantitative way by the technique of *extending*, and might wish to do this in situations such as the following:

*   The materials contain practice in the pronunciation of minimal pairs (bit/bet, hat/hate, ship/chip) but not enough examples of the difficulties for learners with a particular L_1. Japanese speakers may need more l/r practice, Arabic speakers more p/b, Spanish speakers more b/v and so on.
*   A second reading passage parallel to the one provided is helpful in reinforcing the key linguistic features – tenses, sentence structure, vocabulary, cohesive devices – of the first text.
*   Our students find the explanation of a new grammar point rather difficult, so further exercises are added before they begin the practice material.

The point to note here is that adding by extension is to supply more of the same. This means that the techniques are being applied *within* the methodological framework of the original materials: in other words, the model is not itself changed.

Another, more far-reaching perspective on addition of material can be termed *expanding*. Consider these possibilities:

*   The only pronunciation practice in the materials is on individual sounds and minimal pairs, However, this may be necessary but not sufficient. Our students need to be intelligible, and intelligibility entails more than articulating a vowel or a consonant correctly. Therefore, we decide to add some work on sentence stress and rhythm and on the related phenomenon of 'weak' and 'strong' forms in English. A further advantage is that students will be better able to understand naturally spoken English.
*   If there is insufficient coverage of the skill of listening, the reading passage provided may also be paralleled by the provision of listening comprehension material, using the same vocabulary and ideas but presented through a different medium, making sure that it is authentic in terms of the spoken language.
*   Although the new grammar material is important and relevant, the addition of a discussion section at the end of the unit will help to reinforce and contextualize the linguistic items covered, particularly if it is carefully structured so that the most useful points occur 'naturally'.

These kinds of additions are not just extensions of an existing aspect of content. They go further than this by bringing about a qualitative as well as a quantitative change. Expanding, then, as distinct from extending, adds to the methodology by moving outside it and developing it in new directions, for instance by putting in a different language skill or a new component. This can be thought of as a change in the overall system.

Finally in this section, it is worth pointing out that additions do not always have to be made onto the end of something. A new facet of material or methodology can be introduced before it appears in the framework of the coursebook. For example, a teacher may prepare the ground for practice in an aspect of grammar or communicative function determined by the syllabus through a 'warm-up' exercise involving learners talking about themselves and their everyday lives.

Deleting or omitting

Deletion is clearly the opposite process to that of addition, and as such needs no further clarification as a term. However, although material is taken out rather than supplemented, as a technique it can be thought of as 'the other side of the same coin'. We saw in the previous section that material can be added both quantitatively (extending) and qualitatively (expanding): the same point applies when a decision is taken to omit material. Again, as with addition, the technique can be used on a small scale, for example over part of an exercise, or on the larger scale of a whole unit of a coursebook.

We shall refer to the most straightforward aspect of reducing the length of material as *subtracting* from it. The following kinds of requirements might apply:

- Our pronunciation exercises on minimal pairs contain too much general material. Since our students all have the same mother tongue and do not make certain errors, many of the exercises are inappropriate. Arabic speakers, for example, will be unlikely to have much difficulty with the l/r distinction.
- Although a communicative coursebook has been selected as relevant in our situation, some of the language functions presented are unlikely to be required by learners who will probably not use their English in the target language environment. Such functions as 'giving directions' or 'greetings' may be useful; 'expressing sympathy' or 'ordering things' may not.

Deletion in these cases, as with extending, does not have a significant impact on the overall methodology. The changes are greater if material is not only subtracted, but also what we shall term *abridged*:

- The materials contain a discussion section at the end of each unit. However, our learners are not really proficient enough to tackle this adequately, since they have learnt the language structures but not fluency in their use. The syllabus and its subsequent examination does not leave room for this kind of training.
- Students on a short course are working with communicative materials because of their instrumental reasons for choosing to learn English: some of them

wish to travel on international business, others plan to visit a target language country as tourists. The lengthy grammatical explanations accompanying each functional unit are therefore felt to be inappropriate.

Addition and deletion often work together, of course. Material may be taken out and then replaced with something else. Where the same kind of material is substituted, as for instance one set of minimal pairs for another, the internal balance of the lesson or the syllabus is not necessarily altered. The methodological change is greater when, for example, grammar practice is substituted after the omission of an inappropriate communicative function, or when a reading text is replaced by a listening passage. This takes us directly into the next section.

Modifying

'Modification' at one level is a very general term in the language applying to any kind of change. In order to introduce further possibilities for adaptation, we shall restrict its meaning here to an *internal* change in the approach or focus of an exercise or other piece of material. It is a rather important and frequently used procedure that, like all other techniques, can be applied to any aspect of 'content'. It can be subdivided under two related headings. The first of these is *rewriting*, when some of the linguistic content needs modification; the second is *restructuring*, which applies to classroom management. Let us look at some examples of each of these in turn. You will undoubtedly be able to think of many more.

Rewriting   Currently the most frequently stated requirement for a change in focus is for materials to be made 'more communicative'. This feeling is voiced in many teaching situations where textbooks are considered to lag behind an understanding of the nature of language and of students' linguistic and learning needs. Rewriting, therefore, may relate activities more closely to learners' own backgrounds and interests, introduce models of authentic language, or set more purposeful, problem-solving tasks where the answers are not always known before the teacher asks the question. The first two readings listed at the end of this chapter also contain substantial discussion and examples for making textbooks more communicative, as does chapter 9 of Cunningsworth (1984).

It is quite common for coursebooks to place insufficient emphasis on listening comprehension, and for teachers to feel that more material is required. If accompanying audio material is either not available, or cannot be purchased in a particular teaching context, then the teacher can rewrite a reading passage and deliver it orally, perhaps by taking notes from the original and then speaking naturally to the class from those notes.

Sometimes new vocabulary is printed just as a list, with explanatory notes and perhaps the mother tongue equivalent. We may wish to modify this kind of presentation by taking out the notes and writing an exercise that helps students to develop useful and generalized strategies for acquiring new vocabulary.

Equally, a text may have quite appropriate language material for a specific group, but may not 'match' in terms of its cultural content. For example, a story about an English family, with English names, living in an English town, eating English food and enjoying English hobbies can in fact be modified quite easily by making a number of straightforward surface changes.

A last example here is that of end-of-text comprehension questions. Some of these are more like a test, where students can answer by 'lifting' the information straight from the text. These questions can be modified so that students have to interpret what they have read or heard, or relate different sections of the text to each other. Chapter 6 looks at these kinds of tasks.

The point was made in the introduction to this chapter that content changes are not always written down. Adaptation of linguistic content may just require rewording by the teacher as an oral explanation.

Restructuring   For many teachers who are required to follow a coursebook, changes in the structuring of the class are sometimes the only kind of adaptation possible. For example, the materials may contain role-play activities for groups of a certain size. The logistics of managing a large class (especially if they all have the same L_1) are complex from many points of view, and it will probably be necessary to assign one role to a number of pupils at the same time. Obviously the converse – where the class is too small for the total number of roles available – is also possible if perhaps less likely.

Sometimes a written language explanation designed to be read and studied can be made more meaningful if it is turned into an interactive exercise where all students participate. For instance, it is a straightforward matter to ask learners to practise certain verb structures in pairs (say the present perfect: 'Have you been to/done X?'; or a conditional: 'What would you do if . . . ?'), and it can be made more authentic by inviting students to refer to topics of direct interest to themselves.

Modifying materials, then, even in the restricted sense in which we have used the term here, is a technique with a wide range of applications. It refers essentially to a 'modality change', to a change in the nature or focus of an exercise, or text, or classroom activity.

Simplifying

Strictly speaking, the technique of simplification is one type of modification, namely, a 'rewriting' activity. Since it has received considerable attention in its own right, it is considered here as a separate procedure. Many elements of a language course can be simplified, including the instructions and explanations that accompany exercises and activities, and even the visual layout of material so that it becomes easier to see how different parts fit together. It is worth noting in passing that teachers are sometimes on rather dangerous ground, if a wish to 'simplify' grammar or speech in the classroom leads to a distortion of natural language. For example, oversimplification of a grammatical explanation can be misleadingly one-sided or partial: to tell learners that adverbs are always formed by adding '-ly' does not help them when they come across 'friendly' or 'brotherly', nor does it explain why 'hardly' cannot be formed from 'hard'. A slow style of speech might result in the elimination of the correct use of sentence stress and weak forms, leaving learners with no exposure to the natural rhythms of spoken English.

However, the main application of this technique has been to texts, most often to reading passages. Traditionally, the emphasis has been on changing various sentence-bound elements to match the text more closely to the proficiency level of a particular group of learners. Thus, for instance, we can simplify according to

1   *Sentence structure.* Sentence length is reduced, or a complex sentence is rewritten as a number of simpler ones, for example by the replacement of relative pronouns by nouns and pronouns followed by a main verb.
2   *Lexical content*, so that the number of new vocabulary items is controlled by reference to what students have already learned.
3   *Grammatical structures.* For instance, passives are converted to actives; simple past tense to simple present; reported into direct speech.

These kinds of criteria form the basis of many of the published graded 'simplified readers' available for English language teaching.

Simplification has a number of further implications. Firstly, it is possible that any linguistic change, lexical or grammatical, will have a corresponding stylistic effect, and will therefore change the meaning or intention of the original text. This is particularly likely with literary material, of course, but in principle it can apply to any kind of text where the overall 'coherence' can be affected. Widdowson (1979) goes into these arguments in more detail. Secondly, some teaching situations require attention to the simplification of content when the complexity of the subject matter is regarded as being too advanced. This could be the case for some scientific explanations, for example, or for material too far removed from the learners' own life experiences. Thirdly, simplification can refer not only to content, but also to the ways in which that content is presented: we may decide not to make any changes to the original text, but instead to lead the learners through it in a number of graded stages. We shall come back to this notion of 'task complexity' in the chapters on reading and listening comprehension.

Reordering

This procedure, the final one discussed in this section, refers to the possibility of putting the parts of a coursebook in a different order. This may mean adjusting the sequence of presentation within a unit, or taking units in a different sequence from that originally intended. There are limits, of course, to the scale of what teachers can do, and too many changes could result, unhelpfully, in an almost complete reworking of a coursebook. A reordering of material is appropriate in the following kinds of situations:

- Materials typically present 'the future' by 'will' and 'going to'. However, for many learners, certainly at intermediate level and above, it is helpful to show the relationship between time reference and grammatical tense in a more accurate way. In this example we would probably wish to include the simple present and the present continuous as part of the notion of 'futurity', perhaps using 'Next term begins on 9 September' or 'She retires in 2005' as illustrations.
- The length of teaching programme may be too short for the coursebook to be worked through from beginning to end. It is likely in this case that the language needs of the students will determine the sequence in which the material will be taken. There is little point in working systematically through a textbook if key aspects of grammar, vocabulary or communicative function are never reached. For instance, if the learners are adults due to study in the target language environment, it will be necessary to have covered several aspects of the tense system and to have introduced socially appropriate functions and frequently used vocabulary.
- Finally, 'reordering' can include separating items of content from each other as well as regrouping them and putting them together. An obvious example is a lesson on a particular language function felt to contain too many new grammar points for the present proficiency level of the learners.

5.5   A framework for adaptation

There are clear areas of overlap among the various techniques discussed in this section, but it would be beyond the scope of this chapter to try to cover all the combinations and permutations. The intention here has been to offer a workable framework into which the main possibilities for adaptation can be fitted (not to offer some 'how to do' recipes, which are well covered elsewhere). Figure 5.2 shows how the considerations on which the principle of adaptation is based fit together.

1   Choose some materials with which you are familiar, or any others you
    would like to work with. (If you do not have any to hand, look back at
    the unit reprinted at the end of chapter 2.)
2   Decide on any features of the material you would like to change because
    it is not entirely suitable for your own teaching situation.
3   Referring as much as possible to the techniques we have been discussing,
    draw up some suggestions for how to adapt the material to achieve greater
    'congruence'.
4   If possible discuss with other colleagues the reasons for your decisions.

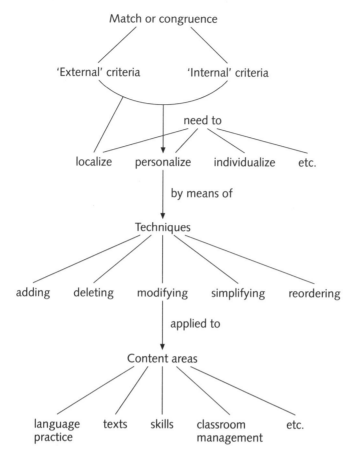

Figure 5.2   A framework for adaptation.

5.6   Conclusion

At one end of the scale, adaptation is a very practical activity carried out mainly by teachers in order to make their work more relevant to the learners with whom they are in day-to-day contact. It is, however, not just an exercise done in self-contained methodological isolation. Like all our activity as teachers, it is related, directly and indirectly, to a wider range of professional concerns. Adaptation is linked to issues of administration and the whole management of education, in so far as it derives from decisions taken about material to be adopted. Further, the need to adapt is one consequence of the setting of objectives in a particular educational context. Finally, adaptation can only be carried out effectively if it develops from an understanding of the possible design features of syllabuses and materials.

This chapter completes our discussion of the principles on which materials and methods are based. In part II we shall show how some of these principles have been expressed in relation to the concept of language skill.

5.7   Further reading

Grant, N. (1987): *Making the Most of Your Textbook*. Grant includes discussion of the principles of adaptation, illustrated by many examples. His book is particularly practical, and focuses on making material developed for the various language skills more communicative.

Part II
Teaching Language Skills

6

Reading Skills

In part I of this book we examined in detail the issues involved in principles of materials design. In this second part of the book, we devote a chapter to each language skill in turn with a final chapter that examines the concept of integrating language skills in the classroom. The division of each language skill into separate chapters is intentional and is *not* intended to reinforce the notion of the skills being taught in isolation, but rather is a way of devoting sufficient space to each one to further our original intention throughout the whole book – that of linking key principles to instances of classroom practice. Cross-referencing (both explicit and implicit) occurs often within this part of the book.

6.1 Introduction

We shall begin this chapter by thinking about the different types of material that we read and how these are linked to the purpose that we have in reading. After this, we attempt to show how advances in our conceptual knowledge about the reading process have changed some of our approaches to designing and using materials for the teaching of reading. We then look at different ways of providing feedback to learners on their reading. The final part of the chapter is devoted to vocabulary and vocabulary teaching.

As a skill, reading is clearly one of the most important; in fact in many instances around the world we may argue that reading is *the* most important foreign language skill, particularly in cases where students have to read English material for their own specialist subject but may never have to speak the language; such cases are often referred to as 'English as a library language'. Even though we are looking at each language skill independently in these chapters, there is clearly an overlap between reading and writing, in that a 'text' has to be written down before we can read it. In many societies literature is still seen as the prime example of writing and therefore one of the first things a student is asked to do is to read. In classroom terms one of the reasons for this is partly practical: it is often thought to be easier to supply a written text to be read than a spoken one to be understood.

6.2   Reasons for reading

Much of the current thinking on reading tends to focus primarily on the purpose of the activity; even if reading is done for pleasure it is still purposeful.

Williams (1984) usefully classifies reading into (a) getting general information from the text, (b) getting specific information from a text, and (c) for pleasure or for interest.

> Think about all the materials you have read during the last week, both in English and in your own L_1. Make a list of them. You may wish to reflect on how your reading of them could be classified according to Williams's categories outlined above. How many of these different types of reading material would you find in your teaching textbook?

The list that you have drawn up may include a newspaper, letters (personal and formal), booklets, leaflets, advertisements, labels on jars, tins and packets, magazines, the telephone directory, train timetables, and so on. Nunan (1999) also adds newspapers on the World Wide Web, email messages, academic texts and some poems written by a colleague. However, if this list could be said to be representative of *actual* reading material, ELT materials in some contexts still have virtually none or very little in the way of newspaper articles, labels or advertisements for students to read, but contain many examples of what we might call more 'traditional' types of texts, especially longer stretches of narrative and descriptions. We shall look at the implications of this later in the chapter.

Rivers and Temperley (1978: 187) list the following examples of some of the reasons that L_2 students may need or want to read:

- to obtain information for some purpose or because we are curious about some topic
- to obtain instructions on how to perform some task for our work or daily life
- to keep in touch with friends by correspondence or to understand business letters
- to know when or where something will take place or what is available
- to know what is happening or has happened (as reported in newspapers, magazines, reports)
- for enjoyment or excitement

Think about your own students' reading purposes in relation to the ones outlined above. Which are similar/different?

6.3   Changes in the concept of reading skills

We have looked at some of the purposes and reasons for reading which we may wish to develop with our learners. Let us now look at how the concept of reading as a skill has evolved in recent years and how this in turn has come to be reflected in the types of ELT materials available.

The traditional way of organizing materials in a unit is generally to begin with a piece of specially written material, which is then 'read' by the student. Such an arrangement essentially focuses on items of grammar and vocabulary that are then to be developed during the unit. This is inadequate if we are attempting to teach reading skills, as students are not being exposed to the variety of styles we would expect with a variety of texts – a scientific report is not written in the same way as a personal letter or instructions on a medicine bottle.

Hence, in reading classes we sometimes have a confusion of aims: often the students are not being taught reading and how to develop reading abilities *per se*, but rather a written text is being used as a vehicle for the introduction of new vocabulary and/or structures. It is fairly common for such texts to begin along the following lines:

It is eight o'clock in the morning. Mr Smith is in the dining room of their house. Mr Smith is sitting at the table reading his newspaper. He is waiting for his breakfast. Mrs Smith is in the kitchen cooking breakfast for Mr Smith, her husband, and their two children. John and Mary . . .

The text would then continue in a similar way.

As reading material it seems artificial because the intention is to draw learners' attention to items of structural usage rather than to the authentic features characteristic of 'real' text, or what makes texts 'hang together'. Many teachers, however, still work with this type of material. In this particular passage the sentences are strung together in isolation with little attempt at coherence. The same structures are repeated several times in a rather contrived way, making the whole text feel awkward and inauthentic. Another problem associated with these specially prepared texts, when it comes to the choice of topic, is that the learners are either presented with overfamiliar material that does not focus on what they can bring to the text, or the content is inconsequential for them. No real interaction takes place between writer and reader as the artificiality of the text means that no real message is being communicated. As we shall see later in relation to the overfamiliarity issue, comprehension questions on a text can sometimes be answered without having to look at the text at all! The essential purpose of all reading generally is to get new information and/or for pleasure,

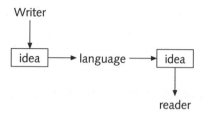

Figure 6.1   The text as object viewpoint.

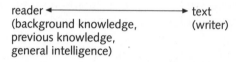

Figure 6.2   The text as process viewpoint.

not to go over what is known already or what is inconsequential to the reader in the first place.

A good many of the so called 'traditional' reading materials do not provide learners with useful texts or effective strategies to improve their reading abilities; and if we are to improve the teaching of reading skills, then research into the reading process may well be of some use. However, research tends to show that we know more about what skilled readers can do, rather than how they do it with any real degree of certainty.

Traditionally, and this is borne out in many of the materials, the reader was seen as the 'recipient' of information or as an 'empty vessel' who brought nothing to the text. This notion of 'text as object' (figure 6.1) is now frequently discredited in reading circles as readers are not entirely passive.

This 'text as object' viewpoint regards the reader as having nothing to contribute to the reading process as such; the writer provides information for the reader who is seen as an 'empty vessel' that merely receives information. We may liken this to a one-way traffic system in which everything flows in one direction only.

In recent years, however, an increasing number of ELT materials that profess to develop reading skills have moved from the 'text as object' viewpoint shown above, to that of the 'text as process', by encouraging close interaction between the reader and the text (figure 6.2).

6.4   *Types of reading skills*

It is generally recognized now that the efficient reader versed in ways of interacting with various types of texts, is flexible, and chooses appropriate reading strategies depending on the particular text in question. Pugh (1978) shows how efficient readers 'switch' styles according to the type of text they are reading.

● READING AND SPEAKING

Pre-reading task

1 What do you think the life of a nun is like? What do they *always* do, *sometimes* do, and *never* do?

2 Which of the following do you think are important to nuns?

> sport   clothes   prayer   food and drink   children
> solitude   hotels   travel   gardening   reading
> television   singing   money

Reading

Now read the text. Which of the things in the list above does she mention?

Sister Wendy, TV Star!

Sister Wendy Beckett has been a nun for nearly 50 years, since she was 16. Most of the time she lives in solitary confinement in a caravan in the grounds of a Carmelite monastery in Norfolk, often not speaking to anyone for 22 hours a day. But every few months she leaves her caravan and travels round Europe, staying in international hotels and eating in famous restaurants. Why is she leading this double life? How does a nun who has devoted her life to solitude and prayer become a visitor to the Ritz?

Sister Wendy has a remarkable other life. She writes and presents an arts programme for BBC television called 'Sister Wendy's Grand Tour'. In it, she visits European art capitals and gives her personal opinions on some of the world's most famous works of art. She begins each programme with these words: 'For over 20 years I lived in solitude. Now I'm seeing Europe for the first time. I'm visiting the world's most famous art treasures.'

She speaks clearly and plainly, with none of the
25 academic verbosity of art historians. TV viewers
love her common-sense wisdom, and are
fascinated to watch a kind, elderly, bespectacled,
nun who is so obviously delighted by all she sees.
They are infected by her enthusiasm. Sister
30 Wendy believes that although God wants her to
have a life of prayer and solitary contemplation,
He has also given her a mission to explain art in
a simple manner to ordinary people. She says:
'I think God has been very good to me. Really
35 I am a disaster as a person. Solitude is right for
me because I'm not good at being with other
people. But of course I enjoy going on tour. I
have a comfortable bed, a luxurious bath and
good meals, but the joy is mild compared with
40 the joy of solitude and silent prayer. I always
rush back to my caravan. People find this hard to
understand. I have never wanted anything else, I
am a blissfully happy woman.'
Sister Wendy's love of God and art is matched
45 only by her love of good food and wine. She
takes delight in poring over menus, choosing a
good wine and wondering whether the steak is
tender enough for her to eat because she has no
back teeth. However, she is not delighted by her
50 performance on television.
'I can't bear to watch myself on television. I
feel that I look so silly — a ridiculous black-
clothed figure. Thank God we don't have a
television at the monastery. I suppose I am
55 famous in a way, but as 95% of my time is spent
alone in my caravan, it really doesn't affect me.
I'm unimportant.'
Sister Wendy earned £1,200 for the first series.
The success of this resulted in an increase for the
60 second series. The money is being used to
provide new shower rooms for the Carmelite
monastery. ■

Comprehension check

1 What do these numbers in the text refer to?

   16   22   20   95%   50   1,200

2 Are the following statements true (✓) or false (✗)?
   Correct the false ones.

a Sister Wendy spends a lot of time alone.
b She travels to art capitals all over the world.
c Her television programmes are popular because she
   meets famous art historians and interviews them.
d She believes that God wants her to lead this double life.
e She doesn't enjoy being alone in her caravan any more.
f She only eats plain food and she doesn't drink alcohol.
g Some of her teeth are missing.
h She loves watching herself on television.
i The other nuns at the monastery always watch her
   programmes on television.
j Sister Wendy is using the money she has earned to
   improve the monastery.

Language work

1 Complete the interview with Sister Wendy.

   I   (a) _____ ?

   SW   When I was sixteen. Goodness, that's nearly
        fifty years ago!

   I   (b) _____ ?

   SW   In Norfolk. In a Carmelite monastery. Well,
        not actually in the monastery but in the
        grounds. I have a caravan.

   I   (c) _____ ?

   SW   No, I don't. Just in Europe—that's far enough!

   I   (d) _____ ?

   SW   I don't really know. I'm not sure why they're
        popular. I feel that I look so silly, but perhaps
        people find it funny to watch a silly old nun!

   I   (e) _____ ?

   SW   Yes, I do. Of course I do. The tours are really
        interesting and everybody enjoys a life of
        luxury now and then. I love good food and
        drink, but you know, I'm happiest on my own
        in my caravan.

   I   (f) _____ ?

   SW   No, I don't! I look ridiculous. I never watch if I
        can help it!

   I   (g) _____ ?

   SW   I'm using it to help the monastery. Some new
        shower rooms are being built. That's good, isn't it?

2 T.14 Listen and check your answers.

Discussion

Work in groups. Look at the list in Exercise 2 of the Pre-
reading task. Which of them are important to *you*? Why?

Source: L. and J. Soars, pp. 20–1 from *New Headway English Course: Intermediate Students'
Book*. Oxford: Oxford University Press, 1996. © Oxford University Press, 1996. Reproduced
by permission of Oxford University Press.

We therefore have to match reading skill to reading purpose. We do not, for example, read seventeenth-century poetry in the same way as we read the television page in our newspaper. Skilled readers scan to locate specific information in a text and skim to extract general information from it. These skills are quite widely practised in many contemporary ELT reading skills courses. The example from a textbook on pp. 93–4 is one of many.

Skimming and scanning are useful strategies for learners to operate; however, there is arguably a limit to their usefulness in the context illustrated above, in the sense that the learner scans for particular information and then does not have to do anything with it. All that we have mentioned thus far tends to confirm the now generally accepted view that efficient readers are not passive and do not operate in a vacuum: they react with the text by having expectations (even though these might in fact have nothing to do with the content of the text) and ideas about the purpose of the text, as well as ideas about possible outcomes.

Efficient readers also interrogate materials of all types by looking for 'clues' in titles, subtitles and within the passage itself. Pre-reading questions can be useful because they focus learners' attention on the types of information that they are about to read.

Classroom teachers often complain that students view reading as tedious and therefore low priority simply because they do not feel challenged or involved in the text. This can be overcome if they can be encouraged to 'dialogue' with the writer by expecting questions to be answered, reflecting on expectations at every stage, anticipating what the writer will say next and so on. Efficient readers appear continually to interrogate the text, forming expectations at every stage.

Ur (1996) suggests various criteria that distinguish efficient from inefficient readers: efficient readers can access content easier by changing reading speed according to text, they can select significant features of a text and skim the rest, they can guess or infer meaning from context, they think ahead by predicting outcomes, they use background knowledge to help them understand the meaning, they are motivated to read the text as they see it as a challenge and the text has a purpose, they can switch reading strategy according to the type of text they are reading and so on.

Getting the learner to interact with different types of text as outlined above does not necessarily mean that learners will have to understand the whole text immediately. They may, for example, be able to understand and to extract specific information from the text as in the example on p. 96.

6.5 Schema theory

Another major contribution to our knowledge of reading, with many implications for the classroom, is provided by Schema theory. Bartlett (1932) first used this particular term to explain how the knowledge that we have about the world is organized into interrelated patterns based on our previous knowledge

---

UNIT 10   **TIME**

30   Looking Forward

1 Some science fiction writers were recently asked what their predictions were for the 21st Century. The article below is about what one person thinks life will be like.

Life in the 21st Century

As for daily life, I think that we will be able to order most of our shopping by computer and this will be delivered to our homes, so in fact there won't be any need to go out to the shops. I'm sure that most of our homes will have a video telephone so we will be able to see the person we are talking to. We will also be watching 'holovision' which will give you threedimensional life-size pictures on your screen – this will replace television. Because of improved technology, there will be no more road accidents. Cars will be guided by computers so people will not have to do any more driving.

I think most of our food will be in the form of pills and liquids which will have all the vitamins and protein that we need for a balanced diet. Only when we go out for social eating will we eat the same food as today, but we will no longer be eating meat.

About once a year our bodies will go into a health centre for a service in much the same way as a car has to be serviced. So, for example, our veins will be cleaned out, our blood purified, our muscles toned up and so on. Any part that is worn out could be replaced by a new plastic part. We will all be much healthier by then anyway, because there will be more leisure time for us to use for exercise. Also a safe medicine will have been discovered which will allow people to lose or put on weight as they need. One exciting development will be the possiblity of being deep frozen for a period of time and then waking up some years later. I would be interested in that myself!

A lot of our wildlife will be conserved in parks but unfortunately I think we will have lost the rhinoceros, the tiger and the panda and a few other species because of ruthless hunting by man. However, most of our energy problems will have been solved by developments in the use of solar energy and safe nuclear energy.

Because of improved media technology, all cultures will become similar and, indeed, everybody will be speaking an international language (English) by 2020.

There will be more women in politics than men – and the world will be a more peaceful place because of this. In fact, women will also be able to run the Marathon faster than men.

2 Write a list of the points you agree with and another list of the points you disagree with.

Agree	Disagree
Shopping by computer	Videophones in homes

Source: B. Milne, Unit 10, p. 60 from *Integrated Skills: Intermediate*. Oxford: Heinemann, 1991. © Heinemann, 1991.

and experience. These 'schemata' also allow us to predict what may happen. This theory takes our idea of the interactive reading process a stage further by proposing that efficient readers are able to relate 'texts' to their background knowledge of the world. Brown and Yule (1983b), McCarthy and Carter (1994), Cook (1997) and Nunan (1999) all provide accounts of how this background knowledge can influence the comprehension process. Clearly it can sometimes be based on previous knowledge of similar texts. For example, if we are reading

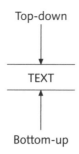

Top-down

TEXT

Bottom-up

Figure 6.3 Top-down and bottom-up processing of a text.

a newspaper, we know from previous experience about the typeface, the layout, the order in which the information is presented and so on. We share cultural background material with others. As Nunan (1999: 256) writes, 'We interpret what we read in terms of what we already know, and we integrate what we already know with the content of what we are reading.' The word 'wedding' in a British context could engender a complete schematic framework to accompany it; that is, 'last Saturday', 'Registry Office', 'Best Man' and so on. This is why reading something written by someone in a language with different cultural assumptions from ours can be difficult. Overseas teachers and students sometimes complain that reading literature in an L_2 is problematic not just because of the language, but also because shared assumptions or different schemata do not always match up.

In many cases an efficient reader appears to use what are called 'top-down' and 'bottom-up' strategies. This means that the reader will not just try to decipher the meaning of individual lexical items but will also have clear ideas about the overall rhetorical organization of the text. The essential features of the bottom-up approach are that the reader tries to decode each individual letter encountered by matching it to the minimal units of meaning in the sound system (the phoneme) to arrive at a meaning of the text, whereas with the top-down approach, the interaction process between the reader and the text involves the reader in activating knowledge of the world, plus past experiences, expectations and intuitions, to arrive at a meaning of the text. In other words, the top-down process interacts with the bottom-up process in order to aid comprehension (figure 6.3).

We might further illustrate this by looking at a speaking/listening analogy first of all. If someone asks us, 'Have you got a light?' and we get stuck at the level of the bottom-up process by working out each individual word, then clearly we are missing the top-down request, that the speaker is in fact asking for a match.

Let us look at a newspaper extract about education in Britain in order to see how some of these principles may operate in reality.

From the title, can you predict what the passage will be about? As you are reading the text think about how you are reading it.

Paying to Learn: Is It Snobbery?

The British social system is probably the most snobbish in the world but that does not necessarily mean – since it is perfectly natural for parents to wish to give their children the same or a better education than they themselves received – that those who choose to educate their children privately are all snobs. Thus, many upper class families who were forced to send their children to boarding schools at the height of the British Empire because they were often out of the country for years, naturally wish to continue the tradition, although nowadays it involves great financial sacrifices. Even today many pupils in boarding schools are still opting out of what may be the best state education system in the world. Some of these are obviously doing this for snobbish reasons – believing that to have been educated privately is to be socially 'one-up' and that children thus educated, whatever their ability, will have an advantage over their state educated contemporaries. The less said about this type of parent the better. Fortunately, most parents who choose private education have very good reasons for doing so.

A good start to a child's education is vital and, since the war, classes in many primary schools have been very large so that nervous children or those of average or below average ability could easily get lost in the crowd and miss out on education altogether. This explains the popularity of the small private preparatory school in which a child has more individual attention and help with particular difficulties. Some children of very good ability certainly do not *need* to be educated privately: my own children have all been educated in the state system and have all gone on to higher education.

However, this is a free country and parents who wish to pay for education are perfectly entitled to do so – they could spend their money much less wisely. There are, nonetheless, two great dangers in having a private system running alongside the state system. One is the development of a privileged class, with the result that people get the top jobs not on the basis of ability but of who they are and where they went to school. If this country is to survive, we must educate our best brains to the highest possible standard – irrespective of their social and financial standing. The other is that we shall need a highly skilled and adaptable workforce capable of dealing with the advanced technology of the future and this will require an efficient state system of education possessing all the necessary advanced equipment.

Where did you look on the line? Did you skim/scan? Did you go backwards/ forwards? Did you stop to look at every word? Did you stop to think at all?

As teachers we may want to offer our learners one effective reading strategy, which might be to approach this text by noting the title first of all. This clearly points ahead to what the writer will be saying and how the argument develops at various stages in the text itself, when the author is giving approval and disapproval to various types of parent. The reader may also put 'schematic' knowledge into operation: in other words an understanding of the background to the British education system, the state-versus-private-education debate, the British Empire, the class system. This 'top-down' processing would interact with the text as would the 'bottom-up' processing at the lexical level. The reader may also get through the passage by means of what are sometimes referred to as the discourse signposts in the text: expressions such as 'However', 'fortunately', and 'there are, nonetheless', which are meant as a useful guide for the reader.

6.6 Implications

Teachers should provide students with a purpose for reading by supplying materials that stimulate interest and do not have an overfamiliar content. Of all the language skills, reading is the most private, and there is a problem in getting feedback on a private process. The notion of privacy in reading can sometimes be related to learner needs: a learner may need material of a different level and topic to other learners in the group, which may involve the teacher in the provision of some individualized reading in the programme. Reading practised with reading laboratories and/or self-access centres may well be more pertinent to some learners' needs. (For a full discussion of individualization and self-access systems see chapter 12.) We also have to be able to assess the difficulty of the materials for our own learners and to grade them according to familiarity of topic, length and complexity of structure and possible number of unfamiliar words/expressions, as overloading learners with too much may involve them in decoding vocabulary at the expense of reading for meaning. We can also develop and foster appropriate skills according to reading purpose, for example by encouraging students to read quickly when it is appropriate to do so. Timed activities or 'speed reading' can be related to the private nature of the reading process that we mentioned earlier. In other words, reading quickly with good overall comprehension does not necessarily have to be made competitive with other students as the individual student and/or the teacher can keep a record of how long it takes to extract information from a given source. Consequently, the transferability of principled flexible skills to different types of reading materials is one of the most effective things to develop in the reading skills class.

6.7 Classroom practice and procedure

On a worldwide level, the format of teaching reading skills may vary according to local circumstances. Many teachers consider dividing reading into intensive, classroom-based work with an adjunctive extensive reading programme to give further out-of-class practice. Some classes will be called 'reading' and will therefore focus primarily on the development of reading skills. Sometimes teachers include reading skills as part of another class either for reasons of expediency – because there is only one timetabled period for English – or for reasons of principle – because they believe that reading is best integrated with the other skills such as writing. The following suggestions for classroom practice and procedure will be of interest to teachers of reading skills.

R. V. White (1981) makes some suggestions about the stages and procedure of a reading lesson that may help us (a) to put the skill into a classroom context, and (b) to see some of its possible relationships with the other language skills:

Stage 1   Arouse the students' interest and motivation by linking the topic of the text to their own experience or existing knowledge. Give some pre-reading/focusing questions to help them to do this.

Stage 2   Give them points to search for in the reading text, or ask the students to suggest the points.

Stage 3   After reading, encourage a discussion of answers.

Stage 4   Develop into writing by using the information gained for another purpose.

> Look at the reading passage 'Paying to Learn' on p. 98. How could you develop it within the framework outlined above?

Beaumont (1983) has developed a scheme for achieving goals and objectives in a reading lesson, which may be summarized as follows:

1   *Text structure* – how is it linked together, how can we work out unfamiliar words?
2   *Text purpose* – what is the text for? Who is it written for? What does it do? How does it fulfil its purpose?
3   *Reading for information* – what are the topic and the main ideas? What are the supporting ideas? How can we distinguish between the main and the supporting ideas?
4   *Interpretation* – what are the opinions of the writer? How can we tell what the writer feels?

Davies (1995) argues the case for providing reading classes and texts that allow students to interact and question the text and to ask about what they do not know, in the belief that this will foster critical readers.

Finally, there are teachers who may want or need to design their own reading course within a particular institution. To this end, Nunan (1999) considers five essential steps involved in designing reading courses:

1   Decide the overall purpose of the reading course within a wider pedagogical framework.
2   Identify the types of texts and tasks that the course requires.
3   Identify the linguistic elements to be covered (consider what is going to be important: grammatical items / lexis/discourse / specific purpose etc.).
4   Integrate texts and tasks into class-based work units.
5   Link reading to other language skills where pertinent (reading as a mono-skill is only taught in some very narrow-angle library language situations. Hence it is useful to think how reading can usefully be integrated with the other language skills. See chapter 10 for further discussion).

Now let us look at a range of ways for developing reading skills in the classroom and the principles behind each of them:

1   Practising specific strategies such as skimming/scanning with a particular text. The idea behind this is to enable the learner to read and select specific information at the expense of other (redundant) information.
2   One effective way of developing reading skills, which gives the learner a reason for reading, is to use the information gap principle often associated with communicative language teaching. Some reading materials, such as those devised by Geddes and Sturtridge (1982) use this principle. In these materials, the information required for the completion of a target task is distributed among two or more sources. Each subgroup only has *part* of the information required to complete the task. The subgroups consequently have to exchange their information so that the information gap is filled and the target task completed. This activity links reading with other forms of communication, e.g. speaking/discussion or listening/writing, and can thus provide a reading-driven integration of the language skills.
3   Several of the more recent materials for reading contain what are sometimes referred to as 'text scrambling' activities. The principle behind this type of material is that students can be taught to have an awareness of the discourse or cohesive features of reading materials. If a passage is clearly written then it can be 'scrambled' and reassembled in the correct order if the learner can recognize the discourse patterns and markers in the text.
4   Some reading materials are constructed along the lines that the learners bring not only background knowledge to reading but emotional (affective) responses as well, and will want to talk about their reactions to various texts.
5   In some instances, depending on the learners and their proficiency, it is feasible to ask the learners themselves to provide reading texts or to research their own material for analysis and discussion in class, particularly in an EAP (English for Academic Purposes) context. Learners often need to read through a lot of material before they select an appropriate piece of material or article. With the advent of the World Wide Web, teachers working in institutions with computers may wish to encourage this. (Refer to chapter 12 for more discussion of Web-based teaching and learning.)
6   Teachers need to think about providing reading passages that provide learners with a way of questioning and interacting with the text (Davies 1995) to ascertain for example what the writer thinks, not necessarily explicitly, about an issue or topic.

1   Examine your own materials for reading. To what extent do they incorporate these principles? Which are different?
2   Decide which types of reading skills you could develop with the following materials. Start with the nature of the text and then look at what kinds of skills could come from it.

9 Tall stories

Here are four 'tall stories' – stories which are probably not true, but people enjoy telling them. Sometime they are called urban myths. Read them and decide whether you think they really happened or not.

Safety first!

Did you hear about the plane which crashed somewhere in South America as it was coming in to land?

Apparently, it was fitted with a device which warns the pilot that he is approaching the ground – a Ground Warning Alarm (GWA) system. Some pilots find this warning irritating so they switch it off.

When the black box was examined, the crash was blamed on pilot error. The decision had been easy to reach. When the plane had been coming in to land, the GWA had gone off, telling the pilot he was too close to the ground. On the tape the pilot can be heard saying, "Shut up, you stupid machine!" Then you hear the sound of the crash.

True story or myth?

What a rat!

Then there was the story of the couple who were in Thailand on holiday. The morning after they arrived, they found a thin little cat sitting on their balcony. They immediately fell in love with it. They cleaned it and fed it. By the time they were ready to leave, they couldn't bear to be parted from it.

They arranged for the cat to come home with them. Waiting at home was their pet poodle. The poodle and the cat seemed to get on together very well, so the couple decided to go out for dinner. When they got back, they found their sitting room covered in poodle hair and the dog halfway down the cat's throat!

It turned out the cat was not a cat, but an enormous Thai water rat!

True story or myth?

Drowned in a drain

A man from Wakefield in Yorkshire went out one night for a few drinks at his local pub. He left his car in the street near the pub. When he decided to go home, he went out to his car, took out the keys, and then accidentally dropped them down a drain in the road.

He could see the keys down the drain on top of some leaves. So, he managed to lift the drain cover, but the key was too far down for him to reach. He lay down in order to reach them. Suddenly, he fell into the drain head first. Just as he did that it started to rain heavily. Nobody heard his cries for help. The next morning he was found drowned, his head down the drain, his legs sticking up in the air.

True story or myth?

Sunk by flying cow

A few years ago, the crew of a Japanese fishing boat were rescued from the wreckage of their boat in the Sea of Japan. They said that their boat had been sunk by a cow falling out of the sky. Nobody believed them.

A few weeks later the Russian Air Force admitted that the crew of one of their planes had stolen a cow in Siberia and put it into the plane's cargo hold.

At 30,000 feet the cow started to run around the plane out of control. The crew decided there was only one thing they could do. So, they opened the cargo door and the cow jumped out, landing on top of the Japanese fishing boat.

True story or myth?

Read one of these stories again at home. You will be asked to tell it to the class at the next lesson. If you like this kind of story, they are all on the Web. Find them under 'urban myths'. Bring one in to class!

Source: H. Dellar and D. Hocking, p. 98 from *Innovations*. Hove: Language Teaching Publications, 2000. © Language Teaching Publications, 2000.

Unit 2 A Treasure Hunt

Stage 1 Introduction

Part 1 People have always dreamed of finding buried treasure. It is not only the hope of finding gold and precious stones which excites them but the search itself – following the clues and piecing together the information. Some people seem to enjoy hiding treasure as much as others enjoy seeking it.

Read the newspaper report. What did the millionaire bury? Did he leave any clues?

Eccentric Millionaire Buries Treasure

It was confirmed by lawyers yesterday that eccentric millionaire Harry Evans who died last month had buried the priceless Hadley jewel. They said that Mr Evans, who had no family himself, felt that the jewel from his private collection should go to 'someone who wanted it enough to search for it'. He left a number of verses as clues to the whereabouts of the buried treasure. The Hadley jewel consists of a gold chain and pendant which contains two miniature portraits. Apparently Mr Evans buried the piece in a water-proof container somewhere beyond the range of metal detectors.

Experts described the piece yesterday as 'unique' and expressed anxiety for its safety.

Just watch these 'snails'

Part 2 Below is an entry from an exhibition catalogue describing the jewel. Why is it called the Hadley jewel?

Chain and pendant (The Hadley Jewel)

Cat. no. 157

Gold and enamelled in black, white, pale blue and red. Set with table-cut rubies, emeralds and pearls.

Height: 6.8 cm.

Condition: the gold suspension ring on the chain is not original and the replacement is 18th century.

History: the Hadley Jewel is so called because it was given as a marriage gift to Catherine Linton on the occasion of her wedding to John Hadley in 1580. It belonged to the Hadley family from Elizabethan times until the twentieth century. The gold miniature case contains portraits of a man and a woman. The lid has floral decorations set into the gold and the whole case is surrounded by a broad band set with gems. Three large irregular pearls hang at the base of the pendant.

Stage 2 Jigsaw Reading Tasks

Read the texts for your group
(Group 1 p. 29, Group 2 p. 39,
Group 3 p. 49):

1 You have only *some* of the clues
that Harry Evans left – read yours
carefully!

2 Name as many things as you
can on the map.

3 In the table below make short
notes about the buildings and
monuments you have marked on
the map.

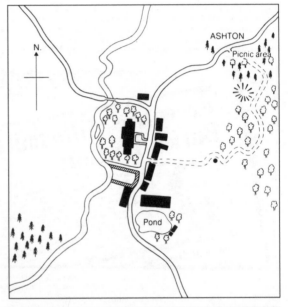

Building or monument	Date	What it looks like

Stage 3 Discussion

1 Find out what the other two groups have named on their maps.

2 Which buildings and monuments have they found out about?

3 Put all your clues together, making sure you begin with the first clue.

4 Mark on the map the exact place where the Hadley Jewel is buried.

5 What happens in your country when someone finds buried treasure?

Unit 2 A Treasure Hunt

Harry Evans buried the Hadley Jewel somewhere in the Ashton-Hadley Hall area. Here are some of the clues he left:

```
Whether it rains or whether it shines
These are the last of the precious lines.

Now you must look for the leaves of the vine
Because what you are seeking is buried under time.
```

Here is an extract from *A Guide to Country Walks.*

Walk 2: Ashton and Hadley Hall (3 miles)

The visitor can leave his car at Ashton picnic area where there are car parking and toilet facilities as well as wooden tables and benches enabling people to picnic in comfort. He can then follow the rough path south and past the ruins of an old castle on his right. This is known as Alfred's castle and is said to have belonged to the old king. The grassy hill commands a fine view of the valley below. Little remains of the castle now because the stone was taken to build the stately house set in the magnificent park that can be seen in the village to the south west. This is Hadley Hall, built about 1690 for the Earl of Swinley.

Hadley Hall may well surprise the visitor as it seems somewhat out of place in this wild landscape. It is indeed elegant and has such proportions that it has been described as a perfect doll's house. Indeed it looks as if some giant's hand has dropped this doll's house into the park. It stands with its west facade looking onto the river while the east faces the village. The visitor can continue on this path, passing on his left the curious Black Mouse stone, and then down into the village emerging between cottages in the village street. Refreshments can be had at the local inn, the Black Lion, a delightful black and white Elizabethan building dated 1590.

Return to Ashton car park by the main road or retrace your footsteps along the path.

2) Unit 2 A Treasure Hunt

Harry Evans buried the Hadley Jewel somewhere in the Emm Valley area.
Here are some of the clues he left:

```
Whether it rains or whether it shines
This is the middle of the precious lines.

If you come early or if you come late,
Go under the three birds that sit on the gate.
```

Here is an extract from *A Visitor's Guide to the Emm Valley:*

If you want to see a really beautiful village you must not miss Harbury. As you enter the village on the B3300 road you see first the village pond which lies beside the old church of St Mary. Shaded with willow trees, the quiet water reflects the church tower as ducks and moorhens swim at their leisure. Opposite the church is one of the finest Elizabethan inns in the country where the tired traveller will find good company as well as refreshment. The inn is built on a far older site as there was originally a hospice there, run by monks and offering food and shelter to pilgrims on their way to Canterbury. Don't miss the remains of the monastic garden which reaches down to the river. This walled garden is now preserved by the villagers as part of the national heritage and is a pleasant place to sit a while. If the sun is shining you can check your watch with the time shown by the old sundial in the centre of the garden. Made in local stone in 1760 the top of the sundial has a fine brass plate where the hours are clearly written and the surrounding metal is decorated with grapes and vine leaves. Delightful though this tranquil scene is, you should press on to see what is perhaps the highlight of the village, the Earl of Swinley's stately home.

Unit 2 A Treasure Hunt

Harry Evans buried the Hadley Jewel somewhere in or near the village of Harbury.
Here are some of the clues he left:

> Whether it rains or whether it shines
> These are the first of the precious lines.
>
> If you are short or if you are tall
> From Alfred's hill you can see it all.
>
> Walk quickly south past the old doll's house,
> Seek a black lion, not a black mouse.

Here is an extract from *The Country Lover's Guide to Villages*:

The River Emm winds its way through the charming village of Harbury, which is well worth a visit. Harbury has more than its fair share of places of historical interest: a stately home, a fine church and a village pub which would look well in any photograph. However, perhaps the oldest building in the village is in some ways the most interesting. As you come into Harbury from the south, the village pond is on your right and a little further on to your left you will see some high walls and a splendid old gateway built straight onto the village street. This is all that remains of the old abbey and the walls enclose a beautiful walled flower garden. The garden and the walls adjoin the old village inn and the walls run round the corner down a narrow land and north-west to the river. The gateway itself has been dated at about 1295 although the walls may be earlier. The visitor who looks up will see an interesting stone carving of a shield above the arch of the gate. On the shield can be seen three birds beautifully carved in white stone. Nothing is left of the abbey itself.

Source: M. Geddes and G. Sturtridge, Unit 2 from *Reading Links*. London: Heinemann, 1982. © Heinemann, 1982.

Task 3 (Pairs)

Work in pairs, A and B.

Student A: Read Text 1. Note briefly in your section of the table the 'orthodox' view on the three aspects of work listed in the text.

Student B: Read Text 2. Note briefly in your section of the table the author's view on the three aspects of work listed in the text.

	Text 1	*Text 2*
NATURE OF WORK		
EFFECT OF WORKING CONDITIONS		
MOTIVATION FOR WORK		

Text 1 'Orthodox' view

THE orthodox view of work which has been accepted by most managers and industrial psychologists is a simple one, and fifty years of industrial psychology and more than a century of managerial practice have been founded upon it. Regarding the *nature* of work, the orthodox view accepts the Old Testament   5
belief that physical labour is a curse imposed on man as a punishment for his sins and that the sensible man labours solely in order to keep himself and his family alive, or, if he is fortunate, in order to make a sufficient surplus to enable him to do the things he really likes.* Regarding the *conditions* of work, it is   10
assumed that improving the conditions of the job will cause the worker's natural dislike of it to be somewhat mitigated, and, in addition, will keep him physically healthy and therefore more efficient in the mechanistic sense. Finally, regarding the *motivation* of work, the carrot and stick hypothesis asserts that the main   15
positive incentive is money, the main negative one fear of unemployment.

Brown, J.A.C. (1954) *The Social Psychology of Industry*, p. 186 (London: Penguin).

Text 2 Author's view

(1) Work is an essential part of a man's life since it is that aspect of his life which gives him status and binds him to society. Ordinarily men and women like their work, and at most periods of history always have done so. When they do not like it, the fault lies in the psy- 5 chological and social conditions of the job rather than in the worker. Furthermore, work is a *social* activity.

(2) The morale of the worker (i.e. whether or not he works willingly) has no *direct* relationship whatsoever to the material conditions of the job. Investigations into 10 temperature, lighting, time and motion study, noise, and humidity have not the slightest bearing on morale, although they may have a bearing on physical health and comfort.

(3) There are many incentives, of which, under normal 15 conditions, money is one of the least important. Unemployment is a powerful negative incentive, precisely because (1) is true. That is to say, unemployment is feared because it cuts man off from his society.

Brown, J.A.C. op cit., p. 187.

Task 4 (Pairs)

Find out from your partner the views expressed in his or her text. Note them in the appropriate section of the table in Task 3.

Now read each other's text to check if anything has been missed out.

Task 5 (Groups)

Work in groups. Discuss your own views and those expressed in the texts. Do you agree with either text? Have your views changed through reading the texts?

Source: E. H. Glendinning and B. Holmström, pp. 105–6 from *Study Reading: A Course in Reading Skills for Academic Purposes*. Cambridge: Cambridge University Press, 1992. © Cambridge University Press, 1992.

6.8   Feedack to learners

Earlier in the chapter we mentioned that reading is essentially a private activity. However, it remains a fact that as we 'teach' reading skills in the classroom this often requires us to have some sort of observable (testable) outcome. In its most extreme form this may be embodied in the materials themselves, which sometimes do little more than test the students rather than helping them to develop different, relevant reading skills.

Questions to learners can be in either written or spoken form and it is generally thought that a balance of the two is appropriate for most learning situations.

One way of thinking about reading comprehension questions is to consider the *form* of the question; for example, yes/no, true/false, multiple choice, non-verbal matrix to be completed, open-ended question and the type of question, what the question is trying to get out of the reader.

Nuttall (1996) identifies five basic question types commonly used for reading. The first of these is literal comprehension. By this she means that if readers do not understand the literal meaning of a particular text, then they are probably not going to get very much else out of that text. The second is reorganizing or putting the information in the text into a different order. Then come questions of inferring or 'reading between the lines'. Writers do not always state explicitly what they mean. An efficient reader can infer meaning not explicitly stated in the passage. This may be seen as an intellectual skill as opposed to a reading skill by some, although there is clearly a measure of overlap. Question types requiring a measure of personal response are often to be found in literary passages where the reader has to argue for a particular personal response supported by reference to the text. The last type of question is quite sophisticated and not all students would need it. Questions of evaluation would require the reader to assess how effectively the writer has conveyed her intention. If the writing is intended to convince or to persuade, how convincing or persuasive is it?

When evaluating questions for use with particular learners there may not be enough of the right type or form to match their purpose or what the teacher knows about their personal background. A variety of different question forms and types that enable learners to use their different reading skills in appropriate ways is of most use.

Look at the following question, which accompanies the passage 'Paying to Learn' on p. 98. What form and type of question is it, according to Nuttall's classification outlined above?
'Complete the following chart with reasons why parents send their children to private schools and state whether the author considers each reason valid or not.'

Reason	Valid? Yes/No
a.	
b.	
c.	
d.	

Asking questions of the learner is not the only way to check comprehension. It is increasingly common to find materials that require the learner to extract meaning from them and then to use that information in order to do something else – such as jigsaw reading or assembling an object from a set of instructions. Successful reading thus enables a certain task to be completed. In many respects this is more akin to what most people do in their L_1 or in the 'real' world; it is rare for people to have to answer questions on what they have read.

6.9 *Vocabulary and vocabulary teaching: Recent developments*

A knowledge and understanding of vocabulary is often considered to be an integral part of a reader's overall competence in a foreign or second language and the explicit teaching of vocabulary (sometimes linked to a reading class) has enjoyed something of a revival in recent years. Some teachers prefer to include vocabulary as part of their reading class as the following material helps to illustrate. Other teachers prefer to think of vocabulary as an area that merits its own syllabus and materials.

---

2 Before reading

After you have matched these words with their meanings, look them up in your dictionary to check that you fully understand them.

1. suspend
2. container
3. controversial
4. motive
5. consent
6. protester
7. pickled
8. formaldehyde

a. permission
b. very likely to cause an argument or protest
c. hang
d. reason for doing something (often criminal)
e. a bottle, can, jar or similar thing
f. a liquid used to preserve things
g. a person who disagrees in a public way
h. preserved (often in vinegar)

ART ATTACK

A man almost destroyed a work of art, worth £25,000, in a London art gallery yesterday. The work of art consisted of a glass container with a dead sheep suspended in formaldehyde.

The protester poured black ink into the case while it was on display at the Serpentine Gallery. Gallery staff were shocked as they saw the protester run away after first changing the name of the work to 'Black Sheep'.

The controversial work was originally called 'Away from the Flock'. It was the latest in a long line of animals pickled by famous British artist Damien Hirst. Neither the police nor gallery staff could think of a motive for the attack, other than the fact that it might be a protest about its controversial nature.

Hirst spent last night emptying the case and cleaning the animal in the hope that it might be repaired. Hirst said recently of the sculpture "I don't think it's shocking. It gets people interested in art. The worst thing is if someone just walks through a gallery without seeing anything." However, he went on to say, "People can't come in and mess about with exhibits without the artist's consent. But it could have been worse. Someone could have come in with a hammer."

Hirst has stated that he intends to pickle his grandmother in formaldehyde when she dies, but only if she gives her consent!

Source: H. Dellar and D. Hocking, p. 113 from *Innovations*. Hove: Language Teaching Publications, 2000. © Language Teaching Publications, 2000.

During the last decade language teachers have been able to benefit from the exponential growth in computer generated corpora, which has provided information about word frequency and how these words can be used in a range of spoken and written situations. The COBUILD Project has already been referred to in chapter 3. Recent examples of dictionaries that evolved from this research include *The Cambridge International Dictionary of English*, 1995; *The Oxford Advanced Learners Dictionary*, 1995; and *The Longman Dictionary of Contemporary English*, 1995. Each of these is based on the new understanding of language that came to light in the 1990s. In the *Longman Dictionary*, for example, the 3,000 most frequent words in writing and speech are given special attention. (Refer to chapter 3 again for a full discussion of the lexical approach.)

Research into vocabulary and vocabulary acquisition shows that we have not explicitly been taught the majority of words that we know in a language (Carter: 2001). This raises some interesting questions for the teaching of vocabulary. Beyond a certain point or proficiency in learning a foreign or second language the acquiring of any new vocabulary is probably going to be implicit rather than explicit. Many practitioners believe that vocabulary development is essentially what is known as an explicit–implicit continuum, where learners may benefit from explicit or implicit learning depending on the stage of their language learning career.

6.10 Vocabulary: what to teach?

What is your overall approach to vocabulary and vocabulary teaching? Do you teach vocabulary in your reading classes or devote separate lessons to it? Why is this?

Teaching vocabulary in its narrowest sense is teaching the individual words of the language that we expect learners to acquire. However, we know from our knowledge of language that an understanding and production of any sort of 'text' normally involves language more than using a simple word in isolation. Hence learners may need to progress beyond the basic grammar of regular and irregular verbs and nouns, for example, and be taught more complex multiword verbs and idioms in context such as 'put someone through on the phone' or someone who 'puts in for a promotion' or 'decides to call it a day'. Lewis (1993) argues that prepositions, modal verbs and delexical verbs (take a swim, have a rest) need to be taught as part of vocabulary development.

Ur (1996: 60–3) advocates a type of 'mini-syllabus' of vocabulary items that ideally need to be taught to the majority of foreign language learners. These items would typically include collocations such as to 'throw a ball' but to 'toss a coin'. Learners could work with dictionaries to see how collocations are listed and treated.

Definitions, connotations and appropriateness

Many learners will need to define various concepts as part of their course. If we define a dog as a common, domestic carnivorous animal to some people the connotation will be friendly and loyal, whereas to others it will mean perhaps dirty and inferior. Taboo words and slang expressions may have their place in some vocabulary classrooms. Stylistic appropriateness is another aspect of vocabulary work than can be stressed: when to use a formal or informal version of a word, for example.

Other areas to look at may include words of the same or similar meaning (synonyms) and those that mean the opposite (antonyms). Superordinates or words used to denote general concepts to cover specific items can also be useful.

Teachers might also need to teach the component parts of words and multi-words, particularly prefixes and suffixes, so that learners can readily interpret words in context such as 'disrespectful', 'ungrateful', 'mismatch'.

6.11 Vocabulary: other possibilities

Depending on the types of learners we are dealing with there is also the possibility of looking at lexical fields in a subject area such as economics or science where associated vocabulary items are linked to a wider picture. New inventions lead to the introduction of neologisms or new words and expressions in the language, which can be a rich source of vocabulary development work. In recent years we have seen the introduction of new subjects and expressions such as 'ecommerce'; 'email virus'; 'surfing the Net'; 'wading through a ton of emails' and so on. Given the nature of English as a global or international language, some teachers may wish to concentrate on aspects of vocabulary that differ in, say, British and American English.

New innovations in learning technologies over the past decade or so have also opened up the possibilities for teachers to link vocabulary work to computers and the Internet. The dictionaries mentioned earlier in this section allow further permutations for teachers organizing classroom work, as learners can work individually or in pairs with online versions of these dictionaries. These online versions often have task sheets or worksheets incorporated so that learners can approach vocabulary from a wide variety of perspectives. (For a full listing of these and other Websites for teaching and learning refer to the appendix.) Learners may also wish to keep a learning diary of their progress and feelings about their vocabulary development. This idea is explored further in chapter 12.

6.12 Conclusion

We began this chapter by examining some of the reasons why we read, as well as the types of material we might typically read in our daily lives. We then considered how our understanding of the reading process and how changes in the concept of reading skills have affected approaches to the design of materials for the teaching of reading, particularly the insights offered by Schema theory. We then looked at these implications for classroom practice and procedure and discussed a range of approaches and materials that feature in reading classrooms. Next we looked at some of the different ways available to teachers for providing feedback to learners on their reading. Finally, we considered some of the different approaches involved in teaching and learning vocabulary.

In what ways might your approaches to the teaching of reading be modified as a result of this chapter?

6.13   Further reading

The following books provide a useful insight into the area:
1   Carrell, F. et al. (eds) (1988): *Interactive Approaches to Second Language Reading* gives a more theoretical overview, whereas the other titles listed here offer background discussion with a practical perspective.
2   Carter R. and D. Nunan (eds) (2001): *The Cambridge Guide to Teaching English to Speakers of Other Languages.*
3   Davies, F. (1995): *Introducing Reading.*
4   Nuttall, C. (1996): *Teaching Reading Skills in a Foreign Language.*
5   Ur, P. (1996): *A Course in Language Teaching.* Module 10.

7
Listening Skills

7.1   *Introduction*

The previous chapter has pointed us in the direction of several themes, both of principle and practice, that will be relevant for the consideration of listening skills to which we now turn. Most obviously, we are dealing with the other key skill under the heading of 'comprehension', and it is simple common sense to assume that reading and listening will share a number of underlying characteristics. The language teaching world turned its attention to listening rather later than it did to reading comprehension. This was due in part to the relevance of quite a large body of research on reading: more importantly, the 'library language' perspective was significant in English language classrooms long before a shrinking world and increased international interdependence led to a greater focus on face-to-face language skills. Even now, however, many learners do not have much opportunity to interact with native speakers, let alone travel to English-speaking countries, so this time lag in the attention given to the different skills is readily understandable.

This chapter will first briefly consider the similarities between reading and listening comprehension, and the ways in which they differ. We shall then examine the nature of listening as a skill and the features of the spoken language to which the skill is applied. Implications for the classroom will be looked at in detail, together with an exploration of how teaching materials reflect the current state of knowledge. As with reading, we shall concentrate somewhat artificially on listening as an individual, discrete skill (although it should be evident that the chapter both looks back to reading and ahead to speaking skills). It is important to be able to pick out the key characteristics of a particular skill, and the integration of skills is to be given explicit treatment in the final chapter of this part of the book.

7.2   Reasons for listening

Pause for a moment and jot down the kinds of things you have listened to in the last few days, both in English and in your own L₁.

The authors' own list is set out here in the order in which the items came to mind:

- Listening to the radio: news, a play, Parliament, a comedy programme (sometimes on a car radio).
- Conversations with neighbours, colleagues, friends.
- Answering the telephone at home and at work.
- Overhearing other people talking to each other: on a bus, in the office.
- Attending a lecture.
- Listening to arrival and departure announcements at the railway station.
- Watching TV.
- Listening to a list of names being read out at a prize-giving.
- While working in the library, trying *not* to listen to other people talking.

(You might like to compare your list and ours with the ones offered by Underwood (1989: ch. 1) or Ur (1984: ch. 1), for example.)

There are several points that we might notice here and that will recur in the course of this chapter. Firstly, there is great range and variety in the type of 'input' – in length or topic, for example. Secondly, in some situations we are listeners only, in others our listening skills form just a part of a whole interaction, and an ability to respond appropriately is equally important. Listening, in other words, may or may not be participatory and reciprocal (Nunan, 1999). Thirdly, there are different purposes involved (to get information, to socialize, to be entertained and so on), so the degree of attention given and possibly the strategies used will differ. A related point is whether we are listening in a face-to-face situation, or through another medium such as the radio or a station intercom system: in some cases interference or background noise may affect our ability to process what is being said. A fifth factor is to consider the people involved in the listening context – how many of them, their roles, and our relationship with them. Finally, we should note that in many situations a visual element gives important clues beyond the words used.

7.3   The relationship between listening and reading

It is useful now to highlight some of the ways in which reading and listening comprehension are both related and different. This short section will therefore act as a bridge, linking our earlier consideration of reading with a framework for thinking about listening skills.

What do reading and listening have in common?

We have seen that the traditional labelling of reading as a 'passive' skill is both misleading and incorrect: this is now well recognized as being equally so for listening. Like the reader, the listener is involved, for instance, in guessing, anticipating, checking, interpreting, interacting and organizing. It is worth quoting Vandergrift (1999: 168) in full to reinforce this point:

> Listening comprehension is anything but a passive activity. It is a complex, active process in which the listener must discriminate between sounds, understand vocabulary and structures, interpret stress and intonation, retain what was gathered in all of the above, and interpret it within the immediate as well as the larger socio-cultural context of the utterance. Co-ordinating all this involves a great deal of mental activity on the part of the learner. Listening is hard work . . .

Rost (1990) even sees the listener in certain circumstances as 'co-authoring' the discourse, not just waiting to be talked to and to respond, but by his responses actually helping to construct it. These are all active verb forms, indicating what people do and not what is done to them. An exception, of course, is when we choose to 'switch off' and pay no attention to what is being said to us, in which case we have decided not to engage our capacity. In other words, we can make the following distinctions, with their reading skill parallels:

Attention	*Recognition*
Listening	Hearing
Reading	Seeing

So just as we might see an object but either not recognize it or regard it as significant, so we can distinguish 'Can you *hear* that man?' from '*Listen* to what he's saying.'

What human beings seem to have, then, is a general processing capacity that enables them to deal with written and spoken input using comparable cognitive strategies. (See, for example, Anderson and Lynch, 1988, for further discussion of this point.) The nature of the processing mechanism for listening comprehension, and how it interacts with what is being listened to, will be discussed a little later. We shall also examine some of the potential difficulties for learners of English: just because a general capacity can be identified does not necessarily mean that the two skills can be activated and 'learnt' equally easily. First of all, we shall look at the most obvious differences between reading and listening.

How do they differ?

The clearest way of distinguishing between listening and reading is to think of the medium itself, and the nature of the language used. The next chapter will be concerned in detail with features of the spoken language, but we can introduce some of them here because they affect the listener's – and especially the learner's – ability to understand:

- The medium is sound, and not print. This self-evident statement has a number of implications. We are dealing, for example, with a transient and 'ephemeral' phenomenon that cannot be recaptured once it has passed (unless it is recorded, or we ask for repetition).
- A listening context often contains visual clues, such as gesture, which generally support the spoken words. More negatively, there can also be extraneous noise, such as traffic, or other people talking, which interferes with message reception.
- Information presented in speech tends to be less densely packed than it is on the page, and it may also be more repetitive.
- There is evidence to show that the spoken language is often less complex in its grammatical and discourse structure. At the same time, however, much speech gives a 'broken' impression, with new starts in mid-sentence, changes of direction or topic, hesitation and half-finished statements. This is obviously more true of informal than of formal speech. (Brown and Yule (1983a) contains a full discussion of the features of spoken English, and is referred to at greater length in chapter 8.)

These are significant distinctions, which were often blurred in traditional language teaching materials that took the written medium to be necessarily dominant. More recent materials claim to be sensitive both to the skill itself and to the spoken medium. Here are some typical instructions for types of activities and exercises taken from two listening comprehension courses that are fairly widely used, *Listeners* and *Intermediate Listening* (Brewster, 1991):

Listening for Gist
You will hear 10 people talking. Listen and write down what you think their jobs are, and one word which helped you decide.

Predicting What People Will Say Next
Listen to the people talking . . . and say if the statements written below are suitable ways of continuing what was said . . .

Guessing About the Speaker
. . . try to identify the situation which is taking place, and who is speaking (this requires the completion of a table).

Listening for Specific Information

Fill In a Column with Your Own Ideas (about what 'an Englishman' looks like) THEN COMPARE YOUR IDEAS WITH WHAT YOU HEAR ON THE TAPE.

Tick the Words that you Hear

Fill In the Gaps for the Missing Words

Make Notes on What the 2 People on the Tape Say . . .

Notice in particular that many of the tasks are based on what people do when they listen – on the processing of meaning that we commented on earlier in relation to both reading and listening comprehension. This may be listening to get the general idea, listening to catch something specific, or anticipating what comes next. Again, although content is clearly important, several of the tasks use tables and other ways of recording information, rather than just requiring a (written) full-sentence answer. Nevertheless, as G. White (1998) reminds us, listening to taped material still tends to treat students as passive 'overhearers', even if task types themselves have become increasingly realistic.

We shall now turn to a more detailed consideration of the skill of listening, and to its pedagogic implications.

7.4   *The nature of listening comprehension*

Product and process

Implicit in what has been said so far is the distinction, already made in chapter 6, between the twin concepts of 'product' and 'process'. This distinction has become an important one for all language skills, particularly those labelled 'receptive', and it signals an increasing recognition that language as a fixed system, a 'finished product', is just one part of the picture. It was a major characteristic of language teaching methodology in the 1980s and early 1990s that much more attention was paid to human beings as language processors than was previously the case, when 'texts' (whether written or spoken) were presented as objects to be understood. It is arguably with the skill of listening that a 'processing' focus is most crucial, given the transient nature of the language material compared with the relative stability of written texts. Later in this chapter we shall look at how process considerations might come together in different ways for different kinds of learners. For the moment, let us review the nature of the product, and then ask ourselves what proficient listeners actually do.

We have already noted some of the features of authentic spoken language. It varies, for example, in degrees of formality, in length, in the speed of delivery, in the accent of the speaker, in the role of the listener, and according to whether it is face to face or mediated in some way. A number of writers (for instance Brown and Yule, 1983a) make a basic distinction between 'transactional' speech, with one-way information flow from one speaker to another, as in a lecture or a news broadcast, and two-way 'interactional' speech. Rost (1990, 1994) makes an important point in relation to the latter: he refers to it as 'collaborative' and argues that, in such a setting, where we are both listener and speaker, the 'product' cannot be entirely fixed, because we have a part to play in shaping and controlling the direction in which it moves.

1   If you overheard the following while you were out shopping, how would
    you interpret it, and what else would you want to hear in order to be able
    to interpret these words?
    'Really? I didn't know that. How long has she been there?'
    And what would be happening if the shop assistant said to you, 'Five?'
2   Look back at the list you made earlier of the kinds of things you have
    listened to recently. Take any one of them, and ask yourself how you came
    to understand what was being said. For example, what aspects do you
    think you concentrated on? It might have been on the vocabulary, or the
    speaker's intonation, or some visual element, for instance. Did you under-
    stand everything and, if not, what interfered with 'perfect' comprehension?
3   How do you think your own learners would have managed listening to
    the same thing in English?

Listening skills

As a proficient listener, you will obviously not have achieved understanding
in any of these illustrative situations by simply 'hearing' the sound: you will
have been processing this stream of noise on a number of levels, which, taken
together, make up the concept of 'comprehension'. Let us now look at each of
these levels in turn. The first two see the listener as a processor of language,
and require a consideration of the micro-skills – the various components of this
processing mechanism.

Processing sound   Full understanding, we have noted, cannot come from the
sound source alone, but equally obviously, it cannot take place without some
processing of what one student of our acquaintance has called a 'word soup'. At
its most basic, a language completely unknown to us will sound to our ears like
a stream of sound.
   Assuming, however, that listeners can identify which language is being spoken,
then they must have the capacity to do at least the following:

*   Segment the stream of sound and recognize word boundaries. This is com-
    plicated in English because of the phenomenon whereby, in connected speech,
    one sound runs into the next. For example, 'I like it' sounds like /ai'laikit/
    ('I li kit'), 'my name's Ann' like /maineimzæn/ ('My name zan') and so on.
*   Recognize contracted forms. 'I'd have gone to London if I'd known about it'
    sounds very different from its 'full' printed form in many grammar book
    examples.
*   Recognize the vocabulary being used.
*   Recognize sentence and clause boundaries in speech.
*   Recognize stress patterns and speech rhythm. English sentence stress is fairly
    regular, and tends to fall on the main information-carrying items (nouns,
    main verbs, adjectives and adverbs) rather than on articles, pronouns,

conjunctions, auxiliaries and so on. Thus 'I went to the town and had lunch with a friend' gives a standard mix of 'strong' forms (marked with stress) and 'weak' forms (and, a) where the sound is often reduced to /ə/. We shall comment later on the language learning difficulties this can cause. Stress patterns can also be systematically varied, to accommodate a particular, intended meaning by the speaker. For example, 'I wás there' (no weak form) carries a tone of insistence; 'Whát did he say?' perhaps suggests surprise or disbelief.

- Recognize stress on longer words, and the effect on the rest of the word. Think of the sound of 'comfortable' or 'interesting', for instance.
- Recognize the significance of language-related ('paralinguistic') features, most obviously intonation. Falling intonation, for example, may indicate the end of a statement; a rise, that an utterance has not yet been completed and the speaker intends to carry on.
- Recognize changes in pitch, tone and speed of delivery.

None of the micro-skills of listening is used in isolation, of course, and those listed so far merge into the second major processing category, the processing of meaning.

Processing meaning If you think back to something you listened to earlier today, perhaps a news item that you found particularly interesting, it is extremely unlikely that you will be able to remember any of the sentence patterns, or much more than the vocabulary generally associated with the subject matter. You will, however, be able to recall in some sense what it was 'about'. (We are not referring here to a stretch of language learned 'by heart', such as a poem.) Research on listening has shown that syntax is lost to memory within a very short time, even a few seconds, whereas meaning is retained for much longer. Richards (1985: 191) comments that 'memory works with propositions, not with sentences', and Underwood (1989) draws a familiar distinction between 'echoic' memory (about one second), 'short-term' memory (a few seconds) and 'long-term' memory. G. White (1998: 55) quotes Kaltenbrook (1994): 'The organisation of a text into message units has an immediate impact on intelligibility . . . Students need to be shown that spoken language consists of *chunks* rather than isolated lexical items and complete sentences' (italics added). What listeners appear to be able to do here is:

- Organize the incoming speech into meaningful sections. This involves the ability to use linguistic clues to identify discourse boundaries. For example, a person giving a talk may signal a new point by explicit markers such as 'Next' or 'My third point' or 'However'; alternatively, a change in direction or topic may be indicated by intonation, or pauses. Related to this is the use of cohesive clues to establish links between different parts of a spoken 'text'. Brown and Yule (1983a) refer to this linguistic context as the 'co-text'.

- Identify redundant material. Speakers often repeat what they say, either directly or by making the same point in different words. Efficient listeners know how to turn this into a strategy to gain extra processing time to help organize what they hear.
- Think ahead, and use language data to anticipate what a speaker may be going on to say. For instance, a lecturer who says, 'So much for the advantages,' is obviously going on to talk about disadvantages; a change in intonation may mark a functional shift in a conversation, perhaps from an explanation to an enquiry.
- Store information in the memory and know how to retrieve it later, by organizing meaning as efficiently as possible and avoiding too much attention to immediate detail.

Finally, processing skills are often discussed under two related headings, which are tabulated below (the equivalences are not exact, but they capture the points made in this section):

Processing sound	*Processing meaning*
Phonological	Semantic
Lower-order/automatic skills	Higher-order skills of organizing and interpreting
Recognition of sounds, words	Comprehension
Localized: the immediate text	Global: the meaning of the whole
Decoding what was said	Reconstruction after processing meaning
Perception	Cognition

We can now summarize the discussion so far. The strategies used for processing meaning are not themselves merely skills of recognition. Although they depend on an ability to recognize key aspects of the sound system, they require the listener to combine, interpret and make sense of the incoming language data. In other words, as we saw in relation to the teaching of reading, we are dealing with the interaction of both 'bottom-up' and 'top-down' processing skills.

In the spirit of the introductory remarks in this chapter and the previous one, the two sets of micro-skills just discussed certainly view the listener as 'active'. However, taken alone they might imply that listening is an internal processing mechanism, a cognitive device disembodied from everyday life. This is clearly not the case, and as social beings we are equipped with other kinds of capacities, which can be thought of as (a) sensitivity to context, and (b) knowledge. Both are to do with the way in which expectations are set up by the non-linguistic environment. For convenience we shall take them together.

Context and knowledge   Most statements, taken out of context, are open to a number of interpretations (and incidentally offer a rich source of humour). A simple 'I spoke to him yesterday' may indicate a justification, doubt, a proof that the other person was where he was supposed to be, straightforward information, a statement on which further action will be based and so on. Its meaning will usually be clear from the context in which it was said. 'Context' here is taken to cover physical setting (home, office, school etc.), the number of listeners/speakers, their roles, and their relationship to each other. Rost refers to this as 'pragmatic context', distinguishing it from syntactic and semantic. He is critical of the information-processing model of comprehension where the listener is seen as 'a language processor who performs actions in a fixed order, independently of contextual constraints' (1990: 7). He pushes the significance of the social context further in an interesting discussion of 'collaborative' or 'interactional' speech (see also chapter 8 of this book). His point, essentially, is that the listener interprets what is being said, constructs a meaning, and responds on the basis of that interpretation. The listener is therefore a key figure in the shaping of the whole interaction: in this view, the listening context is open-ended, likely to change direction, and not fixed in advance.

Finally we turn to the knowledge that listeners bring to a listening experience. This may be knowledge of a topic, or a set of facts. A student following a course in (say) computing, will gradually accumulate a body of information and technical vocabulary to which he can 'refer' in each new class or lecture; if my neighbour has a new grandchild and comes to tell me about it, then I have some idea of the direction the conversation will take. Previous knowledge is not necessarily as detailed as in these examples. Schema theory, as we saw in chapter 6, has shown that we are equipped with pre-organized knowledge of many kinds. It may be that we simply have a set of general expectations when entering a listening situation. If we switch on the TV news, we can probably anticipate both its format and the kind of topic that will occur; if we go to a children's tea party, we expect certain behaviour patterns, and are unlikely to hear a discussion on nuclear physics. These frames of reference are also social and cultural. As members of a particular culture, we have learned the rules of conversational behaviour, and specific topics 'trigger' specific ideas and images.

Listening comprehension, then, is not only a function of the interplay between language on the one hand and what the brain does with it on the other: it also requires the activation of contextual information and previous knowledge. G. White (1998: 8–9) lists under the following headings all the subskills that go to make up the overall skill of listening,

- perception skills
- language skills
- knowledge of the world
- dealing with information
- interacting with a speaker

and comments that 'good listeners need to be able to use a combination of subskills simultaneously when processing spoken language: the skill they will need at any particular moment will depend on the kind of text they are listening to, and their reasons for listening to it'.

At this point you might like to think back to the tasks early in this section, and look at your comments in the light of the present discussion. There is no 'right answer', except to tell you that when the shop assistant said 'Five?' she knew that I always bought a certain kind of bread roll and a certain number. Her one-word query was enough to trigger the frame of reference for both of us, and a simple 'Yes please' was all that was required.

Many of these points are explicitly acknowledged in materials for the teaching of listening. In the Introduction to *Intermediate Listening* (Brewster, 1991: 2), for example, the writer makes the following points:

- We sometimes have an idea of what we are going to hear
- We listen for a variety of reasons
- Important information-carrying words are normally pronounced with more stress
- In face-to-face interaction, gestures and expression are important, as well as the actual words used
- Natural speech is characterized by hesitation, repetition, rephrasing and self-correction

7.5   Listening comprehension: teaching and learning

Before reading on, consider your own situation. To what extent do any of the materials you use to teach listening take into account the components we have been discussing? How might the various components of listening comprehension help your learners to listen more effectively?

In a competent listener, the micro-skills we have been surveying are engaged automatically. Language learners, however articulate in their L_1, are confronted with a rich and complex medium, a daunting array of skills, and a foreign language. We shall first comment briefly on the kinds of difficulties that learners typically experience in relation to what proficient listeners appear to do. We shall then raise some issues about the application of the discussion so far to the classroom environment. Finally in this section, we shall explore the ways in which teaching materials have developed in line with an increased understanding of the nature of the skill.

Learners

There is, of course, no such person as the 'typical learner'. Learners are at various stages of proficiency, and they differ across a range of characteristics –

age, interests, learning styles, aptitude, motivation and so on. The only claim that can be made is that learners, by definition, are not fully competent listeners in the target language. We can suggest, in other words, that they will be operating somewhere on a scale of approximation to full proficiency. With this in mind, several general observations can be made, which at the same time are not true of all learners everywhere.

Firstly, it seems that there is a tendency to focus on features of sound at the expense of 'co-text' – the surrounding linguistic environment. For example, in 'The East German government has resigned. Leaders are meeting to discuss the growing unrest in the country' the learner heard 'rest' and did not notice the prefix, despite the clear implication of national instability coming from the passage. A second, related point is that previous knowledge and/or context may be largely ignored in the interests of a mishearing. One student, rather improbably, claimed to have heard 'fish and chips' in a talk on telecommunications. Celce-Murcia and Olshtain (2000: 103) give a similar example of a student hearing 'communist' when the lecturer had said 'commonest'. This kind of listening error can be difficult to separate, thirdly, from mishearings caused by using an inappropriate frame of reference: another student, possibly thinking of a sadly familiar problem in her own country, heard 'plastic bullets' for 'postal ballots' in a text that was explicitly about electoral procedure. Fourthly, there is sometimes a reluctance to engage other levels of the listening skill to compensate for not understanding a particular stretch of language. For example, a learner may be unwilling to take risks by guessing, or anticipating, or establishing a framework for understanding without worrying about details, perhaps by using, in Rost's terms, 'points of transition relevance' (1990: 100). The most frequently quoted example here is that of a teacher beginning a lesson by saying, 'First of all . . .' If this is not processed phonologically, learners often do not understand at all, or sometimes suppose that a holiday is being announced, having heard 'festival'. Either way, the lesson cannot proceed until the misunderstanding is cleared up.

Underwood (1989) looks at the same points from another angle, and suggests that potential problems arise for seven main reasons:

1   The learner–listener cannot control speed of delivery.
2   He/she cannot always get things repeated.
3   He/she has a limited vocabulary.
4   He/she may fail to recognize 'signals'.
5   He/she may lack contextual knowledge.
6   It can be difficult to concentrate in a foreign language.
7   The learner may have established certain learning habits, such as a wish to understand every word.

What all this amounts to is that learners sometimes 'hear' rather than 'listen'. They appear to suspend their own mother tongue skills, which would allow them to approach a listening task as a multilevel process. Instead there is a marked tendency to depend too much on the lower-order skills, leading to attempts at phonological decoding rather than attention to the wider message.

Classroom applications: some issues

How, then, can the points that have been made in this chapter be reflected, directly or indirectly, in the classroom? Every classroom has its own set of objectives and its own 'climate' and patterns of relationships, all within a specific educational environment. It is therefore not surprising if the principles of language and language processing are taken only variably into account. Imagine the classroom as a filter for some of the following issues, which are set out as questions to consider for your own situation rather than as a 'recipe book' of ready answers. The section on materials will refer to these points again.

- Research into listening comprehension has shown that we are dealing with a complex skill. At the same time, our job is to teach *language*. What is a suitable balance for the classroom between 'tasks' (the skill) and 'text' (the language material)?
- How closely should the classroom attempt to replicate authentic language and authentic listening tasks? As we have seen, a real-life listening experience is highly complex and is unlikely to transfer easily to the classroom, except perhaps with advanced learners. Rixon (1986) makes a useful distinction between the difficulties associated with full authenticity, and the need to preserve the 'naturalness' of the spoken language – see our earlier discussion on sentence stress and strong/weak forms, for example.
- To what extent should spoken material be modified for presentation in the classroom?
- Is it more appropriate to grade tasks (using the micro-skills of listening as a starting point) from 'lower' to 'higher order', or is it preferable to make sure that global understanding has been achieved before focusing on detail? In other words, should we first make sure that learners can listen 'for gist'?
- What resources do we need to teach listening comprehension effectively? Is audio equipment sufficient, or does it leave out the non-linguistic information that video or TV might capture? Is it possible that sometimes the teacher may be more effective in creating a listening environment than the availability of a piece of electronic equipment?
- We can think of the listener's role on a scale of decreasing involvement from participant to addressee to overhearer (adapted from Rost, 1990). Is it possible that the classroom stresses the last of these at the expense of the others? We typically expect our students to listen to (perhaps taped) conversations

between other people. We mentioned White's criticism of this earlier in the chapter. She goes on to propose some extensive possibilities for developing an alternative approach, where students can become participants and even develop their own tasks and materials.

7.6 *Materials for teaching listening comprehension*

What materials, if any, do you have available for teaching listening? Do you have special supplementary materials, or is listening practice incorporated into a main coursebook? Is it necessary to devise your own listening exercises?

Traditionally, much classroom practice consisted of the teacher reading aloud a written text, one or more times, slowly and clearly, and then asking a number of comprehension questions about it. The skill itself was not given much attention, nor were the characteristics of natural spoken English. The objective was to provide an alternative way of presenting language and testing that it had been understood.

There is nothing wrong with this approach in itself, but it could not claim to be teaching listening comprehension. Many current materials, on the other hand, manipulate both language and tasks, and take into account a range of microskills, listener roles, topics and text types. There is space here only to illustrate the main trends. Many more examples will be found in the further reading listed at the end of the chapter (see particularly G. White, 1998).

The first thing to say is that the components of listening – processing sound, organizing meaning, and using knowledge and context – provide a convenient way of laying out the issues, but they are not there to be transferred directly to a teaching sequence. The way they are used depends on the objectives and levels of particular courses, although certain kinds of tasks draw more heavily on some micro-skills than on others.

It is now conventional – and helpful – to divide activities into pre-, while- and post-listening.

Pre-listening activities

The principal function of these activities, which are now common in teaching materials, is to establish a framework for listening so that learners do not approach the listening practice with no points of reference. This perspective is clearly in line with the use of 'knowledge schema' and the establishing of a context. Activities include the following:

A short reading passage on a similar topic
Predicting content from the title
Commenting on a picture or photograph
Reading through comprehension questions in advance
Working out your own opinion on a topic

Any such activity is bound to generate language. However, in some cases more explicit attention is given to language practice, particularly to the activation and learning of topic-related vocabulary. Clearly a reading activity can serve both functions of framework-setting and language practice quite well, provided that it does not become too important a focus in its own right.

Listening activities

By this we mean tasks carried out during or after listening that directly require comprehension of the spoken material. We find here a basic and quite standard distinction between 'extensive' and 'intensive' listening.

Extensive listening practice, or whatever term is used, is mainly concerned to promote overall global comprehension, and encourages learners not to worry if they do not grasp every word. The range of possible activities is enormous, and which ones are selected will depend largely on proficiency. At lower levels, learners cannot be expected to 'organize' mentally what they hear without considerable support. In the early stages, this support may be in a non-verbal form:

Putting pictures in a correct sequence
Following directions on a map
Checking off items in a photograph
Completing a grid, timetable, or chart of information

As proficiency develops, tasks will gradually become more language based, eventually requiring students to construct a framework of meaning for themselves, and to make inferences and interpret attitudes as well as understand explicitly stated facts. (Rost (1990) offers a scale from 'closed' to 'open' tasks.) For example:

Answering true/false or multiple-choice questions
Predicting what comes next (preceded by a pause)
Constructing a coherent set of notes
Inferring opinions across a whole text

Intensive listening, as the name implies, deals with specific items of language, sound or factual detail within the meaning framework already established:

Filling gaps with missing words
Identifying numbers and letters
Picking out particular facts
Recognizing exactly what someone said

Note that sequencing and grading can be carried out using both linguistic and psychological criteria: in other words, grading only according to some notion of syntactic complexity is no longer regarded as satisfactory. Further possibilities for grading include (a) task complexity, whether global → specific or vice versa, or indeed global → specific → global (this last technique is evident in the second sample Unit printed at the end of this chapter); (b) varying the amount of language to be processed, for example, from shorter stretches to longer ones; and (c) using a range of authentic and specially written material.

Language material

Two of our earlier observations are relevant here. Firstly, we distinguished 'interactional' and 'transactional' listening. Secondly, we saw that listeners can have a number of roles, on a scale from participant to addressee to overhearer. Both these elements are represented in listening materials. The most straightforward case is where the learner is an addressee or overhearer in a transactional context, such as:

Attending a lecture
Following instructions or directions
Listening to an interview, or a story, or to people describing their jobs

At the same time, it is clearly important that learners are exposed to the interactional nature of everyday conversation (quite distinct from fixed 'dialogues' to be read aloud). This is rather more difficult to construct in the classroom environment, except artificially. In a way it is a paradox that students may overhear on tape what others say when it would be more 'natural' for them to participate. (This is not always negative, however: learners have the opportunity to listen to the spoken language in an unthreatening situation.)

Post-listening activities

We shall only comment briefly here on these activities, because they are usually not listening exercises as such. The category is open-ended, and looks ahead to our discussion on the integration of skills at the end of this part of the book. Essentially, the post-listening stage is an opportunity for many kinds of follow-up work – thematic, lexical, grammatical, skills developmental and so on. Here are just a few examples:

Using notes made while listening to write a summary
Reading a related text
Doing a role-play
Writing on the same theme
Studying new grammatical structures
Practising pronunciation

7.7   *Conclusion*

Listening comprehension has a number of roles to play within a language course, and its importance clearly depends on the aims of the programme as a whole. It may only be a minor feature, just to give learners exposure to what English sounds like: alternatively, it may have a major function for someone planning to study in an English-speaking country or to interact extensively in the language. Whatever its purpose, we have tried to show in this chapter how views on the learning and teaching of listening have developed from a growing understanding both of the nature of the skill itself, and of the variety and range of language on which it can be practised.

1   A unit from a popular coursebook is printed on the following pages. How closely do you feel that the listening process is mirrored in these materials (at least in so far as you can judge without having the tapes available)? How suitable would they be for your own class?
2   If you had no recorded material available, how could you convert a reading text into a listening exercise? Choose a text originally intended to be read and try to make some practical suggestions.

18 | Planet Earth

A Traffic

1   Traffic congestion in towns causes delays and pollution.
Here are some possible solutions to the problem. Which do you think are good solutions? Mark ✓, ✗ or ? in Column A.

		A	B
1 Improve roads so that traffic moves faster.			
2 Make roads in cities narrower to discourage drivers.			
3 Limit parking places in towns.			
4 Make drivers pay more to use roads.			
5 Spend more money on improving public transport.			
6 Ban private cars from city centres.			
7 Set up a system of 'shared' taxis.			

2   🔊 You will hear part of a radio phone-in programme in which a
government minister, Mrs Fielding, answers questions from two callers.
Which of the opinions above does each caller express? In Column B, mark:
    1(= Frederick Bowles, the first caller) or
    2(= Joanna Briggs, the second caller).
Which solution is favoured by the government?

3   🔊 Here are three ideas expressed in the programme. According to Mrs
Fielding, what are the arguments against them? Listen again and make notes
in the table. Then compare what you have written with another student.

Idea	Argument against
Spend more on public transport	
Make drivers pay more	
Discourage people from using cars in cities	

4   **Extension**   Discuss these questions with another student:
    – Is traffic congestion a problem in your own country? Where is it worst?
    – What is the government doing, and how successful are they?

B Inside the greenhouse

1   Which of these commonly affect
your country?
    – droughts   – high temperatures
    – high winds   – low temperatures
    – heavy rain   – blizzards
    – floods   – sandstorms

Have any of them become more
frequent in recent years?

2   How would you answer these
questions?
    – Is the earth really getting warmer?
    – If so, are there any signs of it?

🔊 You will hear a radio interview in which a man talks about global warming.
Listen to the first part. What are *his* answers to the questions above?

🔊 Listen again and complete these sentences:
    – Most scientists believe . . .
    – In the last 10 years . . .
    – In the next 100 years . . .

3   In the second part of the interview, the man talks about the effects of global
     warming. What do you expect him to say about the topics in the table?

The sea	
Coastal areas	
The USA and Russia	
The Mediterranean	
Food	

     ▣ Listen and see if you were right. Then use the table to make notes
     about what he says.

4   **Extension**   What do you think will happen to the world's climate? Which
     of these opinions do you agree with?
     – The world's climate has always changed. There's nothing special to worry
       about now. In some places, the change might even be for the better.
     – The Earth's climate is changing, but only very slowly. We'll be able to
       adapt to the changes.
     – Very soon, science will find a solution to the problem of global warming.
       Perhaps we will discover a way of reversing the process.
     – In a few decades, life as we know it will become impossible. It's already
       too late to do anything about it.

Source: A. Doff and C. Becket, Unit 18, pp. 44–5 from *Listening 2*. Cambridge: Cambridge
University Press, 1991. © Cambridge University Press, 1991.

7.8   *Further reading*

1   Underwood, M. (1989): *Teaching Listening*.
2   White, G. (1998): *Listening*.

Both these books offer a wide range of examples of listening comprehension tasks and
exercises in the context of a clear discussion of the principles of the listening skill.

8

Speaking Skills

8.1 Introduction

As a language skill, speaking is sometimes undervalued or, in some circles, taken for granted. There is a popular impression that writing, particularly literature, is meant to be read and as such is prestigious, whereas speaking is often thought of as 'colloquial', which helps to account for its lower priority in some teaching contexts.

However, as we shall see in this chapter, speaking is not the oral production of written language, but involves learners in the mastery of a wide range of subskills, which, added together, constitute an overall competence in the spoken language.

With the recent growth of English as an international language of communication, there is clearly a need for many learners to speak and interact in a multiplicity of situations through the language, be it for foreign travel, business or other professional reasons. In many contexts, speaking is often *the* skill upon which a person is judged 'at face value'. In other words, people may often form judgements about our language competence from our speaking rather than from any of the other language skills.

In this chapter we shall look at some of the reasons that we might have for speaking in a variety of contexts. Then we shall examine how our concept of speaking has evolved over the last two decades. Next, we investigate the characteristics of spoken language, including pronunciation and conversation analysis, in order to see what their implications might be for language classrooms, and, finally, we consider various types of activity that we can use to promote speaking skills in the classroom.

What are your learners' speaking needs? Do you feel that your materials fulfil them?

8.2 Reasons for speaking

As a skill that enables us to produce utterances, when genuinely communicative, speaking is desire- and purpose-driven, in other words we genuinely want to communicate something to achieve a particular end. This may involve expressing ideas and opinions; expressing a wish or a desire to do something; negotiating and/or solving a particular problem; or establishing and maintaining social relationships and friendships. To achieve these speaking purposes we need to activate a range of appropriate expressions.

List the different kinds of things you have talked about in the last few days both in English and in your own L_1.

Our own list came out as follows, not in any particular order of priority:

Asking for assistance and advice in a shop
Asking for directions in a different town
Making an appointment by telephone
Discussing and negotiating arrangements
Talking socially to a variety of people
Sorting out arrangements for a car to be serviced

These are just a few of the reasons why people may wish to speak in any language. If we are hoping to make our learners communicatively competent in English as a foreign or second language, then it seems fair to assume that speaking skills will play a large part in this overall competence, although we should point out at this stage that in the early years of communicative language teaching, 'communicative' was interpreted by and large as oral production with the other three skills lagging somewhat behind. However, in recent years there has been a tendency to redress the balance. Speaking is a process difficult in many ways to dissociate from listening. Nunan (1989) points out how successful oral communicators have developed what he terms 'conversational listening skills'. We saw in the last chapter how Rost (1990) developed the idea of 'collaborative listening', whereby the listener can also 'shape' the discourse with the speaker. These two skills often enjoy a dependency in that speaking is only very rarely carried out in isolation; it is generally an *interactive* skill unless an uninterrupted oral presentation is being given. This notion of interaction is often developed in more recent EFL teaching materials. As Widdowson (1978: 58) comments: 'what is said is dependent on an understanding of what else has been said in the interaction', and it is this reciprocal exchange pattern which becomes important for learners to be exposed to and to practise at various stages of their foreign language career.

There is clearly an overlap in the interaction that takes place between the speaker/listener and the writer/reader, for the listener has to interpret the speaker just as the reader has to interpret the writer. The essential difference, though, is that speaker–listener interaction takes place in real time, thereby allowing very little time for the speaker to respond to the listener if the rules of a conversation are to be maintained. In the writer–reader relationship, however, the reader usually has the opportunity of rereading what has been written, time and time again if necessary. This obviously has important classroom implications which will be explored later. Let us now turn our attention to how advances in our understanding of speaking have evolved over the last two decades.

8.3 *Speaking skills and communicative language theory*

In their analysis of the theoretical base of communicative language teaching, Richards and Rodgers (2001: 161) offer the following four characteristics of a communicative view of language:

1   Language is a system for the expression of meaning
2   The primary function of language is for interaction and communication
3   The structure of language reflects its functional and communicative uses
4   The primary units of language are not merely its grammatical and structural features, but categories of functional and communicative meaning as exemplified in discourse

This analysis shows how easily speaking skills can be accommodated within this particular view of language. When we ask our students to use the spoken language in the classroom, we require them to take part in a process that not only involves a knowledge of target forms and functions, but also a general knowledge of the interaction between the speaker and listener in order that meanings and negotiation of meanings are made clear. For example, listeners may give the speaker feedback as to whether or not the listener has understood what the speaker has just said. The speaker will then need to reformulate what was just said in order to get the meaning across in a different way.

We shall shortly see how some recent materials that have been produced for speaking skills often try to encapsulate these views by trying to promote the expression of meaning, interaction and general communicative use on the part of the speaker.

8.4 *Characteristics of spoken language*

It is useful for the teacher of speaking skills in the classroom to look at the characteristics of the spoken language in order to ascertain how native speakers participate in oral interactions. On the one hand, EFL learners require what Bygate (1987) calls the 'motor-perceptive' skills, by which he means what may be broadly termed the correct use of the sounds and structures of the L_2. In the classroom this would involve the learner in such activities as pattern practices, pronunciation development work and so on. On the other hand, with the growth in recent years of fields of enquiry such as discourse and conversational analysis, we now have a much clearer picture of how conversations are structured. In this part of the chapter we shall firstly examine some of the issues involved in teaching pronunciation and then move on to consider how the development of conversation analysis has affected our approach to the teaching of speaking skills. Although the former skills are obviously important, the area of communicative interaction in particular has nourished an approach to the teaching of speaking skills in a communicative way.

8.5   *Teaching pronunciation*

The teaching of pronunciation is carried out in many different ways, and for different reasons. Sometimes whole lessons may be devoted to it; sometimes teachers deal with it simply as it arises. Some teachers like to 'drill' correct pronunciation habits, others are more concerned that their students develop comprehensibility within fluency. No one approach, therefore, is universally applicable. As Dalton and Seidlhofer (1994: 6) write: 'the task of pronunciation teaching . . . is to establish models for guidance, not norms for imitation'. Certainly a native speaker model (itself a complex notion for a language like English) is unrealistic for the great majority of learners, and 'perfection' an unattainable goal.

There are, nevertheless, a number of key aspects of pronunciation and the English sound system that a teacher can in principle attend to. Some of them are 'bottom-up', dealing with both forming and hearing sounds as 'correctly' as possible; others are 'top-down', where a learner's pronunciation is part of a broader communicative approach. This is a balance, in other words, between 'accuracy' on the one hand and 'intelligibility' on the other. In brief, these aspects are as follows:

- Individual sounds, including areas of difficulty for speakers of particular languages (l/r for Japanese, p/b for Arabic speakers, for example), minimal pairs (bit/bat, hit/hate and so on). This may also be accompanied by ear training, and sometimes by teaching students to read the phonemic alphabet – useful of course for dictionary work.
- Word stress, which exhibits a number of key patterns in English.
- Sentence stress and rhythm. In a stress-timed language like English this is of particular importance, because both 'regular' and 'marked' stress patterns essentially carry the message of a stretch of speech: Harmer (2001b: 193) gives the example of 'I lent my sister 10 pounds for a train ticket last week' as spoken with regular stress patterns, and then with varying the stress to emphasize different words. Again, it is useful to link this to listening practice as well.

- Intonation, significant in conveying messages about mood and intention. We might consider the different meanings in varying the intonation in such a simple sentence as 'that's interesting': we can sound bored, ironic, surprised or, indeed, interested.
- Sound and spelling, which in English are in a complex relationship.

More detailed discussion on the teaching of pronunciation is to be found in Kenworthy (1987) and Dalton and Seidlhofer (1994). Popular coursebooks include O'Connor and Fletcher (1989), Rogerson and Gilbert (1990), Hewings (1993), and to practice explicitly the link between spelling and pronunciation, Digby and Myers (1993).

8.6 *Conversation analysis*

Brown and Yule (1983a) have shown that, broadly speaking, spoken communications are essentially 'transactional' or 'interactional'. 'Transactional' language is said to be that which contains factual or propositional information. The language used by the participants is primarily 'message' based. Typically, written language is transactional. Examples of transactional language would be a policeman giving directions to a driver or of someone filing an insurance claim. In each case the message has to be clearly communicated. Spoken language, however, is also used to establish and maintain social roles, and this is termed 'interactional communication'. In certain cases, we may say that the *content* of the conversation may be relatively unimportant; what is important, however, is the ability of the speakers to establish and maintain a relationship. Often when transactional and interactional language need to be used at the same time difficulties can occur – even for native speakers. This is consequently a skill non-native speakers may need to learn and practise at length. An example would be someone trying to ask a bank manager for a loan, where the speaker is trying to conflate serious message oriented language with the language needed to maintain the social roles of the participants.

Brown and Yule (1983a) also examine the various forms of language most frequently used by speakers of the language. These are

- incomplete sentences
- very little subordination (subordinate clauses etc.)
- very few passives
- not many explicit logical connectors (moreover, however)
- topic comment structure (as in 'the sun – oh look it's going down'). The syntax of the written language would probably have a subject–verb–predicate structure
- replacing/refining expressions (e.g. 'this fellow / this chap she was supposed to meet')
- frequent reference to things outside the 'text', such as the weather, for example. This kind of referencing is called 'exophoric'

- the use of generalized vocabulary (thing, nice stuff, place, a lot of)
- repetition of the same syntactic form
- the use of pauses and 'fillers' ('erm', 'well', 'uhuh', 'if you see what I mean' and so on.)

If your L_1 is not English, what similarities and differences would there be to the forms outlined above?

We may also say that spoken language follows certain distinct patterns or 'conversational routines' and rules that must be observed if a satisfactory outcome for each participant is to be achieved, and clearly there has to be something worth talking about in the first place for participants to want to continue a conversation to the end.

Next, within the 'framework' of the conversation, 'turns' have to take place if the conversation is not to be totally one-sided. Certain strategies have to be put into operation by the speaker. In practice, this may mean trying to 'hold the floor' for a while in the interaction, which will also involve knowledge of how 'long' or 'short' the turn can be; interrupting the other speaker(s); anticipating and inferring what is about to happen next; changing the 'topic' if necessary; and providing appropriate pauses and 'fillers' while processing the language.

The essential thing to note from the foreign language teaching perspective is that what may appear to be casual and unplanned in a conversation may nonetheless follow a deeper, organized pattern the learner has to be made aware of.

Do you think it is useful to apply native speaker strategies *directly* to classroom use?

8.7 Classroom implications

If what we have seen above shows native speaker behaviour in conversations, research indicates that the non-native speaker is often reluctant to use some of these strategies when speaking. One such area is the use of pauses and fillers, which, as we have seen, enable the speaker to hold the floor by filling in the silence at that particular moment.

This can often be a cultural phenomenon: some otherwise proficient L_2 speakers find this 'switch' a difficult one to accomplish if they come from an L_1 culture where silences in conversations are more acceptable. Another area that some non-native speakers tend to neglect is that of making encouraging noises to the speaker such as 'really', 'I see', 'aha' during the conversation, which enables the other speaker(s) to see that the conversation is being followed and processed.

One implication of such routines is that there is a need for speaking skills classes to place more emphasis on the 'frames' of oral interactions. We know that conversations have to be started, maintained and finished. The phrases that we use to accomplish this are called 'gambits'. An example of an opening gambit could be 'Excuse me. Do you happen to know if . . .' Within the framework of the conversation the speakers also take 'turns' and, where pertinent, change the topic under discussion. This is not always an easy task to accomplish successfully. However, if sensitivity to how these conversation 'frames' work can be encouraged from the early stages of language learning by exposing near beginners to samples of natural speech to develop their awareness of conversational features and strategies, then learners will find themselves much more able to cope later on when they need or want to take part in real conversations outside the classroom.

9. The Main Problem

The trouble is . . .

The problem is . . .

The real problem is . . .

The point is . . .

The 'awful thing is . . .

Don't forget that . . .

Divide into two teams. The students in one team pick one of the topics from Column A.

A member of the other team has to say a related sentence from Column B, starting with a phrase from the list — within 15 seconds.

Some of the sentences in column B fit more than one topic — or none at all! If in doubt, ask the players to explain any choices you don't understand.

Example
Highjackers

The trouble is, nobody knows how to handle them.

Round 1

A	B
Raising children	It makes saving a waste of time.
The rising cost of living	Nobody knows how to handle it.
Learning a language on your own	It's an uphill struggle.
Living together	The further away you are, the worse it is.

Round 2

A	B
Television	It wears you out before the day is over.
Mother-in-law for the weekend	Nobody knows how to handle it.
Jogging	It makes you feel so depressed.
Smoking	It bores you to tears.
	Everybody gets on everybody's nerves.
	You need will-power to stop.

Round 3

Try again. This time the topics are given, the other team has to make up a suitable response using one of the phrases.

Topics. Drugs, football hooligans, unemployment, famine, forgetting to do your homework, flying, computers, politics, learning English.

1. Alternatives to *awful* are *terrible, worst.*

10. A Surprising Fact

Speaking

Sometimes the best way to support an argument is to come up with an unexpected fact.

The following paragraph contains some surprising facts (given in *italics*).

Read the paragraph aloud and introduce each of these facts with one of the phrases from the top list, and add a qualifier from the bottom list.

Example

TV plays a very large part in British life. (There were 2.3 TV's per household in Britain in 1987.)

— Do you realize that there were, on average, 2.3 TV's per household in Britain in 1987? Normally TV is an important part of British life.

TV has a tremendous effect on children. (*Children spend more time watching TV than doing anything else in their waking hours.*) Early in life, children learn from TV to influence their parents about what to buy — not just in the area of toys, but also at the supermarket. (*Women buy more snack foods when accompanied by children.*) Also, when parents don't limit their children's TV watching, they become so dependent on television for their entertainment that they begin to lose their potential for creativity. (*A study has shown that children without TV who are left to themselves develop their own creative powers.*) Many people are also worried about the high percentage of programmes that highlight violence. (*Children have been shown to learn violence from TV.*) In short, the negative effects of TV probably outweigh its possible positive influence in presenting the world to the growing child.

Writing

Write out the sentences in italics — each with its opening phrase and its qualifier.

Discussion

Do you agree with the text you read?
If not, give your arguments and try to include some surprising facts which you know.

Start:

Do you realise that . . .

Believe it or not,

You may not believe it, but . . .

It may sound strange, but . . .

¹The surprising thing is . . .

¹Surprisingly,

²Oddly enough,

²Funnily enough,

End with:

Generally

By and large

As a rule

Normally

Usually

On the whole,

1. These relate to a point you have already made — they come in the middle of what you are saying.

2. These connect what you say to what has just been said — usually they introduce a *coincidence*. All of these expressions are rather informal, and will sound natural used to somebody you know rather well.

Source: E. Keller and S. Warner, pp. 16–17 from *Conversation Gambits*. Hove: Language Teaching Publications, 1988. © Language Teaching Publications, 1988.

> Look at the extracts 9. & 10. above from materials designed to introduce learners to conversation 'gambits'. How effective might it be for your own learners?

What has happened in materials and classrooms in recent years has clearly been influenced by a number of the findings we have outlined above. In what might rather loosely be termed 'pre-communicative' language teaching, dialogues were often used in class, but the purpose was not to teach the rules of communication, appropriateness and use: the focus was nearly always a structural one, and learners were rarely given an information gap task that would have enabled them to engage in some real communication. No account was offered as to how a sentence takes on meaning from its relation to surrounding utterances and to non-linguistic factors. It was also rare for attention to be drawn to who was actually speaking to whom and the consequences of this are obvious. Pattison (1987) comments on how students lacked the 'transfer skills' to then say anything meaningful *outside* the classroom.

> In the light of what we have mentioned above, look at the following examples. How would you characterize each as *spoken* language? How do they differ?

Example 1:
A: Well, in this job we do er a lot of cradle work you see, and, er on different tower blocks in Birmingham.
B: A lot of what did you say?
A: Cradle work. That's ou, outside work, on the er blocks of flats, where you can see the outside cradles up the outside of the tower blocks.
B: Oh, I'm with you now, you sort of sta, hang in a basket to clean the windows then?
A: Yeah, that's right, I do, yeah! Good job we're well insured isn't it!
(From *Listeners*, Underwood and Barr, 1980.)

Example 2:
JOHN: Hello, how are you?
TOM: I'm fine thank you. How are you?
JOHN: I'm also fine thank you.
TOM: How's your wife?
JOHN: She's very well thank you. How is your wife?
TOM: She's also very well thank you.

The first example shows two people who have a desire to communicate; they have a purpose; there is an information gap to fill in because B does not understand at first what A is talking about. They are also selecting appropriate language for their needs. The second example is rather artificial as conversation and sounds more like a script than a piece of spontaneous language.

In the precommunicative speaking skills classroom, therefore, learners were expected to respond to teacher prompts by using instances of language that were usually predictable. In the communicative classroom, however, interaction is far less teacher-centred and focuses on learners speaking to each other for a specific reason in order to achieve a specific outcome.

From the materials point of view, within the precommunicative framework, there is far more control of the form of the language. Sometimes only one item will be the focus of a particular lesson; it might be practice in the use of the pronouns 'it' and 'one', or conversations specially written to drill comparative forms. Brumfit (1984) writes about language activities designed to foster accuracy and those designed to foster fluency. When applied to language tasks these do not necessarily have to be seen as 'opposites', but can be complementary, depending on the actual aims and purpose of the speaking skills class in question. Within the precommunicative framework it is evident that the speaking skills were accuracy-focused to a large extent. Within the more communicative framework, however, the emphasis is far more open-ended with the whole target language being a potential vehicle for communication and not just a restricted object of study: hence activities are designed to develop fluency in the learner.

Nunan (1999) suggests that teachers need to be aware that motivation is a consideration in determining whether or not learners are willing to communicate. Clearly the more meaningful the materials and tasks are for the learners involved the better the outcome will be.

Ur (1996) develops this further by suggesting that good speaking skills classrooms are ones where learners talk a lot, participation is even, motivation is high and the language is at an acceptable level.

Tsui's (1996) research into what she calls the 'reluctant' speaker in the language classroom revealed five main reasons why learners are unwilling to participate: the students perceive themselves to be at a low proficiency level, they worry about making mistakes and the resultant derision from peers, teachers may be intolerant of silence, turn-taking is uneven across the class and input is incomprehensible. The implication for teachers, therefore, seems to be to devise meaningful activities that will motivate students to speak within a supportive environment.

1 Consider your own speaking skills classes with respect to the information above. Does this tell you anything about *your* approach to teaching speaking skills or the approach favoured by the materials?

2 The titles, with dates of several popular speaking skills courses, are listed here. Pause for a moment to look at them and ask yourself what significance the titles might have. How do the dates of publication approximately parallel what you know of changing perspectives on language and language learning?

OPEAC Oral Drills Workbook (1970)
Between You and Me: Guided Dialogues for Conversation Practice (1974)
It's Your Choice: Six Role Playing Exercises (1977)
Communicate (1979)
Discussions That Work (1981)
Interact: An Interaction Workbook (1982)
Eight Simulations (1983)
Speaking Personally (1983)
Conversation Gambits: Real English Conversation Practice (1988)
Speaking Out (1988)
Study Speaking (1992)
Conversation Lessons: The Natural Language of Conversation (1997)

These are *speculative* questions in a sense and we do not want to suggest that there is a rigid relationship between titles, dates and a 'movement' in language teaching.

8.8   Types of activity to promote speaking skills

In this section of the chapter we examine some activities used in the classroom to promote the development of speaking skills in our learners. For focusing purposes, we shall begin by looking at an example of some 'pre-communicative' materials and then move on to consider what might broadly be termed 'communicative' activities or games. After this we shall examine some oral problem-solving activities, role play and simulation materials for decision-making, and materials requiring personal responses from the learners. We finish this section by discussing materials designed to teach the rules and patterns of conversation.

In recent teaching materials a lot of attention has been paid to designing activities that focus on tasks mediated through language or that involve the negotiation and sharing of information by the participants. The idea behind this thinking is that learners should be provided with the opportunity to use the language they know in meaningful activities they feel motivated to talk about. There are obviously going to be different levels of 'authenticity' in the materials, depending on whether they are concerned with what Rivers and Temperley (1978) call 'skill getting' or 'skill using'. In the former, activities can be designed that are more controlled, or are what we might call 'pseudo-communication'. In the latter, the idea is to stimulate genuine interaction. By way of contrast, before looking at some different types of activities to further illustrate the genuine interaction principle, we shall have a brief look at an example of precommunicative speaking skills.

Many of the precommunicative materials used guided dialogues as a way of trying to develop oral practice with learners. Conversations were frequently structurally graded. Let us look at an imagined example designed to practice the 'not enough' structure:

A: Can John paint the ceiling?
B: No. He can't reach. He isn't tall enough.
A: What about if he uses a ladder? Will he be able to do it then?
B: I should think so.

The pattern practice that learners have to follow, which can then be applied to other conversations, is as follows:

A: Can X do Y?
B: No. He/she isn't tall enough.
A: What about if he/she uses a Z? Will he/she be able to do it then?
B: I should think/imagine so.

In contrast to this we now turn our attention to materials for the teaching of speaking skills that form part of the communicative approach, beginning with communication games.

Communication games

Speaking activities based on games are often a useful way of giving students valuable practice, especially, although by no means exclusively, where younger learners are involved. Game-based activities can involve practice of oral strategies such as describing, predicting, simplifying, asking for feedback, through activities such as filling in questionnaires and guessing unknown information. Even though these activities are called games, thereby implying fun, they are also communication based and require the learners to use the information they find out in a collaborative way for successful completion of a particular task.

One such activity based on questionnaires can be found in *Interact: An Inter-action Workbook* (Aston, 1982), where learners have to decide what constitutes job satisfaction. They have to decide first of all what criteria would lead to job satisfaction and then the class is divided into four or eight equal groups, A to D or A to I, for example. Each group then decides which jobs are going to be discussed (own parents', husband's, wife's and so on). Each group has to interview members of another group and then learners have to discuss which interviewee has the best job. The questionnaire can include details of job, the approximate salary, the hours worked, distance to work, holiday entitlement, what fringe benefits are included and so on.

At the end of the activity each group can tell the rest of the class about the best job that they found. They then compare these and decide which is the best in the whole class and why. Successful completion of this type of activity clearly depends on the effective communicative use of the language and of the sharing of information amongst the participants.

The 'describe and draw' principle is based on a series of plans and diagrams one student has to describe to another so that the latter can complete the task. The idea behind this 'describe and draw' communication activity is to give learners practice in handling, by means of oral description and drawing in pairs, a core of material of non-verbal data, that is, maps, plans, shapes, graphs. The activities are motivated by the fact that many EFL learners have difficulty when trying to handle these sorts of data in the spoken form. This activity is also a useful way of developing Nunan's (1991) notion of conversational listening skills in that the 'listener/drawer' can ask for further clarification if something has not been understood. A typical example would be as follows:

> Learner A has a plan of a town centre containing the High Street, churches, school, library, shops, houses or the floor plan of a building such as a school or a company. Learner B then has to draw the plan as accurately as possible from the description given by learner A. For further examples of these activities see Jordan (1982).

Ur (1996: 124) has some variations on the picture idea, but in this instance learners are issued with pictures everyone can see. They then have to describe the pictures by saying as many sentences about them as possible. A 'secretary' then marks down the number of utterances. After this, a second picture is provided and learners have to try to beat their first number of sentences produced.

Problem solving

Many speaking skills materials start from the premise that a communicative purpose can be established in the classroom by means of the information gap we mentioned earlier in the chapter. An example of an information gap principle using the 'jigsaw' materials can be seen at work in materials developed by Geddes and Sturtridge (1980). The materials, primarily for listening in this case, nevertheless include purposeful speaking activities. By getting students to listen to different chunks of information on a tape, the authors set up an information gap whereby the students have to share with other groups the information their group has acquired in order to build up a complete picture of that particular situation. Another problem-solving activity is provided by Gairns and Redman (1998). In this case the learners are given the character profiles of four different people, each of whom wishes to be elected as a local leader. It can be seen from the contents of the material provided (see p. 146) that each person possesses some negative qualities and learners have to discuss and decide in pairs or small groups whom they would wish to elect, giving their reasons in each case.

Think of how you might set up speaking skills activities with an information gap in your own classroom.

Simulation/role-play materials

One way of getting students to speak in different social contexts and to assume varied social roles is to use role-play activities in the classroom. Materials are generally aimed at the more proficient EFL learner, although this is not always the case, as they can be set up in a highly structured way with a lot of teacher control. At the other end of the spectrum, however, a considerable amount of choice may be exercised by allowing the students more freedom in what they will say. Role-play activities are also a pertinent way of integrating skills in the language classroom and therefore we examine them from this perspective in more detail in chapter 10.

Role-play materials are often written specifically to get learners to express opinions, to present and defend points of view and to evaluate arguments based on the notion of what Prabhu (1987) calls an opinion gap, in that the activity involves the learner in formulating an argument to justify an opinion for which

3 Now read the profiles of four people who are candidates for election as your local leader (this could be a mayor, or council leader or other type of local official).

1. Doctor Rennison: local GP with 20 years' experience. Respected by broad cross-section of local population. Close links with all social service agencies. Intelligent, eloquent but is known to support euthanasia and was once involved in a police investigation about the mysterious death of an elderly patient. No firm evidence discovered.

2. Martha Holdsworth: solicitor with a lot of experience with the Citizens' Advice Bureau. Known for liberal views on legalising soft drugs. As a student was convicted of a minor drugs offence. Has been in a wheelchair for five years following a car accident. Is now a campaigner for better facilities in public buildings for disabled people. Extremely hardworking.

3. Eleanor Brown: gave up early career in journalism to bring up her three children. Now they have left home, is writing again for the local evening paper and runs a local charity organisation and AIDS support group. Became well-known locally when her home was burgled and she shot and wounded the burglar as he was trying to escape. This occurred shortly after the break-up of her marriage.

4. Tom Adams: local farmer/businessman with a reputation for getting things done, but known to upset people and make enemies. His business partner was charged with bribery of an agricultural official to gain special grants and subsidies, but Adams was not charged. Local man who loves the town and wants to preserve its character and traditions.

Which of them would/wouldn't you support or vote for, and why? Discuss in small groups, using the language in the box, and give your reasons.

I'd be I wouldn't be	willing happy reluctant/unwilling prepared very happy	to vote for someone who ...
I'd I wouldn't	support ... because ...	

4 Have a ballot in the class to find the most popular candidate.

Source: R. Gairns and S. Redman, p. 59 from *True to Life*. Cambridge: Cambridge University Press, 1998. © Cambridge University Press, 1998.

there is no one objective way of demonstrating the outcome as right or wrong. For example, learners may be asked to consider the planning of a new motorway that would have to go through farmland, some countryside of outstanding beauty, as well as through the outskirts of a large town, as in Lynch (1977). The learners' role cards would be written from the various points of view of all the parties concerned in the planning project and each learner (or pair or group, depending on the number of people in the class) would be asked to prepare notes to speak from in a meeting. As we suggested above, there is not one answer to this type of negotiated activity, and in this sense the outcome of the discussion is very much up to the learners themselves. There are many subject topics available for role-play purposes, including the re-enacting of the trial of an accused person in a courtroom, or compiling and presenting a news magazine programme for radio or television. For a younger group, Ur (1996) suggests organizing a summer camp for blind children on an insufficient budget, with learners having to think how they would raise the money.

With reference to the types of materials we have examined thus far, Littlewood (1981) makes a distinction between what he calls 'functional communication activities' (which could include problem solving; questionnaires and describe and draw activities) and 'social interaction activities' (such as role play and simulation). This distinction could be seen as reflecting the transactional/interactional distinction we examined earlier in the chapter, because the functional language activities require learners to use the language they know to get the meaning across as effectively as possible. The social interaction activities, on the other hand, also require learners to pay more attention to the establishment and maintenance of social relationships.

Materials requiring personal responses

Some speaking materials have been designed in order for learners to become more closely involved with the materials so that they can have more meaningful things to talk about and thereby learn more readily and efficiently. A logical extension of this would then be to get outside the materials themselves and to use the learners' own backgrounds and personalities in speaking classes so as to give them more genuine reasons for wanting to communicate with each other. One example of materials is *Speaking Personally* by Porter-Ladousse (1983), which contains twelve units of fluency practice that have been devised along these lines. The aim of these materials is to encourage learners to react individually to questions concerning many aspects of their daily lives, on such topics as their image as seen by others, their futures, views on honesty and truthfulness and so on. The extract below is taken from the unit 'Life's tensions'.

Read the extract and consider how you might organize the learners and the classroom in order to use the material effectively.

5   Life's tensions

5.1   How stress-proof are you? ☆

Study the following situations and consider what your reaction would be in each of them. If you think you would have any of the reactions listed beneath each situation, place a tick in the box beside it.

Example
You have been invited to dinner with your boss to meet some very important business contacts. During the meal you knock over an almost full bottle of wine. Would you blush? Would you stammer? If so, fill in the boxes as in the example. Would you:

feel embarrassed?	☐	feel calm?	☐
blush?	☑	feel amused?	☐
stammer?	☑	be indifferent?	☐

You may sometimes find yourself ticking columns on the left and the right. For example, you might feel embarrassed but calm in the situation above.

---

1 You have driven through some traffic lights as they were turning red. You are stopped by a policeman who senses that you are in a hurry and seems to be taking his time deliberately. Do you:

feel uneasy?	☐	behave in a friendly manner?	☐
start perspiring?	☐	act coolly?	☐
behave aggressively?	☐	look detached?	☐

2 At a friend's wedding you are unexpectedly asked to make a speech. Do you:

blush?	☐	feel amused?	☐
feel your hands trembling?	☐	feel composed?	☐
begin to stutter nervously?	☐	feel pleased and flattered?	☐

3 You have just finished dining in a restaurant and have asked the waiter for the bill. You suddenly discover that you have left both your wallet and your cheque book at home. Do you:

feel embarrassed?	☐	remain calm?	☐
start stammering?	☐	simply tell the waiter what has happened?	☐
have a nervous laugh?	☐	have a natural laugh?	☐

4 You are caught travelling on a bus without a ticket. Your reaction is:

a feeling of shame?	☐	a feeling of indifference?	☐
a forced smile?	☐	an amused smile?	☐
a shortness of breath?	☐	a look of imperturbability?	☐

5 Travelling down the motorway at 70 m.p.h. (approx. 113 km.p.h.) you have a flat tyre. You manage to stop on the hard shoulder. Do you:

feel rage?	☐	remain unflappable?	☐
feel at a complete loss?	☐	feel quite able to cope with the	
become exasperated?	☐	situation?	☐
		reflect calmly on what to do	
		next?	☐

6 You are caught between floors in a lift. You are alone. Do you:

get damp palms?	☐	keep your composure?	☐
grow pale?	☐	feel not particularly worried?	☐
panic?	☐	wait patiently to be rescued?	☐

7 You are returning from a holiday abroad and have more cigarettes and spirits in your suitcase than are permitted by the regulations. A customs officer asks you to open your suitcase. Do you:

get worked up and agitated?	☐	keep your self-control?	☐
feel afraid?	☐	behave with resignation?	☐
find your hands trembling?	☐	consider that you have lost this	
		round in a fair game?	☐

8 At a party you meet someone who greets you very warmly as an old friend, but you cannot remember his name, or even where you have met him before. Do you react:

with embarrassed		by bluffing your way out of the	
self-consciousness?	☐	situation?	☐
with anxiety?	☐	by honestly avowing the	
with a sinking feeling in your		inadequacy of your memory?	☐
stomach?	☐	by laughing the matter off?	☐

9 You are walking out of a department store when you suddenly realise you are clutching an article that you have forgotten to pay for. You see someone who looks as if he might be the store detective looming up. Do you:

lose your sang-froid?	☐	behave in a friendly manner?	☐
wish the ground would open up		remain completely unruffled?	☐
and swallow you?	☐	act nonchalantly?	☐
have palpitations?	☐		

➡→

Source: G. Porter-Ladousse, Unit 5.1 from *Speaking Personally*. Cambridge: Cambridge University Press. © Cambridge University Press, 1983.

This is how Porter-Ladousse (1983: 106), the author of the book, sees the materials being used:

> The material in this book is to a great extent designed to be used by students working in pairs or in small groups. Consequently, the role of the teacher is not so much to give a model of fluency in the target language as to encourage fluency in the learner. It is less to explain words and grammatical structures than to act as a facilitator, enabling the learners to work these things out for themselves. The teacher will present the material, organize the classroom, keep the students working and smooth out the difficulties they meet. The kind of classroom in which there is an empty space or in which the furniture can be moved is particularly suitable for the material in this book. In a traditional classroom, students will work with their immediate neighbours, on both sides as well as in front and behind.

Another example where the learner has to provide a personal response is provided by Dellar and Hocking (2000). In a unit on personal relationships the 'talking point' after a passage on 'partner shopping' invites learners to comment on various aspects of this topic.

Partner shopping

You are a busy executive with little free time on your hands. You are single. You are looking for a partner, but where do you start? The obvious answer is your local supermarket. That's where you go once a week to stock up on everything you need for the coming week, so why not use it to find a partner?

There's nothing new in that, you might say. You might already be one of those single guys who hang around the washing powder lane, looking as if you've never washed a shirt in your life, hoping that the woman of your dreams will take pity on you and explain the difference between soap powder and fabric softener.

Or are you the innocent blonde who picks up a passionfruit and asks that tall dark handsome guy you've been following since your eyes met over the skimmed milk if he's ever tried one?

The British supermarket chain, Asda, recently invented 'singles nights', recognising the fact that their stores were one of the best places in town to meet a partner. It's certainly the warmest and cheapest! But the prize for marketing brilliance must go to another chain, Sainsbury's. They have imported an idea from the Japanese which looks as if it might catch on. As you enter the store you take a 'love bleeper'. You key in your likes and dislikes

– a 25-year-old brunette of medium height who is into rock music, or maybe what you're after is a bodybuilder who likes quiet evenings in front of the TV. If you come close to another shopper who is looking for someone like you, both bleepers will start bleeping and flashing at each other.

Crazy? Maybe! But for people living in big cities, working late every night, this idea may not be as silly as it sounds. Where DO you go to meet people? If it works, just think how romantic it'll sound when you tell your children that you met their mum over the vegetable counter!

11 Talking point

Where did the 'love bleeper' idea come from originally?

Where did you meet your partner? Would you take a love bleeper if you went to a store with that system? What would you say to the person whose bleeper bleeped at you?

Is this a sad story for sad people? Or is it the way forward in the modern world?

Source: H. Dellar and D. Hocking, p. 82 from *Innovations*. Hove: Language Teaching Publications, 2000. © Language Teaching Publications, 2000.

Thinking of this material, are there other ways in which you can use the background of your own learners to get them to communicate with each other?

Materials illustrating rules/patterns of conversation

At the moment of writing, very few of the speaking skills materials available on the market emphasize the patterns and rules of conversation that we mentioned and illustrated earlier in the chapter. *Conversation Gambits* by Keller and Warner (1988) is one of the exceptions, however. Their book aims to introduce learners to the effective use of gambits in conversations. The materials are divided up into opening gambits (starting and introducing ideas into a conversation), linking gambits (linking your ideas to what someone else has just said), and finally responding gambits (agreeing/disagreeing at different levels).

The authors stress throughout that a lot of the misunderstanding between people comes from *how* they speak, not necessarily *what* they say. The overriding principle behind this type of material is to try to make learners sound more natural when participating in conversations and discussions. People who never use gambits when they are speaking may be interpreted by the other participant/s as being abrupt, direct or even rude in some cases. For example, we do not generally go into a shop and ask, 'How much is this?' but would probably say, 'Could you tell me how much this is please?' Similarly, we may want to introduce a piece of surprising news with 'You may not believe this, but...' If we are in a shop and wish to leave without purchasing something we may say 'I'm afraid I can't make up my mind at the moment,' or, 'I'll have to give it some thought.' The materials contain mini–conversations that allow learners to practise the gambits as they speak.

Materials to enhance academic speaking skills

The materials we have examined thus far have been largely within the general language teaching framework. However, some learners need to speak in an academic community, especially if they are studying their specialist subject in an English-speaking country. *Study Speaking* (Lynch and Anderson 1992) is widely used in this pedagogical context and provides speaking tasks on topic areas such as types of courses, accommodation, teaching and research and health issues.

Have another brief look at the activity types in this section. What are the organization principles behind each of them?

8.9 Feedback to learners

In all of the activities outlined above teachers may wonder how to correct errors produced by learners during the oral skills class. Generally we tend to correct oral mistakes through speech, but the 'how' and 'when' obviously requires a great deal of sensitivity on the part of the teacher. If we are trying to encourage our learners to become fluent in the spoken language, correcting regularly during oral work will tend to inhibit further those learners who may already be rather taciturn in class. Most teachers feel that correcting a student in mid-sentence is generally unhelpful unless the student is floundering and is giving the teacher signals that she wants some help. Some teachers prefer to 'log' oral mistakes in writing and hand these to a student at the end of a class in the belief that learners may 'learn something from their mistakes'. Learners are individuals and it may be helpful for teachers to work out the kinds of corrections students find most useful, perhaps even linking these to tutorials and diary work (see chapter 12). Ur (1996: 246) contains a sensible discussion of this topic.

8.10   Conclusion

We began this chapter by examining the needs that learners may have to speak in a foreign language in the first place. Then we discussed some of the background to speaking skills by emphasizing speaking as an active skill. Subsequently we looked at the ways in which speaking and listening interact and how research into communicative language theory and the characteristics of spoken language has had important classroom implications over the last two decades. Finally, we offered a brief overview of the design principles underlying some of the speaking skills materials that have been produced over the last 20 years.

8.11   Further reading

1   Bygate, M. (1987): *Speaking*, gives a very useful insight into the nature of the speaking skills within a broad pedagogical framework.
2   McCarthy, M. and R. A. Carter (1994): *Language as Discourse*, offers a useful insight into this area from a teacher-friendly perspective.

9
Writing Skills

9.1 Introduction

Writing in the language class – the last of the skills that we discuss here as 'discrete' – reflects many of the recurrent themes of this book so far. We shall need, for instance, to call on various communicative criteria; on the concepts of 'product' and 'process'; and on the role of formal language practice, to see how, along with other skills, writing too has developed and has accumulated many insights into the nature of language and learning. However, as well as having much in common with other skills, we shall see that writing differs in some significant ways to do with the purpose of writing in class and in everyday life, and the relationship between these two settings.

   This chapter will first survey the reasons for writing and the different types of writing associated with them. The central section will focus on a number of approaches to teaching writing, particularly as expressed in teaching materials, and will try to show how perspectives have gradually changed. We shall then move on to the classroom environment itself, including some possibilities for writing-related activities, the issue of error correction and the role of the teacher.

9.2 Reasons for writing

1   At this point it would be helpful to note down your reasons for needing – or wishing – to write in the course of a typical week, and the form that your writing takes. Try to think of all possible contexts. Can the kinds of writing you do be grouped together in any way?
2   How do you think your own list might compare with that of other people you know: perhaps a friend who isn't a teacher, or your students?

Our own list included the following, not in any particular order:

Shopping list	Notes from a book	Official forms
This chapter	Parts of a prospectus	Letter requesting tourist information
Telephone messages	'Reminder' lists	An essay
Letter to a friend	A meeting agenda	Business letters
Comments on student work	Invitations	Diary (narrative and appointments)
Birthday card	Office memoranda	Map showing how to get to our house
Writing emails		

We can now make a few initial observations arising directly or indirectly from thinking about the kinds of writing we do. The implications of these points for the teaching of writing are taken up below.

1.   A typical 'writing profile' covers a great range of styles. We may just write a list of nouns, or a number, or even simply a visual representation (a list, taking a phone message, drawing a map). Alternatively, taking notes from a book or a verbal message will require some facility with reducing language structure into note form in the interests of speed and efficiency. Discursive writing has many different functions (narrative, persuasion, setting out an argument and so on) and makes considerable demands on our ability to structure an extended piece of writing carefully. Email writing is more often conversational, even when done for professional purposes, and is more immediately interactive.

Moreover, in some cases we ourselves initiate the need to write – different kinds of letters, a shopping list, or a short story, perhaps – whereas in other cases the writing is a response to someone else's initiation, as when we respond to an invitation or a letter. The final point to make here is that our writing has different addressees: family, colleagues, friends, ourselves, officials, students and many more.

Reasons for writing, then, differ along several dimensions, especially those of language, topic and audience.

2.   In straightforward terms of frequency, the great majority of people write very much less than they talk and listen, although the amount of writing may be increasing as people have more access to computers and to email communication. It is, for example, not unusual to find emails taking over from telephone calls. Nevertheless, it is still the case that many adults do not need to write much in their everyday lives: and if there are few 'real-world' reasons for writing in our L_1, there are even fewer for doing so in a foreign language. Writing for most of us only happens to any significant extent as part of formal education. This dominance of oral/aural over literacy skills holds even for those of us for whom writing is an integral part of our professional lives.

Types of writing

Personal writing	Public writing	Creative writing	
diaries	letters of – enquiry	poems	
journals	– complaint	stories	
shopping lists	– request	rhymes	
reminders for oneself	form filling	drama	
packing lists	applications (for memberships)	songs	
addresses		autobiography	
recipes			

Social writing	Study writing	Institutional writing	
letters	making notes while reading	agendas	posters
invitations	taking notes from lectures	minutes	instructions
notes – of condolence	making a card index	memoranda	speeches
– of thanks	summaries	reports	applications
– of congratulations	synopses	reviews	curriculum vitae
cablegrams	reviews	contracts	specifications
telephone messages	reports of – experiments	business letters	note-making
instructions – to friends	– workshops	public notices	(doctors and other
– to family	– visits	advertisements	professionals)
	essays		
	bibliographies		

Source: T. Hedge, p. 96 from *Resource Books for Teachers: Writing*. Oxford: Oxford University Press, 1988. © Oxford University Press, 1988.

3. Some ways of classifying types of writing can be suggested. R. V. White (1980: 14–15), for example, proposes a simple and useful two-way distinction between *institutional* and *personal* writing, each of which he subdivides further. 'Institutional' includes business correspondence, textbooks, regulations, reports; 'personal', for White, covers the two main areas of personal letters and creative writing. Hedge (1988) offers a more detailed breakdown under the six headings of *personal, study, public, creative, social* and *institutional*. Her checklist is self-explanatory, and is reproduced above in full. We shall refer back to it when discussing the 'products' of writing appropriate to the language classroom. In the meantime, you will certainly recognize some elements of your own list here. You might like to see whether your writing fits into the categories that Hedge uses.

9.3   *Writing materials in the language class*

It is now time to ask what part writing can and does play in the language class, given its more limited role for most people outside an educational setting. We have seen in previous chapters that some attention to 'real-world' language and behaviour is regarded as increasingly important in the current English language teaching climate. It would be difficult to argue the case that writing in the language class should only mirror the educational function (writing essays and examination answers, taking notes from textbooks and so on) except perhaps in certain 'specific-purpose' programmes. At the same time, it is not immediately obvious how the notion of 'authenticity' and the opportunities for transfer from real world to classroom can be maintained to the extent that this can be done for speaking and listening skills.

These two issues – the possibilities for reflecting communicative criteria, and the treatment of the skill of writing resulting from its general educational role – have been significant in the development of materials and methods. We shall now go on to look at how writing has been handled in English language teaching, attempting as we do so to pick out the major trends.

> The titles, with dates, of several popular writing courses are listed below. Pause for a moment to look through the list. Then, as you read the rest of the chapter, ask yourself what significance the titles might have. For example, can you discern a shift in the approaches to the teaching of writing? Do the dates of publication approximately parallel what you know of changing perspectives on language and language learning? (It might even be interesting to compare your ideas here with the similar task in chapter 8.)

These are speculative questions, and we certainly do not wish to suggest that there is a rigid relationship between a title, a date and a 'movement' in language teaching. We shall make a few comments in the conclusion to this chapter.

Guided Composition Exercises (1967)
Frames for Written English (1966/1974)
Guided Course in English Composition (1969)
Guided Paragraph Writing (1972)
From Paragraph to Essay (1975)
Think and Link (1979)
Communicate in Writing (1981)
Writing Skills (1983)
Pen to Paper (1983)
Freestyle (1986)
Word for Word (1989)
Outlines (1989)
Feedback (1994)
Reasons to Write: Strategies for Successful Academic Writing (2001).

'Traditional' writing activities

There are a number of types of writing task that most of us will be familiar with, both as teachers and from our own language learning experience. Simplifying for the moment, they can be listed under three broad headings:

Controlled sentence construction   If the focus of a language programme is on accuracy, then schemes for controlling learners' writing output will obviously predominate. The range of activity types is considerable, and typical approaches include

- providing a model sentence and asking students to construct a parallel sentence with different lexical items
- inserting a missing grammatical form
- composing sentences from tabular information, with a model provided
- joining sentences to make a short paragraph, inserting supplied conjunctions (but, and, however, because, although . . .)

Free composition   Apparently at the other end of the spectrum, a 'free writing' task requires learners to 'create' an essay on a given topic, often as part of a language examination. Sometimes students are simply invited to write on a personal topic – their hobbies, what they did on holiday, interesting experiences and the like. Other materials provide a reading passage as a stimulus for a piece of writing on a parallel topic, usually with comprehension questions interspersed between the two activities.

Although 'controlled' and 'free' writing appear to represent very different approaches, they are not in fact mutually exclusive, and many writing schemes lead learners through several stages from one to the other. A typical example is provided in Jupp and Milne's *Guided Course in English Composition* (1969): each 'composition' begins with structure practice, continues with a sample composition, and then uses this material as a basis for students' own compositions.

The 'homework' function   Particularly in general coursebooks (as distinct from materials devoted specifically to the skill of writing), it is quite common to find writing tasks 'bunched' at the end of a unit, either as supplementary work in class or set for homework and returned to the teacher for later correction.

This brief and generalized summary indicates several trends in the 'traditional' teaching of writing from which current views have both developed and moved away:

- There is an emphasis on *accuracy*.
- The focus of attention is the *finished product*, whether a sentence or a whole composition.
- The teacher's role is to be *judge* of the finished work.
- Writing often has a *consolidating* function.

In other words, in many earlier materials the 'product' did not on the whole reflect the kind of real-world writing discussed earlier, and the 'process' was not really the concern of anyone except the writer: certainly it was not given much explicit attention. Byrne, however, rightly points out that 'many such schemes were carefully thought out and, although no longer fashionable, produced many useful ideas on how to guide writing' (1988: 22). This is well borne out by Moody, who devised one of the better known schemes (*Frames for Written English*, 1974). Moody argues that the advantage of controlled practice is that it leads to automaticity in grammatical usage, and he certainly does not claim that a structured scheme provides a comprehensive view of writing. Furthermore, we should note that these approaches to writing drew on key language teaching and educational traditions: as such they fulfilled important pedagogical and practical functions. We shall also find that many of them contain the seeds of later developments.

This said, materials have gradually come to reflect both the diversity of written texts and the ways in which writers approach a piece of writing. We shall take each of these in turn.

9.4   *The written product*

We commented earlier that any piece of writing we do can be seen from a number of different perspectives that clearly take us beyond a concern for accuracy alone. Whilst few teachers are likely to be satisfied with written work full of grammatical mistakes, at the same time notions of 'correctness' are now felt to have a broader base, and to be embedded in a more integrated view of the skill of writing. Raimes's suggested techniques for teaching writing 'stem from the basic assumptions that writing means . . . a connected text and not just single sentences, that writers write for a purpose and a reader, and that the process of writing is a valuable learning tool' (1983: 11). She lists nine areas of relevance: excluding 'process' considerations, the concern of our next section, these are as follows:

1   Syntax (sentence structure)
2   Grammar
3   Mechanics (handwriting, spelling and so on)
4   Organization (paragraphing, cohesion)
5   Word choice
6   Purpose
7   Audience
8   Content

A comparable approach is taken by Hedge, who refers to the production of a piece of writing as 'crafting', 'the way in which a writer puts together the pieces of the text, developing ideas through sentences and paragraphs within an overall structure' (1988: 89). She uses the term 'communicating' to examine specifically the need for a writer to develop a sense of audience.

We shall now look at some selected examples of activities to be found in materials for the teaching of writing: many more examples will be found in the books listed under 'Further reading' at the end of the chapter. Within the overall framework of the need for an awareness of purpose, we shall modify Raimes's and Hedge's categories and use just the headings of (a) levels of writing, and (b) audience.

Levels of writing

Look back again at your personal list of writing activities. Most teachers, for example, write comments on student work as a regular part of their jobs. You may well recognize this style:

> This is quite a good summary, but it would have been a good idea to include more of your own opinions. Think more carefully about tenses. Your hand-writing is also sometimes difficult to read.

From a different sphere, in a letter home from holiday you will probably in-clude something about what you have been doing, details of people and places, and perhaps some information about travel arrangements. As you write, you will certainly have been operating on a number of different and interacting levels, not necessarily consciously, of course, and moving between 'top-down' and 'bottom-up' strategies discussed in chapter 6.

We saw in chapter 2 how the advent of the 'communicative approach' had far-reaching implications, including an extension of the size of language stretches that can be dealt with from sentence to discourse level. The two outer layers on figure 9.1 will certainly require consideration of both 'cohesion' – linking devices – and 'discourse coherence' – the ways in which a text forms a thematic whole. Such criteria are now well-established in the teaching of writing. Typical organizational principles for materials include paragraph structuring, particu-larly related to functional categories, and the use of a range of linking devices. Sentence-level and grammar practice is not omitted but, as the diagram suggests, is set in the context of a longer and purposeful stretch of language. Writing, then, is seen as primarily message-oriented, so a communicative view of language is a necessary foundation.

Some of the trends in the teaching of discourse-level writing, and the tech-niques used, are readily discernible from a glance at many of the published materials of the last two decades or so. Functional categories include

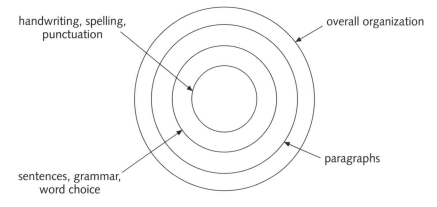

Figure 9.1 Levels of writing.

sequencing; chronological order
comparison and contrast
classification
cause and effect
description: of objects, and processes
definitions
writing instructions
predicting and speculating
expressing opinion
expressing reasons
discursive essays
writing narratives: e.g. of events

Nunan (1999: ch. 10) makes a number of proposals for developing what he terms 'discourse writing'.

Linking devices covered include the various connectives associated with these functional categories, and the notions of lexical cohesion, referencing using pronouns and the article system, ellipsis and substitution that we looked at in chapter 2.

The techniques used are many: you will notice that they usually require learners to understand the overall purpose of a piece of writing, not just the immediate sentence-bound grammatical context. Here is a small selection of some of the possibilities:

- Providing a text to read as a model for a particular function.
- Answering questions on a text, then using the answers as the basis for a piece of writing.
- Using non-verbal information in many forms. This may be a simple visual, such as a picture or a drawing; or a table, a graph, a diagram. Alternatively, the overall structure of a text may be represented visually, as an 'information-structure' diagram. The last of these is particularly common with classifications.
- Selecting appropriate connectives in a paragraph.
- (Re)constructing a paragraph from sentences given in the wrong order, or a whole text from a set of jumbled paragraphs. This technique is usually referred to as 'unscrambling'.
- Paragraph or story completion, which can be done by adding an ending, but also a beginning or a middle section.
- Parallel writing.
- Choosing an appropriate title for a piece of writing, such as a newspaper article.
- Working on identifying and creating 'topic sentences' as the basis for developing paragraphs.

Many other techniques are developed from pre-writing tasks carried out in the classroom: we shall look at these a little later in this chapter.

Audience

Several authors on writing (Byrne, 1988; Hedge, 1988; Tribble, 1996) make the important point that writing is a process of *encoding* (putting your message into words) carried out with a reader in mind. Certainly the outermost layer of figure 9.1 – the overall organization – is best considered in relation to audience and purpose. The degree of 'crafting' that needs to be done, and at what level, will also be determined to some extent by the addressee. Stylistic choices, in other words, depend on why and for whom we are writing.

   It is likely that, in the great majority of situations, our students still write primarily for their teachers, or perhaps for an examiner, both acting in the role of evaluator. Grant (1987) makes the very useful point that, although transferring real-life writing directly to the classroom is problematic, what we should be aiming at is at least the creation of 'plausible contexts'.

> Would you say that your students do most of their writing for their teacher, or are there other 'plausible contexts' that you have introduced into your classroom? When you have read through the following suggestions for extending the range of possible recipients for your students' writing, consider to what extent your own materials or classes could be adapted to accommodate them.

As we have noted several times, the classroom has its own purpose and structure, and is not simply a reflection of the outside world. In this sense, we can think of writing activities both from the 'instrumental' perspective of what is useful for external purposes, but also in terms of their educational function and the reality of the classroom itself. The following audience suggestions reflect this dual aspect. We have listed addressees along with a few suggested topics, but of course the possibilities are considerably greater than this. Our students, then, can write

- to other students: invitations, instructions, directions
- for the whole class: a magazine, poster information, a cookbook with recipes from different countries
- for new students: information on the school and its locality
- *to* the teacher (not only *for* the teacher): about themselves, and the teacher can reply or indeed initiate (see Rinvolucri, quoted in Hedge (1988), who suggests an exchange of letters with a new class to get to know them)
- for themselves: lists, notes, diaries (for a fuller discussion of diary writing see chapter 12)
- to penfriends
- to other people in the school: asking about interests and hobbies, conducting a survey
- to people and organizations outside the school: writing for information, answering advertisements

- If the school has access to a network of computers, many of these activities can be carried out electronically as well. (We comment on this point later.)

So far we have looked at the 'what' of writing, particularly at the nature of text and the importance of writing with a readership in mind. Writing continues to serve as a vehicle for language practice, and necessarily so, but this function is integrated into a broader and more diversified perspective. As Byrne puts it, teachers need to make students aware that 'any piece of writing is an attempt to communicate something: that the writer has a goal or purpose in mind; that he has to establish and maintain contact with his reader; that he has to organize his material and that he does this through the use of certain logical and grammatical devices' (1988: 14).

We now turn to the 'how'.

9.5 The writing process

One of the aims of this book is to trace the changes of focus in materials and methods for English language teaching, and to show how different approaches have gained prominence at different times. A characteristic of the last decade in particular has been a growing interest in what a language *skill* entails. Initially, attention was focused on the receptive skills, especially reading: more recently, research into writing – much of it concerned with writing in the mother tongue – has become more accessible to second-language teachers, and is beginning to have a significant impact on the design of materials and on attitudes to teaching writing. Stylistic factors, whether grammatical, discoursal, or lexical, are now set alongside a concern for how writers go about the performance of the task itself. A detailed discussion of the research base is outside the scope of this chapter: readers interested in pursuing the L_1/L_2 parallels further are referred to Grabe and Kaplan (1996); descriptions of some of the procedures used to elicit information from writers, such as retrospective reports, behaviour protocols, directed reports and thinking aloud protocols are described in Hayes and Flower (1983). We shall now look at the writing process from the two related points of view of the writer and the classroom.

The writer's perspective

Try to note down the various stages that you think you go through when producing a piece of continuous text, such as a letter, a report, an essay, a story and the like.

Except perhaps with something as straightforward as a shopping list, it is unlikely that your text will appear directly on the page in its final form without any intervening stages. Even with a shopping list you may decide to reorder it, and categorize items in terms of different types of shop or different sections of the supermarket. Writers, it seems, do a great number of things before they end up with the final version – the 'finished product'. For instance, they jot down ideas, put them in order, make a plan, reject it and start again, add more ideas as they go along, change words, rephrase bits, move sections around, review parts of what they have written, cross things out, check through the final version, write tidy notes, write on odd pieces of paper as thoughts occur to them, write directly into a typewriter or a word processor if they are lucky enough to have one, look at the blank page for a long time, change pens, refer back to something they have read – and many more things, some of them quite idiosyncratic.

If all this is what writers do 'naturally', then Raimes (1983) is right to refer to the English language writing class as very often 'anguish as a second language'. This 'anguish' must be particularly severe if students are expected to turn in a perfectly polished piece of work. Even if accuracy is an important and legitimate requirement, it is only achieved after a rather untidy and stumbling set of procedures, and the nature of the process itself needs to be acknowledged. We shall return to this point from a different angle when looking at attitudes to the correction of written work.

Hedge refers to all the components of the process taken together as 'composing' (taken alongside 'communicating' and 'crafting'). She suggests the following as a representation of the stages of writing (adapted from Hedge, 1988: 21):

Getting ideas together → planning and outlining → making notes → making a first draft → revising, redrafting → editing → final version.

Byrne (1988) has a similar set of steps:

List ideas.
Make an outline ('scaffolding').
Write a draft.
Correct and improve the draft.
Write the final version.

One of the most explicit schemes for 'process writing' was developed by White and Arndt (1991). They are critical of traditional – institutional – approaches to writing that merely reinforce the learning of the language itself, requiring students to demonstrate knowledge of linguistic structures. Their own proposals are more concerned to help learners develop the cognitive strategies involved in writing, and their own list of strategies is as follows:

Generating
Focusing
Structuring
Drafting
Evaluating
Reviewing

For most of us, even this is still rather idealized: as Hedge points out, writing is not linear, but is more like a recursive, even messy, activity, where we move around among the different stages and carry out each stage several times, with great personal variation. However, although 'stage' is in principle contrasted with 'process', for pedagogic purposes it is useful to use the 'stage' idea as a framework for teaching, because of the need for a systematic procedure in the classroom context. Some researchers have also tried to isolate the strategies used by 'good' writers, but for our purposes it may be more useful to think of 'typical' strategies for attacking a writing task, rather than the less accessible ideal.

Nevertheless, out of the complexity and untidiness a set of procedures emerges, which for teaching purposes can be reduced to three (following Hedge):

1   Pre-writing: jotting down ideas and preparing provisional plans.
2   Drafting and redrafting, involving reviewing and revising; in other words, working out what to say and then how best to say it.
3   Editing the pre-final version, including assessing clarity for the intended reader and checking accuracy.

Materials for teaching writing are increasingly beginning to incorporate these process-based insights in various ways. An early example can be found in *Writing as a Thinking Process* (Lawrence, 1972), a course aimed mainly at people studying English for academic or professional purposes and based on a view of writing whereby learners are able to articulate their own thought processes. The emphasis is on paragraph construction in functional categories, and students are expected to manipulate data and make inferencing statements according to explicit cognitive criteria. For example, a task on chronological sequencing may require learners first of all to arrive at a correct sequence, then to make deductions by relating the different stages in that sequence. It is only much more recently, however, that the broader 'process' spectrum that we have been discussing here is taken more fully into account. *Outlines* and *Perspectives* (Hopkins and Tribble, 1989; Hopkins, 1989), for instance, include drafting, checking, improving for a second draft, editing and rewriting as central activities in each unit. *Practice Writing* (Stephens, 1996) balances out activities between the product (formal and informal language, layout of letters, newspaper articles, stylistic comparison, paragraphs, topic sentences, linking devices and so on, as well as language accuracy) and process (planning, drafting and redrafting, editing).

Writing in the classroom

Writing, like reading, is in many ways an individual, solitary activity: the writing triangle of 'communicating', 'composing' and 'crafting' is usually carried out for an absent readership. However, we must remember that our students are language learners rather than writers, and it would not be particularly helpful to have them spend all their time writing alone. Although process research points to a need to give learner-writers space and time to operate their own preferred individual strategies, the classroom can be structured in such a way as to provide positive intervention and support in the development of writing skills. We shall comment only very briefly here on possible classroom activities – they look directly ahead to the next chapter on the integration of language skills, and to the management of classrooms that will be the focus of the third part of this book.

The classroom can provide an environment for writing at each of the three main stages of (1) gathering ideas: pre-writing and planning, (2) working on drafts, and (3) preparing the final version. The primary means by which this can be done – leaving aside for the moment the teacher's role of marking and commenting – is by establishing a collaborative, interactive framework where learners work together on their writing in a 'workshop' atmosphere. A few typical examples, all involving oral skills, must suffice:

- 'Brainstorming' a topic by talking with other students to collect ideas.
- Co-operating at the planning stage, sometimes in pairs/groups, before agreeing a plan for the class to work from.
- 'Jigsaw' writing, for example using a picture stimulus for different sections of the class to create a different part of the story (Hedge, 1988: 76–7).
- Editing another student's draft.
- Preparing interview questions, perhaps for a collaborative project.

Ur (1996, Module 11: 164–8) has an extensive list of writing activities. Additionally, the range of possibilities for using computers in writing (and in language teaching more generally) is increasing rapidly, and there is potential for students to work collaboratively as well. Clearly there are advantages in having available both spellcheckers and fast editing packages; but students can also use email both within the school, to network with each other, and outside, for example to write to penpals ('mousepals', to use Harmer's (2001b) term. Howarth and Hetherington (2000) provide further examples for the use of personal computers, including setting up 'virtual classrooms', when it may be difficult to get learners together at the same time, and developing online courses. Kanan and Towndrow (2002) have a practical discussion of the use of online feedback. (For further discussion, see chapter 12.)

In the multidimensional view of writing explored in this chapter, there are clearly a number of different possibilities available for the sequencing of materials and activities. We can reduce these to three:

1 Varying/increasing the size of the linguistic 'building blocks', from single lexical items → sentences and sentence joining → the construction of paragraphs and finally → whole texts. This requires attention to all levels of language, from sentence and text structure to a sense of the coherence of a completed piece of writing. This is related, of course, to the more traditional progression through a writing scheme from 'controlled' to 'guided' to 'free',

though we now have a much wider range of descriptive tools available for the language material.

2 Paralleling the stages in the process of putting a whole piece of writing together. Although writing processes have little in themselves to do with proficiency – an elementary learner can in principle plan, draft and redraft, and edit as well as an advanced one can – the degree to which the process can be put to use obviously does have.

3 Task complexity. It can be argued – although it is a point that needs further exploration – that personal (expressive) writing is in some sense 'easier' than its institutional or professional counterpart. A letter to a friend, or a short story, while they obviously have their own structure, nevertheless are not as constrained by rules as, say, a business letter or a report or an essay.

9.6   *Correcting written work*

1 What is your usual and preferred method for correcting student work?
2 What do you see as your main role in relation to the writing your learners produce?

Obviously teachers' attitudes and methods are determined to a certain extent by their approach to language teaching (whether chosen or imposed), and by the whole educational climate in which they work. We commented earlier that the most common role for the teacher is to be a judge, a critical evaluator of the finished product. Work is returned to students with mistakes indicated or corrected: the legendary red pen has always been a tool of the teacher's trade. However, the approaches to writing that we have looked at, from the perspective of both 'product' and 'process', inevitably lead to a much more varied view both of the role of the teacher and the classroom environment, and of the criteria for marking and assessing students' written work.

Firstly, process considerations suggest the usefulness of intervention at all stages of writing, not just at the end. It is unlikely that a draft will need to receive a grade, so the teacher, by commenting and making suggestions, becomes a reader as well as a critic. Harmer (2001b: 261–2) regards the teacher as 'motivator' and 'feedback provider'. The feedback given to students is in this view both 'formative' – concerned with a developmental process – as well as 'summative' – the evaluation of the end-product. Raimes suggests no less than thirteen stages, from topic selection to the assignment of follow-up tasks (1983: 140–1). Secondly, this feedback, whether summative or formative, takes place at a number of different levels of writing, and sentence grammar is not the only subject of attention. We need to take into account the appropriateness of the writing to its purpose and intended audience as well as topic and content criteria. Several marking schemes along these lines are now used by individual teachers, in materials, and by some examination boards. A useful example is proposed as a 'writing profile' by Hopkins and Tribble (in *Outlines*, 1989) under the headings

Communicative quality
Logical organization
Layout and presentation
Grammar
Vocabulary
Handwriting, punctuation and spelling

You might like to 'weight' these in terms of their importance in your evaluation of your own students' writing.

Thirdly, the red pen method is inherently negative, but there is no reason why feedback should not be positive as well. The *Outlines* scheme, for instance, commends as well as criticizes ('communicates effectively', 'excellent control of appropriate vocabulary' and the like). The issue here is what we see to be the overall function of correction. A distinction should be made between 'mistakes', when learners are not using correctly the language they already know, and errors, which, as we have seen, are largely the outcome of a learner's developing competence. Mistakes will require direct feedback and remedial treatment, and will largely relate to language points already covered; errors may be more appropriately used for the planning of future work.

In passing, there is an interesting further dimension to the notion of 'correctness' that derives from research into the notion of 'contrastive rhetoric' (Connor, 1996). This refers to the idea that, at least to some extent, thought patterns are culturally determined, and that these will be expressed in styles of writing. Ballard (1984), for example, has some interesting data on how her Thai and Japanese students were perceived to be writing 'incorrectly' in an English-speaking environment because of a tendency to approach points indirectly; many Arabic speakers overuse 'and' to concatenate propositions, not so much because of impoverished language knowledge but because of cultural predispositions. This fascinating field is relevant to teaching because it raises obvious questions about the sources of apparent 'error'.

Finally, there are implications for the role of people other than the teacher in the feedback process. Using other class members as addressees, and the classroom as a co-operative working environment, automatically means that students are involved in the production of each other's written work. There is then a natural extension to peer editing and revision, as well as the more established procedure of peer 'correction'. Clearly all these aspects will only be effective with guidance and focus, but potentially they can help students to develop a critical stance towards their own work as well. Several other procedures might be developed to involve learners in what is presumably the ultimate aim of *self*-monitoring and *self*-correction. These include marking schemes that indicate mistake type, leaving the learner to identify the specific problem; the establishing of personal checklists, which of course change as proficiency grows; and the technique of 'reformulation', in which the teacher suggests another wording for what the student is trying to express. It is important to recall that self-evaluation too will require different criteria at different stages in the writing process: there is little point in too great a concern for accuracy when gathering ideas, formulating a plan and establishing readership, whereas correctness has a vital role as the final draft takes shape. Hedge (1988) prefers to think of 'correction' under the more general heading of 'improving', a cover term that stresses the interacting of marking procedures with processing categories.

9.7 Conclusion

Earlier in this chapter we asked you to consider the titles of some published teaching materials to see if any trends were discernible. Although it is much too simplistic to suggest that the date of publication can be directly linked to a particular approach, it is probably true to say that there is a gradual shift from guiding learners through grammatical patterns against the background of 'composition' requirements, to a concern with paragraph and text structure from a communicative perspective, to titles that reflect ways in which we think about the activity of writing – 'outlining', 'putting pen to paper' and so on – and to those that refer explicitly to strategies, and to the role of the teacher. Materials for the teaching of writing, then, do not neglect the basic skills, but are increasingly likely to see writing in terms of purpose, audience, and the development and organization of thinking, for real-world, for learning and for educational purposes.

1 If you are a regular user of email, make a list of the main ways in which email differs stylistically from more conventional writing. If you use (or plan to use) email writing in your own teaching, in what ways might your attitude to 'correctness' change?
2 Consider the unit provided here from as many angles as possible, for example: subject matter; 'authenticity'; level; types of writing task; sequencing of activities; suitability for your own students. If it is not suitable, what would you wish to change?

9.8 Further reading

1 Hedge, T. (1988): *Writing*. A rich source of ideas for the teaching and learning of writing skills, using a framework that includes both 'process' and 'product' considerations.
2 Tribble, C. (1996): *Writing*. Covers the teaching of writing from the perspective of both principle and practice.

UNIT 10

A formal job application

1 Before you read the job advertisement, think about the following questions.

If you are still a student.
1 What job would you like to do in the future?
2 Do you think you have the right personal qualities and skills for the job?
3 Which of the items in the lists below would be most important in your job?

If you have a job now.
1 What job do you do?
2 Why did you choose it?
3 What sort of personal qualities and skills do you need for your job? (Some of the words below may help you.)

1	2	3	4
patience	humour	good manners	good communication skills
honesty	ambition	leadership qualities	
intelligence	initiative		
independence	stamina	a sympathetic manner	a sense of humour
reliability	enthusiasm		
efficiency	energy	ability to work under pressure	ability to cope in a crisis
confidence	imagination		
	creativity		

2 Now make adjectives where possible from the nouns in lists 1 and 2.

3 Look at these job advertisements. Which job would you prefer? Why?

TOURIST GUIDE

Do you want to work for one of the most up and coming companies in International Tourism? Do you:

- know this area well?
- have experience in dealing with groups?
- speak at least two languages?

We have a vacancy for a Tourist Guide.

You will need patience, good humour and excellent communication skills. A smart appearance is essential.

Excellent prospects and salary.

Apply in writing to:
Personnel Manager, Eurotours, Granada, Spain.

Trainee Sales Manager Required

A confident, enthusiastic young person is required to train as a Sales Manager in our foreign book sales department. You will need excellent communication skills, plus a good command of English. A smart appearance and pleasant manner are essential. Prospects are excellent for applicants who can take responsibility and who really want to get to the top.

Apply in writing to:
Shortman Publishing House
9, Clifton Street
Kensington,
London WC6 8LP

WORK FOR NTV RADIO!

New world service radio station is looking for

talented young people

for a variety of opportunities, both as presenters and behind the scenes.

> •Applicants must be imaginative, reliable and self-confident.
> •Training will be given where required but a high degree of
>   hard work and commitment will be demanded in return.
> •Ability to keep cool in a crisis essential!
> •Applicants must speak good English.

Salary negotiable, depending on experience.

Apply, in writing, to:
NTV Radio, PO Box 892, London W1

4 What are all the qualities you think you would need for each of the
   jobs? Make some notes under these headings:

   Tourist Guide   Sales Manager   Radio Presenter

5 Look at the Tourist Guide advertisement. Underline the most
   important details which you should refer to in a letter of application.

6 Now imagine you are the Personnel Manager of Eurotours. What sort
   of person are you looking for? What do you need to hear from a good
   applicant? How formal would you expect their letter to be?

Pairwork

Student A: Imagine you are going to interview someone for a job
like the one in the first advertisement (Tourist Guide). Use the ideas
in the box to write some questions. When your partner is ready,
begin the interview.

Student B: Imagine you are applying for a job like the one in the
first advertisement. Note down some (imaginary) details about
yourself. Use the questions in the box to help you. When you are
ready, begin the interview.

EXPERIENCE
Have you ever ....?
How long have you ....?   When did you ....?
                                 In your last job, did you ....?

LANGUAGES
How many ....?
How well ....?   .... certificates?
                 .... ever lived abroad?

KNOWLEDGE OF AREA
How well ....?
What do you think a group of .... people might like to visit?

PERSONAL QUALITIES
How ..... with customers who complain about everything?
What ..... your best qualities?

HOBBIES
What ....?
              .... belong to any clubs?

WHAT IF?
What would you do if ....?

WHY?
Why do you think we .... you the job?

A letter of application

This is the letter one of the applicants wrote for the job of Tourist Guide.

1 **Do you think Eurotours will be impressed by his/her letter? Has he/she supplied all the details requested? Is the language and style he/she uses formal or informal? Is this appropriate? Has he/she included any unnecessary information?**

2 **The words in bold type are important because they help to link the text together. They refer back to words or information given earlier in the text. Mark the words they refer to, as shown in the example.**

```
                                        4 Green Street
                                        Kensington
                                        London

                                        5 August, 199-

Personnel Manager
Eurotours
Calle Principal
Granada
Spain


Dear Sir/Madam,
I saw your advertisement for a Tourist Guide in this week's edition of
'Travel' and would like to apply for the post.
As my c.v. shows, I am very well qualified for this job. I studied Tourism at
London University from 1992-5 and obtained the enclosed Diploma. As you can
see, this included a special course on tourism in Europe. Since leaving
University, I have also done a number of training courses in different aspects
of the tourist industry (certificates enclosed).
For the past year, I have been working as a courier here in England. In this
job, my main responsibilities include guiding groups around the city and
dealing with bookings and accommodation.
Before that, I had a job with Smith's Travel Agency in London. There, I
answered telephone enquiries and dealt with holiday bookings.
My mother is Spanish and I therefore have a perfect understanding of Spanish
people, their language and the country. I know Andalucia especially well as I
have spent most of my holidays around this region.
As regards languages, I speak Spanish and French fluently. In addition to
these, I am at present taking classes in German.
I would now like to broaden my experience as a courier. I would also welcome
the chance to work for a large company like yours, with the chances for
promotion this would provide.
In my spare time I play basketball for a local team of which I have recently
been made captain. I also help out with the local youth club.
As you can see from my references, I have plenty of patience and good humour.
In fact I have been named 'Courier Of The Month' by our local tourist board on
two occasions.
I would be able to come for interview at any time.
I look forward to hearing from you.

Yours faithfully,

Chris Jones

Chris Jones
```

Verbs and prepositions

Complete the sentences with an appropriate preposition and the correct form of the verb (gerund or infinitive).

1 I am interested ..... (*apply*) for the post.
2 I would like the chance ..... (*widen*) my experience.
3 I am looking forward ..... (*meet*) my colleagues.
4 I have got a lot of experience ..... (*deal*) with groups.
5 This job would give me the opportunity ..... (*travel*).
6 I hope ..... (*hear*) from you soon.

Written tasks

1 Study this spidergraph. It is the plan the candidate made before he/she wrote the letter of application you saw earlier.

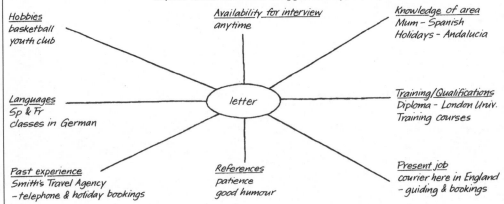

Hobbies
basketball
youth club

Availability for interview
anytime

Knowledge of area
Mum – Spanish
Holidays – Andalucia

Languages
Sp & Fr
classes in German

letter

Training/Qualifications
Diploma – London Univ.
Training courses

Past experience
Smith's Travel Agency
– telephone & holiday bookings

References
patience
good humour

Present job
courier here in England
– guiding & bookings

2 Write a letter of application for one of the jobs advertised at the beginning of this Unit.

> **USEFUL TIPS**
> STYLE/REGISTER
> Remember to use very polite, formal language for letters of application.
> TENSES
> The Present Perfect Simple and Continuous are useful if you are talking about recent work and experience.
> LINKING YOUR TEXT TOGETHER
> Check back to the exercise on text linking that you did in this Unit. Try to do the same with your text.
> DRAFTING
> Nobody writes a perfect text the first time. There are always words that need changing or errors to correct. After you have written a first draft of your letter, exchange your work with your partner. Check each other's work for errors in spelling, punctuation and paragraphing. Then rewrite the text with any other changes you need to make.

Source: M. Stephens, Unit 10, pp. 48–51 from *Practise Writing*. Harlow: Eurocentres/ Longman, 1996 © Addison Wesley Longman Ltd, 1986, 1996. Reprinted by permission of Pearson Education Ltd.

10

Integrated Skills

10.1   *Introduction*

So far in this section of the book we have been devoting a chapter to each of the four language skills in order to give each one some in-depth treatment. In this final chapter of part II we consider some of the different ways in which these language skills may be taught in an integrated way in the classroom. Some of the natural overlap of the language skills has already been examined in chapters 6 to 9, particularly with regard to speaking and listening and to reading and writing, although there are situations where either three or all four language skills can be integrated effectively, and in this chapter we intend to examine some of these. We start by examining situations that require an integration of skills in order for them to be completed successfully. After this, we consider some different approaches to the integration of language skills in materials. Finally, we look at skills integration in the classroom by discussing a broad range of different materials from the teaching of general English to the teaching of English for academic purposes. We also consider project work and role play/ simulation in relation to the concept of integrated skills.

Let us begin by trying to clarify the concept of integrated skills by looking at the definition provided by the *Longman Dictionary of Applied Linguistics*. According to Richards, Platt and Weber (1985: 144) it is 'the teaching of the language skills of reading, writing, listening and speaking in conjunction with each other as when a lesson involves activities that relate listening and speaking to reading and writing'. If we look around us in our daily lives we can see that we rarely use language skills in isolation but in conjunction, as the definition above suggests and, even though the classroom is clearly not the same as 'real' life, it could be argued that part of its function is to replicate it. If one of the jobs of the teacher is to make the students 'communicatively competent' in the L_2, then this will involve more than being able to perform in each of the four skills separately. By giving learners tasks that expose them to these skills in conjunction, it is possible that they will gain a deeper understanding of how communication works in the foreign language as well as becoming more motivated when they see the value of performing meaningful tasks and activities in the classroom. As Morrow (1981: 61) states in his second principle of communicative methodology:

> One of the most significant features of communication is that it is a dynamic and developing phenomenon. In other words, it cannot easily be analysed into component features without its nature being destroyed in the process. It is of course possible to identify various formal features of the way language is used communicatively, and these can be studied individually. But the ability to handle these elements in isolation is no indication of ability to communicate.

Lubelska and Matthews (1997: 16) provide seven statements relating to integrated skills for teachers to brainstorm with other teachers:

1 Integrating skills involves using some or all of Listening, Speaking, Reading and Writing to practice new material (vocabulary, pronunciation, grammar, text/discourse).
2 All four skills must be practised in every lesson.
3 As listening and speaking naturally go together, it is always desirable to integrate these two skills.
4 The sequence hear–speak–read–write is the most appropriate for integrated skills work.
5 A common topic, such as holidays or pets, is a device linking the separate activities in integrated skills lessons.
6 If we want to develop specific subskills (reading for gist, guessing unknown words etc.), it is necessary to focus on individual skills in some lessons.
7 Integrated skills may be fine with a small group of adults, but it is difficult to do with large classes and in lessons lasting only 35 minutes.

It is obvious that teachers may have very different ideas regarding integrated skills in the classroom and there are no clear black and white answers to these statements. It could be argued that much will depend on the context. However, these 'think about' points may be useful in getting teachers to reflect on what they do or on what they would like to do in the future.

10.2 Situations requiring skills integration

Let us now examine some situations that require an integration of at least two language skills in order for the task to be completed successfully.

As you are reading, note down the different language skills involved at each stage.

From the skills integration point of view the situations may be quite limited – such as speaking on the telephone and taking down a message or taking part in a conversation – or, alternatively, they may be much longer and involve more skills integration, as we can see in the following examples:

1   We may read about a film or a concert in a newspaper or magazine:

We ask a friend if they would like to go
We phone the box office to reserve tickets
We drive to the cinema / concert hall with the friend
We ask the clerk for the tickets
We watch the film/concert
We discuss the film/performance with the friend on the way home

2   We may need to read lecture notes / articles / a paper in order to write a composition or an essay:

We discuss it with other learners / the teacher
We compose a draft
We rewrite it until we have a final version
We read the teacher's feedback
We speak to other learners / the teacher about the feedback

The two situations we have illustrated above show how, in our daily lives, we are constantly performing tasks that involve a natural integration of language skills. They also show that none of these stages is completely predictable. For example, in the first situation described above, all the seats may have been sold for that particular performance or our friend may reply that she cannot go to the film or the performance on that evening for whatever reason. However, at each stage there is a *reason* for using that particular skill.

Exposure to this type of 'natural' skills integration will hopefully show learners that the skills are rarely used in isolation outside the classroom and that they are not distinct as such, but that there is considerable overlap and similarity between some of the subskills involved (for example in previous chapters we saw how the subskills of reading and listening involved purpose and anticipation).

The notion of 'appropriacy' will, we hope, be developed in learners if they can see how the four skills can be used effectively in appropriate contexts. As we said earlier in the chapter, overall competence in the foreign language is going to involve more than performing in the four skills separately: it will also involve them in effective, combined use of the skills, which will depend on the nature of the interaction taking place. We might also argue that as integrated skills materials are more likely to involve learners in authentic and realistic tasks, their motivation level will increase as they perceive a clear rationale behind what they are being asked to do.

Let us consider one more example of the integration of skills in a real-life situation: we may see an advertisement for a product that interests us in a newspaper or in a magazine; then we may wish to talk to a friend about it to see if she thinks it would be a good buy. If after some discussion she thinks not, we might decide to leave it there, or we might decide to phone the company offering the product to get further details. Next we might write a letter (enclosing a cheque) that will be read by somebody at the company who will despatch the product, possibly with a covering letter.

We can break this down into the different language skills that it would generate: reading, speaking/listening, writing, reading, writing. Again, one important point to note is that none of the events in this particular scenario is entirely predictable, but will depend very much on individual circumstances as to how and when the outcome will be reached.

Another variation on this theme is provided by Harmer (2001b) who introduces a seven-stage activity for integrating skills, which involves the following sequence:

1 Learners read an advertisement for a public relations job with a major airline.
2 Learners write an application.
3 The teacher divides the class into small groups and distributes letters from the other learners.
4 Each member of the group reads each letter and scores each one from 0 to 5 depending on the quality of the letter.
5 The scores are added up and the winner chosen.
6 The group writes a letter to the winner and another letter to the unsuccessful applicants.
7 The letters are read out to the class and feedback and comments are obtained.

The overall aim and rationale of the activity is to provide solid integration of skills plus the notion that learners are writing for a purpose.

> If you teach integrated skills in your own situation, pause for a moment and think about how you do it. In what ways are your integrated skills activities similar to / different from the ones outlined above?

Byrne (1981), with respect to integrated skills, makes a useful distinction between skill integration viewed as synonomous with 'reinforcement' on the one hand, and skill integration where the four skills are introduced and established naturally, or as naturally as is possible within a classroom context, on the other hand. In the former, integration typically involves linking the language skills in such a way that what has been learned and practised is reinforced/ extended through further language activities. In some cases this would involve a focus on listening and speaking first, followed by reading and writing, as this would provide a convenient class-plus-homework pattern. However, this would not expose learners to contexts where the four skills are established naturally and could deny learners the opportunity to use the four skills with a measure of appropriacy. Let us look at how this might occur in an example from a typical EFL textbook where a writing activity is rather artificially 'grafted on' to the rest of the unit as an extension activity rather than being designed to fit in with the rest of the unit as a whole as illustrated below:

MAN: What do you do Miss Jones?
SALLY: I'm a secretary.
MAN: Oh, a secretary.
SALLY: That's correct.
MAN: Where?
SALLY: At Midtown Council.
MAN: I see.
SALLY: I'm looking for a small one-bedroom flat near my office.
MAN: Now let's see. Ah yes, here's one. It's in Billington Road, and it's a one-bedroom flat.
SALLY: Billington Road? Where is Billington Road exactly?
MAN: Here, look at the map. Billington Road is just here, next to the Town Hall.
SALLY: Oh, that's wonderful.
MAN: Yes. Well here's the address and the telephone number. 23, Billington Road, London, NW7. 234-8181
SALLY: Thank you very much. Goodbye.
MAN: Goodbye.
MAN: (phones) Hello, hello! 234-8181, Mrs Johns? A young woman called Sally Jones is coming to view the flat this afternoon. She's a secretary at Midtown Council. Thank you Mrs Johns. Goodbye.

And the extension:

Sally's mother, Mrs Jones, is in London. She wants to see Sally for lunch. Sally invites her for lunch. Sally writes her a message:

Mum, Please meet me outside the Shakespeare pub at 1pm. You can't miss it. It's next to the Odeon cinema.

Love, Sally.

If we contrast this example with those we examined earlier in the chapter it does not really focus the learner on examples of authentic skills integration.

Recently, however, some materials have been produced that aim to provide learners with a balanced approach to integrated materials graded from elementary through to advanced. The *Integrated Skills* series from Heinemann (Bell, 1990), for example, claims to offer 'a new approach to skills teaching, in which integrated skills activities bring together reading, writing, listening and speaking in a natural and realistic way, and provide a balanced method for students to practise and develop their language skills'. Ten units form the basis of each book, each unit containing three lessons linked to the main theme of the unit. Typical themes in these units are health, earning a living, the unconscious mind, education, protecting wildlife.

> 1 Look at the materials provided on pp. 179–82 from one of the textbooks in the series. The section giving information on the breakdown of the skills from the map of the book has been deleted.
> 2 From your reading of the materials, try to decide which skills are being practised at each point. What language is being practised at the same time? Do you feel that there is a natural progression of skills through the unit?

10.3   Integrated skills in the classroom

Nunan (1989) suggests how an effective language lesson can incorporate a range of different factors that ought to maximize language learning potential: he calls it 'the integrated language lesson'. Developing a unit of material to practise the integration of language skills in the context of a restaurant, he includes the following seven design principles:

1 *authenticity:* A tape containing authentic interaction between a waiter and a restaurant customer for learners to listen to.
2 *task continuity:* One activity builds on what went before; for example, listening leads on to reading and discussion.
3 *real-world focus:* The materials make an explicit link between the classroom and the 'real' world.
4 *language focus:* Learners are systematically exposed to the language system and are encouraged to identify patterns and regularities through discovery learning.
5 *learning focus:* The tasks develop the skills of self-monitoring and self-evaluation.
6 *language-practice:* The activities give the opportunity to learners to (e.g.) have controlled oral work practice.
7 *problem solving:* Learners work in pairs or in small groups to try to facilitate language acquisition.

As teachers we thus have a variety of ways of integrating the language skills in the classroom and in this section of the chapter we shall be examining some of the possibilities for different types of EFL classroom. We shall begin by looking at examples of general EFL materials; then we shall look at an example of skill integration from some EAP (English for Academic Purposes) Study Skills materials. Then we shall proceed to look at suggestions for developing listening and note-taking skills, giving oral presentations, project work, and role play and simulation.

UNIT 3   **JOB**

7 Which Job?

1 Look at the list of jobs below and choose the one that you would most like to do and the one that you would least like to do.

nurse
journalist
shop assistant
manager of a football team
policeman/woman
air steward/stewardess
cook
car mechanic
disc jockey
farmer

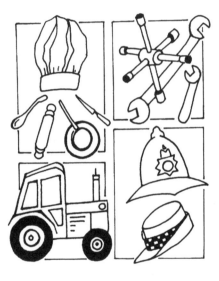

Compare your choices with another student and explain your reasons.

2 Which of the following qualities do you think are important in an air steward/stewardess?

good looks
intelligence
knowing several languages
good eyesight
physical fitness
a technical knowledge of aeroplanes
smart clothes
the ability to swim
patience
knowing how to look after babies
a knowledge of First Aid

3 Listen to Mark's conversation with the recruitment officer at Virgin Atlantic, an airline which carries passengers from London to America. What are the job requirements? Fill in the chart below.

Age

_____

Height

_____

Other requirements

_____

4 Read the article opposite in which an air stewardess talks about her work. Match the titles below with the right paragraph.

Training
The Route and my Job
Getting the Job
Working Hours
Introducing Debbie Mason
Social Life and Family Life
Health Problems

WORK MATTERS

There's more to being an air hostess than serving packaged meals to overweight businessmen.

* * *

Debbie Mason, 24, has risen through the ranks to become an in-flight purser (head stewardess) with Virgin Atlantic. She told Sue Wheeler about her life on Richard Branson's airline and what it takes to get on in this high-flying job.

* * *

Some time ago I was working in an office when I saw a picture of Richard Branson and read about him starting a new airline, Virgin. I sent him a letter saying I was interested in working for him. After a successful interview with a recruitment officer, I began their four-week training course. The personnel officers say it's usually obvious at the start whether somebody has the right qualities or not. Personality is very important. You have to be flexible, attractive, very well-groomed and able to smile when duty calls – even if you don't feel like it. Obviously you don't need airline experience, but nursing, or other work with people, is useful.

* * *

The training course is really common sense although the practical side includes things like life-boat sessions in a swimming pool, fire fighting in a smoke-filled room and learning how to deliver a baby. In reality, though, you end up dealing mainly with travel sickness. The point is you have to be prepared for everything.

I had to pass exams in safety equipment procedures and first-aid which are required by the Civil Aviation Authority (CAA), plus Virgin's own cabin services course.

* * *

I work on flights from Gatwick to New York or Miami. And I'm definitely not a glorified waitress! Only 10% of my work involves serving people. The emphasis is on safety and that's what we're here for. Before every flight there's a briefing where the crew are asked questions on first-aid and safety.

* * *

I think this job ages you. On flights to New York I'm on board from 2.15 in the afternoon until nearly midnight our time. I'm supposed to drink eight pints of water per flight to prevent my body

from dehydrating, but it's nearly impossible to get through that much. So my skin is probably suffering. But I think these are minor disadvantages. When we go to New York it's only 6.55 pm American time and we usually go out and have a party!

* * *

I fly about four or five times in a 28 day roster, which means I work hard for two or three days, then take time off. I get at least eight days off every month, so it doesn't feel like most other full-time jobs. I get four weeks holiday a year, three of which have to be in the winter. But as one of my perks is being able to fly with any airline for 10% of the normal cost, I can afford to go to far away places in search of winter sun.

* * *

It's a sociable job on board and off. There are only 220 crew members in total so we do know each other pretty well. This means things are very friendly and I think it's obvious to the passengers that we're having a good time, which helps them relax. When people leave Virgin to work for other airlines they often miss the intimacy of a small company and come back. But although the social life with Virgin is fabulous, outside it's non-existent. Friends and family know my time off is precious, but even at home I'm sometimes on standby. The job puts a strain on any romance. Happily my boyfriend works for Virgin too, and we chose to work a 'married roster' which means we fly together all the time. It's either this or take a chance you'll bump into each other once in a while.

5 Decide whether the following statements are true or false. If they are false, correct them.

a   She enjoys working for Virgin Atlantic.
b   Serving food takes up most of her time.
c   Virgin Atlantic recommends that she drinks a lot of water during flights.
d   She has less free time than people do in most other jobs.
e   She can get cheap flights on any airline.
f   She doesn't see her boyfriend very often.

HOMEWORK

Choose the job that you would most like to do. Write a paragraph describing the requirements for the job and what the job involves.

Map of the book

	TOPIC	SKILLS

UNIT 1 LIVING

LESSON

1 Around the World	Different lifestyles Hobbies and interests	Reading: Getting specific information from a magazine article Vocabulary: Finding synonyms in a text Speaking: Discussing hobbies and interests Writing: Writing a profile
2 Living at Home	Home life Relations with parents How to bring up children	Speaking: Answering a questionnaire Listening: Listening for gist Writing: Drawing up a set of rules for parents
3 Another Country	The problems of living abroad Impressions of Britain	Speaking: Discussing why people live abroad Reading: Reading a magazine article for gist Listening: Making notes from an interview Writing: Writing first impressions of a country

UNIT 2 THE POLICE AT WORK

4 Missing People	Reporting a missing person Physical descriptions	Writing: Predicting questions Vocabulary: Labelling a diagram Listening: Listening for specific information: physical descriptions Writing: Writing a physical description for a poster
5 Accident	Car accidents	Reading: Deducing meaning from context Speaking: Discussing accidents and how to reduce risks Writing: Writing a report of a road accident from notes
6 Burglary	Protecting your house Describing objects	Vocabulary: Objects found in the house Identifying objects from descriptions Listening: Listening for specific information: detailed descriptions of objects Writing: Writing a list of instructions

UNIT 3 JOB

7 Which Job?	Different jobs An air stewardess talks about her work	
8 Applying for a Job	Choosing holiday jobs Applying for a job	Reading: Reading intensively: job advertisements Listening: Listening for specific information: choosing a job Writing: Writing a letter of application
9 The Interview	Going for an interview	Speaking: Discussing interviews Reading: Making notes from an article Listening: Predicting questions. Making notes from interviews

	TOPIC	SKILLS
UNIT 4 HOLIDAYS		
LESSON		
10 Going Places	Holiday advertisements	Listening: Listening for gist and for specific information Speaking: Interviewing people about holidays Writing: Writing a holiday advertisement
11 Ballooning	Dangerous sports A ballooning holiday	Speaking: Discussing sports Reading: Reading for specific information Vocabulary: Labelling a diagram (parts of a balloon)
12 Complaining	Making complaints about a short holiday	Speaking: Discussing reasons for complaint Listening: Making notes from a phone conversation Writing: Completing a letter of complaint
UNIT 5 PEOPLE		
13 Choosing Partners	Marriage partners Personal activities and interests	Speaking: Discussing what makes a happy marriage Reading: Reading an advertisement for specific information Writing: Writing a description of an ideal partner
14 Judging People	Character	Vocabulary: Character adjectives Speaking: Expressing opinions about people Writing: Writing a character outline Listening: Listening to voices and matching them with photographs
15 Predicting Character	Analysing character Psychological tests	Listening: Listening for specific information Speaking: Discussing methods of character analysis Writing: Writing horoscopes
UNIT 6 SURVIVAL		
16 In the Antarctic	Survival in the Antarctic Going on expeditions	Vocabulary: Labelling a diagram Reading: Reading for specific information – intensive reading of extracts. Writing: Writing a leaflet advertising a trip
17 Ky Ho	The escape of a Vietnamese boat boy	Reading: Reading a newspaper article for specific information Deducing meaning from context Listening: Listening for specfic information Making notes from an interview Writing: Writing a newspaper article
18 Castaway	Survival on a desert island Favourite things	Vocabulary: Labelling a diagram (things on an island) Speaking: Discussing how to survive on an island Listening: Listening to a radio interview for specific information Writing: Writing a message
UNIT 7 HOUSE		
19 Renting a Room	Having lodgers House rules	Speaking: Discussing renting a room Establishing the house rules Listening: Making notes from a conversation Listening for details Writing: Writing instructions

Source: B. Milne, Map of the Book and Unit 3 from *Integrated Skills: Intermediate*. Oxford: Heinemann, 1991. © Heinemann, 1991.

READ, THINK AND DISCUSS

What do you think she is talking about?

This is part of an interview with a young woman. Can you guess what she is talking about?

It was always the same. Always. I was in a house, a strange house, and I knew somehow that I shouldn't have been there; that I shouldn't have gone in. But there was some strange force, pushing me. There were some stairs ... very steep stairs ... and I started climbing them, and ... and then quite suddenly I fell. Then, when I was at the bottom of the stairs, I suddenly realised that there was someone ... or something else there in the house with me, and that these eyes had been watching me all the time, and ... I knew then that something terrible ... something awful ... was going to happen to me ... that I was going to be punished ... because I'd done something I shouldn't have done. I didn't know what it was I'd done; only that it was wrong, very wrong. Then I could hear it ... this thing ... whatever it was in the house with me ... coming closer in the darkness, because everything was dark, you see ... and it came closer and closer. And there was nothing, absolutely nothing I could do to avoid it ... nothing. I was trapped! Trapped in that dark house at the bottom of the stairs. There was no way out!

FREE STYLE

What do you think?

Choose the answer you think is best. Then give your reasons for the choice. She must be talking about:

a some terrible thing that really happened to her.
b a dream she had more than once.
c something she only imagined but which never really happened.

LISTEN AND FIND OUT

Now listen to the full interview. Then answer these questions:

1 What was she talking about?
2 What was she really afraid of?
3 How did she find out what her real fear was?
4 Have you ever had the same kind of fear?

In what kind of situation would you be afraid? It doesn't have to be a situation you have really been in. For example, it could be like this: 'I think I would be very afraid if I was walking down a dark street late at night all alone and suddenly I heard footsteps behind me.'

Then see if you can describe it to someone else.

Source: R. O'Neill with P. Mugglestone, p. 64 from *The Third Dimension*. Harlow: Longman, 1989. © Longman, 1989.

General materials

In chapter 3 we looked at how *The Third Dimension* and *The Fourth Dimension* (O'Neill, 1989) cultivate the dimension of 'expressivity' in language, and how these materials are designed to allow learners to express what they want to say and to give some depth to expressing it. From the integrated skills point of view the 'read, think and discuss' sections of a unit as the one illustrated on

p. 183 build up the learner's sense of anticipation through a reading passage that moves on to a listening exercise and then moves on to discussing (speaking plus listening). One skill is dependent on another skill being practised before a full outcome can be achieved. The materials lead the learner, while reading the passage, to build up some anticipation that can only be satisfied by listening to an interview to find out the full picture. Hence, the skills are integrated across topics that the authors have attempted to 'personalize' for a wide range of learners.

EAP materials

Materials practising the integrated skills of listening and note-taking (writing) can be very useful in a number of academic and educational contexts, particularly for English for Academic Purposes students who will be going on to study their specialist subject through the medium of English. Materials such as *Panorama* (Williams, 1982), *Study Skills for Higher Education* (Floyd, 1984) and *Campus English* (Forman et al., 1990), *Study Speaking* (Lynch and Anderson, 1992), *Study Reading* (Glendinning and Holmstrom, 1992), *Learning to Study in English* (Heaton and Dunmore, 1992), *Study Tasks in English* (Waters and Waters, 1995) all include material under the broad umbrella of 'study skills', are based on target analysis of needs and are designed to try to replicate as far as possible the skill areas that learners will find most useful in educational/academic contexts. Some of these materials focus directly on the types of study skills learners will need. For example: using your time effectively, dictionary skills, library skills, reading skills, note-taking skills, writing skills, quoting skills and examination skills. Others attempt to integrate the four skills into topic areas that have a 'wide angle' appeal to EAP learners. Such topics might include the legal system, renewable energy, food for thought, our brave new world, health and the world of education.

> Look at the following instructions based on materials from a section of *Campus English*. Decide which language skills the instructions require and consider the extent to which the skills are integrated in this section. (From Unit 8: 'What's it all for?' section 1: 'The World of Education'.)

A   *Consider the following questions*:

Why are you continuing your education?
What benefits will your education bring you?
Try listing them in order of importance
How do you see yourself in ten years time?
What influence will your education have on this?
Discuss your ideas on these questions with other students. Can you pinpoint any common objectives?

B1 *Tomorrow Talking* A television team conducted a survey recently to find out the attitudes of pre-university students in Britain.

    a)   Read through the beginning of the report on this survey and note how it was organized in terms of target group selected and the way it was organized.

    b)   Read on through the report and make a note of the actual questions that were posed by the interviewers.

B2 To find out more about the attitudes of students in your learning environment towards today's society, it might now be interesting to conduct a similar survey.

    a)   Decide on the composition of the group you want to investigate.

    b)   Decide on the manner in which the survey is to be conducted.

    c)   Decide on the areas to be examined and the questions to be posed.

    d)   Decide on the way in which you will collate and interpret the data.

B3 Conduct the survey and present the results in an appropriate way.

B4 Write a brief report on the findings.

Listening and note-taking using audio/video materials

It is possible for teachers wishing to incorporate listening and note-taking skills into their classrooms to use audio/videotape material available on the market or, if recording equipment is available, to record a short sequence on a topic relevant to the needs of their own learners, thereby motivating them further. As Kennedy (1983) writes, this would then provide a realistic context in which the activity of note-taking could take place. It may be possible to work within the framework of existing materials by developing this principle to fit in with the ideas/topics covered in a particular textbook (we refer the reader to chapter 5).

> Think about how a lesson based on audio/video input might proceed.

One suggestion might be to ask learners what they know or think about the topic in the first instance, clearing up any ambiguities or terminology beforehand. Next, the teacher can play a short sequence (5–10 minutes) of the tape and ask them to take guided notes on a sheet provided, or ask them to note down the most important points that they hear/see. When they have finished, the learners can be asked to compare their work with that of other students. A natural follow-on activity from this would be discussion work where learners should be asked to discuss points they found interesting or, if the material is suitable, some aspects of the tape that may be more open to question (as happens in 'real' life). Then the students could be asked to reconstruct the overall 'message' of the tape from their own notes. A transcript of this section of the tape can be handed out afterwards for immediate feedback and self-correction. Natural integration of skills – primarily listening, note-taking (writing) and speaking, but also reading through notes to reconstruct the text – can thus be achieved.

Oral presentations

Preparing learners to give short oral presentations in class to the rest of the group is another useful way of achieving skills integration in the classroom. One way to begin this activity is to take cuttings from newspapers, magazines and topics presented (but not developed in this way) in existing teaching materials. In some cases reading material can be used as an initial stimulus and the activity can be graded to give lower proficiency learners an opportunity to work with less exacting materials. The learners can then take notes and try to pinpoint aspects of what they have read that will be worth discussing. They are then given time to prepare a short talk in front of the class and are encouraged to use maps, diagrams, charts and overhead projector slides if these can help to make the talk clearer to the group. During the presentation, the other learners are required to take notes so that they can ask questions and/or raise pertinent points during a plenary discussion after the talk has finished.

As teachers we can sometimes experiment with student assessment at this stage by asking the students to assess each other's work (peer assessment). It is possible to devise a fairly rudimentary evaluation sheet where small groups of students are asked to answer questions that might cover the following: what they thought of the presentation; was it well organized and were they able to follow the main points; could they summarize the talk for someone who was not present; did the speaker make effective use of visual support material; what advice would they give to the speaker for future presentations. This activity can thus interrelate the reading, writing, speaking and listening skills in a motivating way.

Project work

Projects with integrated 'themes' that entail integrated skills can provide a pertinent way of giving learners an effective forum in which to develop these skills. Let us consider an example that takes the overall theme of 'Civilization' as its starting point and examines how it may be seen from opposing points of view. Viewpoint A is concerned with becoming better acquainted with it; viewpoint B is concerned with escaping from it, as shown in figure 10.1 below.

One suggestion for reading materials for viewpoint A would be magazine articles or books and booklets on the 'Grand Tour', a popular phenomenon in the eighteenth century, when certain young men visited classical areas and cities in Europe. For viewpoint B, materials from magazines and newspapers on 'getting away from it all' and 'living on a desert island' could be provided. The

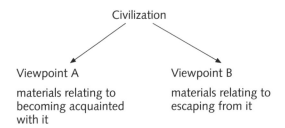

Figure 10.1 Different interpretations of civilization for materials selection.

reading component could be designed so that a 'jigsaw' pattern is established (see chapter 6), which would enable learners to piece together information from both parts to get a complete picture of the theme.

Possible listening activities might include interviews with a man on his reactions to the Grand Tour and a woman/group on living a communal experience on a desert island. Speaking could involve discussion prompts such as 'what problems do you think people would have on a Grand Tour / desert island?' (reference might be made to health, money and safety, for example); and 'is living on a desert island escaping responsibility?' The level of difficulty and amount of guidance offered could be varied according to the level of the learners.

For a more advanced group Gairns and Redman (1998) suggest producing a magazine of short stories as a class project with learners having to decide in pairs or small groups the topics to be included. They also comment that learners might wish to divide tasks into some to be carried out in class and others to be accomplished at home. The final outcome of the project might be a wall display or in booklet form or indeed a combination of both.

Think of some ways of integrating writing skills into the project work outlined above.

The scheme outlined above is relatively teacher-led. In some cases it may be possible to allow learners to work on projects by collecting data themselves and, where they have access to native speakers, to devise questionnaires and interviews they can then feed back into the group. Skills integration should develop naturally from the tasks that the learners are asked to complete.

Role play / simulation

Role play and simulation activities are often thought to be one of the most effective ways of integrating language skills in the language classroom. Though the terms 'role play' and 'simulation' have been interpreted in many different ways by both teachers and textbook writers, both activities offer a flexible yet principled way of tailoring integrated skills to learner needs.

What are the advantages to learners and to the teacher of using role play /
simulation activities in the classroom? Are there any potential problems to
using them?

It is generally the case that role-play activities involve the learner in 'role
assumption'; in other words, the learner takes on a different role (and perhaps
identity) from his or her normal one by 'playing the part' of a different person.
Role play is used more frequently in the general EFL classroom, that is, in the
teaching of English for General Purposes (EGP), where the ultimate goals for
learning the language are not necessarily specified in advance, if at all. It may be
desirable, however, to give learners more practice in language 'use', even though
it may be argued that the communication which ensues is not entirely natural,
as the learners may not really empathize with the character whose role they
have been asked to assume.

Simulation work, on the other hand, usually requires the learners to take part
in communication that involves personal experience and emotions. Because of
this, simulation is often seen as being central to English for Specific Purposes
(ESP) situations where the task/s to be worked upon can be related directly to
the learner's actual or intended occupation. As a consequence, the learners will
not only learn more about the communicative use of language in the L_2, but will
learn more about the setting/scenario relevant to their occupational field. For
example, as well as building up competence in the use of the foreign language,
a business person taking part in a meeting may well learn more about negotiation strategies in an international context.

Both types of activity clearly have their place in the classroom – be it for general
purposes or for learners with more specific goals in learning the language –
as they offer a flexible approach to integrating the skills, and involve learners
at all stages by stimulating their creativity and responding to their needs and
interests. According to Jacobs (1988: 99) these types of group activity encourage positive student attitudes towards the target language, their peers, and the
teacher, since 'the mutual dependence that co-operative structured activities
require would lead to more communication among students because they need
to exchange information and advice in order to succeed in achieving their goals'.
They can also release the teacher from the centre stage position for a lot of
the time, thereby allowing the possibility of more individual help if necessary.
If we manage the activity effectively we can possibly overcome problems of
introversion and lack of fluency in learners by designing tasks that all learners
can participate in. A model for structuring simulation (and role-play) activities in the classroom is offered by Herbert and Sturtridge (1979). Their
structure incorporates the flexibility mentioned above with respect to how tasks
can be graded, the role of the teacher during the activity, and to the type of
material to be used. They suggest a three-phase sequence for staging a role-play /
simulation in the classroom. In the first phase learners are given the informational input and/or the linguistic input necessary to carry out the simulation. In

the second phase the learners work on the activity by discussing the task or the problem set. In the third phase the teacher gives learners feedback on the activity just performed, possibly discussing errors and suggesting follow-up work if necessary.

In the first phase, for example, the informational input can either be in the form of a memorandum to read or perhaps it could be listening based. The linguistic input can be graded so that preliminary work can be done on the material in class before the role-play / simulation activity proper or, if the teacher thinks that the learners have had enough training, they can be presented with a 'deep-end strategy' in which they are given informational input but then move straight into the second phase, the language work being dealt with as an 'outcome' in the third and final phase.

As an illustration of this, let us consider a role play / simulation in which learners have to discuss some cost-cutting measures in their firm, company or school – a fairly typical situation. A task for the first phase of the simulation may involve the reading of a memorandum regarding an imminent meeting for the heads or representatives of different divisions/departments/sections in the company or school. The participants can be divided into small groups for each division or section (or run separate simulations), and are given a memorandum to read and think about, plus some notes that summarize the present situation in their own division.

However, all participants could be given different information about their respective divisions and a 'jigsaw' is thus established, which will be pieced together when this information becomes disclosed during the second (main) phase. For example, what might be an effective measure to implement in one section of the school or company could prove disastrous for another section. Ensuing interaction is therefore going to focus heavily on negotiating suitable outcomes for as many parties involved in the discussions as possible.

The information that the other learners have will be similar with respect to some of the measures above, and very different in other cases. Hence much of the meeting will focus on the negotiation and management of potential conflict. In the first phase it may be an idea to 'tease out' some of the language that the participants will need in the second phase. In this second phase the simulation itself takes place and the main focus is one of fluency. The teacher may wish also to take notes, operate audio/video equipment, or intervene in the simulation if so required. At the conclusion of the meeting, one of the managers can be asked to write a report to head office summarizing the decisions that were agreed upon in the meeting. This type of simulation is thus a highly effective way of integrating reading, listening, speaking and writing skills.

The third phase, that of 'feedback', has to be handled carefully so as not to become a negative account of what went wrong. For error analysis it might be possible to give a report on general types of mistakes made in the group, or where and how communication broke down, as well as giving individualized feedback to learners. The simulation should also provide many ideas to the teacher for future language work. Other types of role-play / simulation work might include setting up a committee to consider the applications of several candidates for a grant or scholarship, which only one of the candidates can obtain. In another type of activity, students could enact roles in an imaginary courtroom by trying to solve a particular crime.

> If your textbook does not provide any material for role-play / simulation work, would you be able to incorporate some of the above suggestions into your lessons? Refer back to chapter 5 if necessary.

10.4   Conclusion

This chapter has attempted to unify some of the issues raised in previous chapters by considering different permutations of integrating language skills in the classroom. First of all we attempted to define integrated skills, and the advantages to the learner of working with integrated skills materials. We saw that some tasks and materials only develop the skills in an 'additive' way and are somewhat removed from the ways in which we might use the skills in the 'real world'.

Finally we considered some class activities which offer different permutations of the skills: listening and note-taking using audio- and video-based materials; making oral presentations and role-play / simulation activities. This chapter concludes the second part of the book. In part III we shall examine different ways of organizing the resources and management of the classroom.

> In chapters 6–9 we looked at each language skill in turn. Review these chapters and see what implications there are for the integration of skills across the chapters.

10.5   Further reading

The following provide background discussion to integrated skills with some practical examples.

1   Byrne, D. (1981): 'Integrating Skills'. In Johnson and Morrow, *Communication in the Classroom*.
2   Sequence 1A of Supplementary material in Lubelska, D. and M. Matthews (1997): *Looking at Language Classrooms*, has some useful information about skills integration in different types of classroom.

Part III
Aspects of Classroom Methods

11

Groupwork and Pairwork

11.1 Introduction: structure and content

One of our key themes in the earlier part of this book has been the effect of 'communicative' approaches on the design of materials for English language teaching. Provided that the term is not taken to imply a single methodology, it is clear that the development of a broader view of the nature of language and language learning has permeated language teaching over the last three decades or so. From the perspective of methods used in the classroom, asking students to work in groups or pairs has come to be taken for granted as a natural, integral part of language learning behaviour and of communicative methodology. Most teachers are now familiar with these kinds of instructions in their coursebooks:

'Practise the dialogue with a partner'
'Ask your classmates . . .'
'Work in a group of four . . .'
'Give your story to someone else in the class to read'
'Do the quiz in pairs'
'What could happen next? Discuss in groups'
'Discuss your answers with other students'
'Choose a question, and ask as many other students as you can'

We shall see later that, although the relationship between materials and methods is in a sense an obvious one, it is not quite as clear-cut as it might seem, as indeed some of the examples just quoted here imply. We can consider not only the frequency with which a particular activity is used in the class-room, but also to what extent that activity grows out of the materials themselves.

Check through the coursebook you most frequently use. How often are learners expected to work in pairs or in small groups? What kind of language material is being practised during pairwork and groupwork activities? For example, is it a written dialogue? grammar? free speaking on a given topic?

It will be useful at this point to make a general distinction in language teaching between *content* and *structure*. By 'content' we here mean the materials themselves – the language items selected for practice, whether structural or functional; whether subject matter, situations and so on. 'Structure', on the other hand, is concerned with how classes are managed, and thus with decisions about various classroom options as to who works with whom and in what possible groupings. In Richards' words (1990: 10), 'Classroom management refers to the ways in which student behaviour, movement and interaction during a lesson are organized and controlled by the teacher to enable teaching to take place most effectively.' Wright (1987) makes a three-way distinction between 'language data' (for example topic), 'method' (for example practice) and 'classroom organization' (for example 'work in groups') but we have chosen to put the last two together for the purposes of this chapter. 'Structure', in other words, is procedural, and can be thought of as being content-independent.

This chapter is the first of a pair in which we look at a variety of organizational possibilities for the classroom and the first in a part of the book in which we look, very selectively, at aspects of classroom methods. Here we discuss, first, the functions of groupwork and pairwork. We then go on to consider the implications of various classroom structures for patterns of interaction between teachers and learners, and of learners with each other. The final section will examine possible advantages and disadvantages in different styles of classroom management. The first part of the chapter is mainly descriptive; the second part, evaluative.

11.2   The classroom setting: functions of groupwork and pairwork

The social organization of the classroom

Managing classes so that learners 'work in pairs' or 'divide into groups' is now so much part of the everyday professional practice of large numbers of English language teachers that the instructions leading to these activities sometimes seem to be 'switched on' automatically, occasionally with a frequency difficult to justify. It happens with all kinds of content – dialogue practice, sharing opinions, reading aloud, comparing answers to questions, doing grammar drills, formulating questions in an information-gap task – the list could be extended considerably.

While all these can undoubtedly be practised in a number of different ways, at least two kinds of objections can be made. The first is the possibility that imposed classroom structures may not always be congenial to the learning styles of individuals in the class: we shall come back to this point in the chapter on individualization that follows this one, and again when considering how teachers, by observing what goes on in their classrooms, can become more sensitive to their students' preferred ways of working. The second objection is that a mechanical organization may pay insufficient attention to the relationship between an activity and its purpose. For example, it may be unhelpful to practise reading aloud in groups or pairs if students are unable to check each other's accuracy. If, however, the aim is to encourage learners to discuss a topic more freely, then a paired format may be the most useful one. As Morrow (1981: 59) writes, 'A consistent methodology is more than just a collection of activities or techniques. It requires an underlying set of principles in the light of which specific procedures . . . can be evaluated, related and applied.' Brumfit (1984) is similarly critical of a methodology that sees groupwork as a mere management device, preferring it to be a means of developing real communicative competence. (We shall comment on a possible modification of this view below.)

A more coherent picture of management structure is provided by the notion of the classroom as an aspect of 'social organization'. Seen from this perspective, any procedural decision by a teacher – asking students to work in pairs, or to divide themselves into groups, or nominating group membership directly – leads to a specific set of interaction patterns and to control of those interactions. The classroom, as we saw in chapter 1, does not operate in a vacuum, and this patterning is closely related to the role relationships of teachers and learners, and of learners with each other; and thus by extension to the nature of the school and to the whole educational, even socio-cultural, context. We shall need to bear this wider setting in mind when discussing the pros and cons of pair and groupwork. We have already noted similar considerations in relation to some of the cultural implications of communicative language teaching more generally, and its appropriacy (or not) both in principle and practice. Wright (1987) explores the social organization of the classroom in detail, focusing particularly on organizational patterns, social relationships and role differentiation in relation to pedagogic purposes and outcomes.

Functions of groupwork and pairwork

As we have just noted, Brumfit is typical of many writers on language teaching methodology who see a necessary connection between the organizational structures available to teachers and a 'communicative' methodology. In many ways it is logical to assume a natural link between the learning of functional aspects of language use and a classroom-based behaviour that requires class members to exchange and share information and ideas. Such a link, for instance, may mean that students learn how to give and follow instructions in a paired format; while to respond appropriately in a typical range of practical social situations, or at a more advanced level, may involve the exchange of opinions within a small group. The methodological implications are pointed up even more sharply by task-based learning (TBL), a great deal of which is predicated on the use of pairwork and groupwork.

We can, therefore, take communicative purposes to be a valid and important aim of groupwork or pairwork. However, it would be limiting to think of this as the sole function of such 'alternative' methodological patterning. We need to remind ourselves that the language classroom does not only exist as a reflection of the 'real world' or, to be more precise, the world outside the school: it has its own rationale and frame of reference. As such, Morrow's criterion of a 'consistent methodology' can comfortably encompass the use of various patterns of interaction, firstly, for language practice and problem-solving activities within a modified communicative framework. Issuing invitations to one's classmates, reaching a conclusion in discussion using roles assigned by the teacher, or working with a partner to book a hotel room (as in Watcyn-Jones's *Pairwork*, 1981, for example) obviously require as much a linguistic as a social outcome. Again, as we have seen, it is TBL that makes the most explicit link between communicative interaction and outcomes on the one hand, and accuracy within language development on the other (J. Willis, 1996). Secondly, such procedures can also allow for work on language content that is not functionally based at all: in a large class, practising drills will give individual learners more chance to speak than they might otherwise have. Wright gives the example of a blank-filling task that can become interactively interesting 'if groups of learners are instructed to identify correct answers and to speculate on the reasons for the incorrectness of the other alternatives in a multiple choice exercise' (1987: 143–4).

This takes us directly to the final point to be made here. The classroom is clearly a place where people have to work together, essentially requiring a compromise between their own individuality and the dynamics of the whole group. In other words, it is ideally a co-operative environment where structuring activities in different ways (quite apart from the primary language learning function) can allow for the establishment of a cohesive and collaborative working atmosphere. Wright (1987) captures this distinction by referring to both the 'instructional' and the 'enabling' functions of classroom organization.

Pairwork and groupwork

Pairwork and groupwork are not synonymous terms: just as they obviously reflect different social patterns, so the ways in which they are adapted and applied in the classroom also have distinctive as well as similar functions. Pairwork requires rather little organization on the part of the teacher and, at least in principle, can be activated in most classrooms by simply having learners work with the person sitting next to them (although other kinds of pairing – for example, according to proficiency – may be more suitable depending on the task). The time taken for pairwork to be carried out need not be extensive, and there is a very large range of possible tasks throughout the whole spectrum of functions we have identified, from fully communicative, 'simulated', structure and vocabulary practice, to those where an important aim is to set up co-operative working habits. Chapter 8 of this book ('Speaking Skills') has a number of examples, as does Harmer (2001b, ch. 8), Littlewood (1981, chs 4 and 5, and 1992).

A group, on the other hand, even though it can have a comparable range of functions, is by its very nature a more complex structure, which will probably require greater role differentiation between individuals as well as a certain amount of physical reorganization of the classroom. This role differentiation may refer to 'assumed' roles, particularly in a 'communicative' setting (having learners enact a courtroom scene with a variety of 'characters', for example, or 'pretend' to be a town council trying to negotiate a decision about building priorities), or to the structure of the group itself, with members being assigned tasks of chair-person, reporter/note-taker and so on. The timescale often needs to be more extended, to allow for the greater number of interacting participants. Ur (1996: 232–3) makes the point comprehensively: 'The success of groupwork depends to some extent on the surrounding social climate, and on how habituated the class is to using it; and also . . . on the selection of an interesting and stimulating task whose performance is well within the ability of the group. But it also depends on effective and careful organisation.'

Finally, groups and pairs are not mutually exclusive, and there are a number of variations that bridge these two basic structural activities. For instance: individuals out of a pair can re-form to make a different pair; or pairs can 'snow-ball' by joining other pairs until eventually the whole class may have re-formed.

At this point in the chapter, it will be useful to consider briefly these two issues, one of which summarizes the discussion so far, the other of which looks ahead:

1   Looking at your comments on the first task in this chapter, to what extent does the use of pair and groupwork in your own materials reflect the different functions we have discussed? Try to distinguish particularly between 'co-operative' purposes and different kinds of language practice, as well as between pairs and groups.
2   How much flexibility do you have in your own teaching in the 'management' of your classroom?

11.3   *Interaction and classroom structure*

Arranging the class

Readers may well recognize one or more of the following possibilities for the physical arrangement of their classroom, as shown in figure 11.1 (where

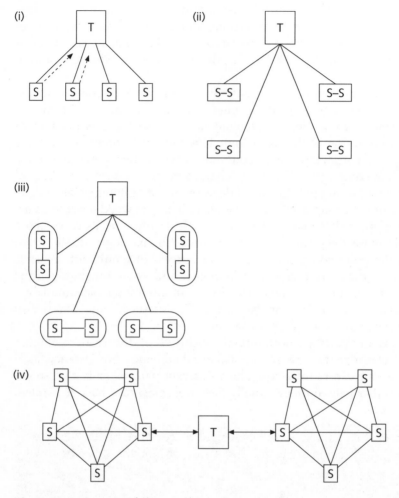

Figure 11.1 Patterns of classroom organization.

T = teacher, S = student, and the lines = main directions of interaction). Not all possibilities can be covered here, but we have tried to show a representative sample. Wright (1987: 58) sets out patterns in a comparable way, but also includes the relationship of individuals, pairs, groups and the whole class to the product, or learning outcome. He also sets out the layout in more detail. These arrangements are not necessarily static, and in a flexible classroom may change during the course of one lesson, both physically as well as in terms of roles and interaction. There may, of course, be straightforward physical restrictions on the possibilities, such as room size or the nature of the classroom furniture (tables, benches, worktop space, mobility). Space considerations not only act as obstacles to the establishment of a more communicative and co-operative classroom: a room that is too small for the number of students may actually force participative working patterns even where they are not appropriate.

Interaction patterns in the classroom

Just as a great deal has been written about different organizational structures in everyday classroom practice, so there is a large and rapidly growing research literature concerning the effects of various types of patterning both on aspects of classroom behaviour and on learning outcomes. The research comes particularly from studies in the psychology of second language acquisition, and from work in social psychology and the sociology of small-group behaviour. Here we can only set out very selectively a few of the topics of potential interest to teachers, just to give a flavour of the debate. The bibliography gives several references that go into these topics in more depth, and teachers may wish to evaluate the relevance of these studies to their own classrooms (and ways in which the nature and requirements of research converge and diverge from those of teaching and learning).

The 'lockstep' class   The area that has received by far the most attention to date is that of the quantity and quality of verbal interaction in the plenary class as opposed to the smaller group setting. The former is represented in simple terms by figure 11.1. (i) The principal researchers have been Long and his colleagues (for example 1975, 1985; Pica and Doughty, 1985), whose basic premise is that *pedagogical* reasons for group work can be supported by *psycholinguistic* research.

These researchers make a basic distinction between, on the one hand, a 'lockstep' organization of classroom interaction, where activities are 'teacher-fronted', and, on the other, a small-group format. Lockstep is explained in terms of a simple sequence of teacher stimulus → student response → teacher evaluation of student response (a traditional pattern of teacher question → student answer → teacher comment). This is, in other words, a situation where the whole class is moving along together, where all the students are 'locked' into the same activity at the same time and at the same pace and where the teacher is the primary, even the only, initiator. Nunan (1999: 70) uses the terms 'high-structure' and 'low-structure' tasks to distinguish between the teacher and learner respectively as the locus of control. Long (1975: 216) comments more critically, 'The teacher who attempts to conduct a large, heterogeneous group of . . . 30 secondary age EFL students through a language programme as one unit is obliging all students to cover the same ground at the same time, at the same pace, via the same approach, method and technique, and using the same material.' In such a context, he argues, 29 out of 30 people will be 'unemployed' at any one time, at least as far as observable learning behaviour is concerned.

It follows from this that breaking the class down into smaller size units (groups, pairs) should in principle lead to a greater amount of language being spoken by each individual, and to a wider variety of language functions being used as a result of increasing role differentiation. Long quotes research by Barnes on 'exploratory' language in the small-group setting, though whether L_1 use can be assumed to have direct relevance for the learning of a foreign language is debatable. Finally, Malamah-Thomas (1987: 7) isolates 'action' and 'reaction' as characteristics of traditional lockstep arrangements, and stresses the need for 'interaction', 'a constant pattern of mutual influence and adjustment', whether between learners, or teacher and learners. We shall comment in a little more detail on the implications for teaching of this kind of research in the next section. Before leaving this point, however, we must be careful not to assume that a whole-class, teacher-fronted methodology is necessarily undesirable. Harmer (2001b: 114–15) offers a common-sense antidote to some of the more negative comments by enumerating a number of positive advantages of the lockstep class, including its practical usefulness when teachers need to give instructions and explanations, but also its affective role in reinforcing a sense of 'belonging' and, for many educational settings, in creating the security of the familiar.

Group structure   Discussion of the nature of classroom organization also draws on very extensive research into the 'social' structure of groups of participants working on specific tasks. It is interesting to speculate what might happen if we simply tell the whole class to divide into small groups in any way they choose: will they do so randomly, or with friends, or with people of similar proficiency? Furthermore, if we imagine giving a free discussion topic to a subgroup consisting of, say, six or seven of our students, and we then leave them to talk with only a small amount of monitoring, it is probable that some will talk more than others, one or two will want to dominate and control, others will react by withdrawing into silence and so on.

   These kinds of 'natural' grouping, and relatively spontaneous speech and behaviour patterns within an unmonitored group, are clearly quite different from the other end of the spectrum of control, where the teacher specifies both the group and the nature of the task in detail (a dialogue rehearsal, for example). The majority of classes fall somewhere between the naturally occurring and the completely structured. Harmer (2001b: 120–2) lists the principles of friendship, streaming (by ability) and chance, as ways of dividing a class into groups. Jacobs describes how he investigated co-operative behaviour in small groups in his writing classes, and relates it to research in social psychology on 'goal structure'. He found it necessary to *construct* groupings to achieve a co-operative rather than a competitive or an individualistic goal structure, on the argument that 'when I put students into groups, I hoped they would just naturally co-operate with each other. But my experience . . . showed that *groups* did not necessarily equal *co-operation*' (1988: 97). Wright (1987) cites more detailed research on how natural groupings evolve, and identifies four stages:

Forming
Storming (conflict behaviour in the group)
Norming (group cohesion starts to develop)
Performing (the group solves a task)

Finally, some recent empirical research by Storch (2001) examined the question of how collaborative pairwork really is. Looking at three pairs of ESL tertiary students working on composing tasks, she was able to show both that patterns of collaboration vary, and that task performance is thereby affected in certain ways. She places these different behaviours on a collaborative/ non-collaborative spectrum.

Learning styles

It is often argued that, in lockstep classes, learners are unrealistically assumed to learn what teachers choose to teach them, leaving no room for the kinds of individual differences that we touched on in chapter 3. We can, however, make a general distinction between overt behaviour – what learners appear to be doing, whether in groups or in the whole class – and covert learning processes that are not so easy to observe directly. Clearly as teachers we would wish to bring these two aspects in line as closely as possible: research on learning styles is a developing area that is beginning to contribute to our understanding, and one to which teachers, with their rich knowledge of classrooms and learners, have much to contribute.

One basic distinction in learning style research is between 'cognitive' factors (to do with the way people think) and 'affective' factors (to do with emotions and what we feel). There is some attempt to relate these to different types of teaching. Although there is an assumption that all learners will do better if they are in a setting where learning by discovery is encouraged, it is not clear that such preferences are universal. There is now quite a long research tradition on the strategies apparently used by 'Good Language Learners' (Naiman et al., 1975), and on the various cognitive and personality types that affect learning (Skehan, 1989). A number of writers are now trying to relate methods, not just to ideas about the nature of communication, but also to what is known about these kinds of psychological variables. Willing (1988), for example, directly relates cognitive style to methodology by looking at research into 'field-dependent' and 'field-independent' learners, claiming that the former will be more likely to prefer team problem-solving situations in groups, whereas the latter tend to favour situations that call for more individual work. This is only speculation, but it does point to the direction in which research on learning is moving. There are still many questions that have to be answered: it is not clear whether styles are teachable, nor how preferences might affect the practical organization of a class.

So far, we have looked at groupwork and pairwork in the classroom from a number of angles as a procedural, organizational concept, and at some of the related research background. It is now time to turn to an examination of the potential advantages and disadvantages of such procedures.

11.4   *Groupwork and pairwork: benefits or drawbacks?*

Before you start to read this section (and looking back at some of your
comments earlier in this chapter), consider the feasibility and appropriacy of
groupwork and pairwork as 'organizational frameworks' for your own classroom. What are the possibilities and limitations? And to what extent do you
need to take into account external views and guidelines, rather than organize
your class according to your own preferences?

We must be clear that any discussion of the advantages and disadvantages of
particular methods is relative. There can be no absolute pros and cons, and we
say again that what is appropriate in Mexico may not be appropriate in Japan.
This is why the headings in this section are all printed with a question mark
against them, to indicate the difficulties of making generalizations. We have
stressed many times that any individual teacher with a single class has to be seen
in the wider context of the school and its educational and social environment.
In many parts of the world, and in the perceptions of many people, the status of
'teacher' commands great respect, and it would not be regarded as appropriate
behaviour for the teacher to take a strongly interactive role. In other words,
there are many different notions of 'authority' and 'social position', and the
expectations of behaviour that go with them. Wright (1987) comments that
such expectations directly affect our awareness of 'social distance', and points
out that, on the whole, the greater the assigned status, the greater the sense of
social distance and therefore the likelihood of a very formal working framework. The implications of this for whole class versus small group work in the
language classroom are clear.

Again, it is often the case that 'knowledge' is regarded as content to be
transmitted, so that language becomes a curriculum subject similar to history,
or physics. In such a context it is unlikely that exploratory, problem-solving
activities will fit naturally into educational philosophy and practice. The picture
can become very complex when teachers and learners with different backgrounds
and preconceptions meet in the same classroom. Consider, for example, the
mutual difficulties of a teacher trained in the 'communicative' tradition with an
instinctive preference for small group work, and a learner who believes that a
teacher's role is to be an explicit instructor. Neither side is right or wrong, but
a process of adjustment will certainly be necessary.

At the same time, we have also noted that 'the wider context' will include not
only local conditions but also the English language teaching profession as a
whole. From this perspective, research and practice are not static, and what is
appropriate at a particular point may well be superseded a few years later.
Wright (1987) reminds us that such concepts as 'power' and 'distance' can in
certain circumstances vary even during the course of a single lesson. To deny
the possibility of change, then, is to assume that all development is irrelevant.

Neither position – the universal application of certain methods on the one hand, or a lack of openness to new ideas on the other – is realistic.

A final consideration in setting out the framework for discussing the pros and cons of groupwork and pairwork is the question of whose perspective is taken into account. Any teacher will have a view; but so will learners, parents, colleagues, head teachers and education authority personnel, and these views will not always necessarily be in harmony.

We now enumerate, first, some of the more frequently heard points in favour of groupwork and pairwork, and then some of the points against. There is insufficient space here to present argument and counter-argument for each of these points, and readers are invited to consider each argument critically and from their own perspective.

Advantages?

Our earlier discussion of the research base put forward a number of reasons why getting learners to work in subgroups in a plenary class is often to be preferred to 'lockstep' (while also acknowledging that certain kinds of practice may best be handled with the whole class paying attention at the same time):

1   In a lockstep framework, there is little flexibility. Students are frequently 'observers' of others, and work to an externally imposed pace. In small-group and pairwork, on the other hand, the possibility of an individual's learning preferences being engaged is correspondingly increased. (We shall see in the next chapter how the individualization of instruction can take learners even further along this path.)

2   Groupwork in particular is potentially dynamic, in that there are a number of different people to react to, to share ideas with and so on: exchange of information is sometimes more 'natural' in smaller-scale interaction. The extent to which this is so, however, clearly depends closely on the nature of the task set.

3   Different tasks can be assigned to different groups or pairs. This may lead to a cohesive whole-class environment if these tasks can be fitted together, perhaps in a final discussion. Alternatively, a teacher working with a mixed proficiency group may have the flexibility to allocate activities according to learners' levels.

4   Each student has proportionally more chance to speak and therefore to be involved in language use. Furthermore, the more varied the types of activity, the greater the variety in types of language used. This takes us back to Long's earlier point concerning improvement in both quantity and quality.

5   Groupwork can promote a positive atmosphere or 'affective climate' (Long and Porter, 1985), as distinct from the more public and potentially threatening 'performance' environment of the lockstep classroom. Motivation, too, is often improved if learners feel less inhibited and more able to explore

possibilities for self-expression. Arguably, too, co-operation in the classroom is encouraged. These are undoubtedly positive factors, but the individual classroom still needs to be 'in tune' with its educational environment.

6　There is some evidence that learners themselves favour working in smaller groupings. Student opinions recorded on the *Teaching and Learning in Focus* series of videos (Thematic module: *Learners*) claim to like group work, because it provides 'variety'; interestingly, less enthusiasm is shown for pairwork in some cases, one student saying that she does not feel she can 'take enough' from just one other person. Willing's (1988) research in Australia on learning styles amongst adult migrants to the country bears out these comments: from a long list of learning styles, groupwork was rated as best in 35 per cent of questionnaire responses as against only 15 per cent for pairwork. Nunan (1988), commenting on Willing's work, gives teachers food for thought by showing how much *teachers'* ratings of the usefulness of activities differ from *learners'* preferences. For instance, although 'conversation practice' is rated as 'very high' on both sides, pairwork comes out as 'very high' for teachers but low for learners. (Spratt (1999) and J. McDonough (2002) have comparable data.) It has to be stressed here that published research data are somewhat patchy, and different contexts might produce differential results. In chapter 13 we shall be looking at some of the small-scale investigations that teachers can carry out in their own classrooms, and the theme of 'learner preferences' provides us with a good example.

Disadvantages?

Many readers will recognize these kinds of stated objections to groupwork and/or pairwork, and as usual such objections must be evaluated critically and according to context. Some are practical and straightforward classroom management problems, whereas others are deeper in the sense that they impinge on attitudes to teaching and learning and the whole cultural setting of the classroom.

1　There is some concern that other students will probably not provide such a good 'language model' as the teacher, though this problem, of course, has to be balanced against the richer interactive possibilities that a non-lockstep environment can provide. Certainly feedback from the teacher requires a more complex arrangement when multiple groupings are involved, as does the necessary 'control' to ensure that quieter students are not dominated by more talkative individuals.

2　There are several possible institutional objections to rearranging the classroom and to an increased communicative environment. Furniture, for example, may be impossible to move around or may encourage static interaction patterns (such as students sitting in rows on long benches fixed to the floor). Sometimes, too, school authorities or other colleagues may react negatively to what they perceive to be the increased noise levels that come from an active class.

3   Some monolingual classes readily use their mother tongue instead of the target language, particularly where discussion is animated and even more so when the teacher shares the same L_1. It is not surprising that interacting in English in these circumstances may initially be perceived as artificial.

4   Learners – as Willing's research shows – often have strong preferences, and it is not unusual to find a stated wish for teacher control and direct input of language material. It is even an expectation in many cases, and there is a point at which a teacher's doubts about its pedagogical effectiveness need to be matched by learners' perceptions of the 'best way' to learn.

5   If the class is divided into smaller units, there may be problems of 'group dynamics' where, for example, students may not wish to work with those of their peers assigned by the teacher to the same group. This may be compounded by feelings of being 'better than' or conversely 'worse than' others.

6   By far the most commonly heard objection to 'alternative' classroom arrangements, and in some ways underlying all the others listed here, is that of class size. It is all very well, the argument runs, to conduct groupwork and pairwork if you have only a small, multilingual class of co-operative adults working in a comfortable, modern environment, but 'try doing it with a class of forty!' This is the title of an article by Nolasco and Arthur (1986), in which they try to meet the 'large class' objection head on. Using their experience of teacher training in Morocco, they first of all list nine reasons for teacher resistance to what were perceived as 'new' ideas and techniques. These reasons, some of which we have already met, were as follows:

Students not interested in unfamiliar materials and methods
Discipline problems
Physical constraints
Problems of duplicating material
Students prefer grammar and exam practice
School administration objects to noise
Students talk in L_1 in pairs
Students complain they are 'not being taught'
Enthusiasm causes problems of class control

The authors are sympathetic and sensitive to these objections, and go on to sketch out a phased plan whereby teachers and learners can gradually be introduced to the advantages of groupwork and pairwork. The plan starts from the basis of familiar materials and working patterns, and slowly increases learner responsibility, initiation and control. A more detailed discussion by the same authors of the direct relationship between the large class and communicative methodology is listed in the 'Further reading' section of this chapter: the perceived problems are wider than just the methodology of groupwork and pairwork.

11.5   Conclusion

In this chapter we have tried to show that dividing a class into small groups, asking learners to work in pairs or, by implication, any kind of 'structuring' decision by the teacher, are not merely a set of alternatives that can be mechanically applied. However sound their justification in principle, all such arrangements have to be assessed in terms of the teaching situation in its widest sense – the existing syllabus and materials, expected roles of teachers and learners, the practicalities of physical space, the institution, and the whole educational system. At the same time we argue again that no teaching environment can be regarded as fixed for all time. New syllabuses are introduced, often in line with shifting perceptions of national and international needs; attitudes of teachers and learners to materials, methods and to each other change; the expectations of individuals develop, both for themselves and alongside wider social changes. As we shall see in the remaining chapters, all these considerations have direct implications for the training and development of both teachers and learners.

1   Draw up a table for your own classroom of the things you like about groupwork and pairwork, and the things you don't like. You will probably be able to think of more points than we have included in our discussion here.
2   If possible, compare your ideas with those of a colleague – it would be particularly interesting if you could work with someone from a different background to your own.
3   What factors do you think influence your opinions? It may be the materials you use, your learners' attitudes, school policy, your view of your own role, and so on.

11.6   Further reading

1   Nolasco, R. and L. Arthur (1988): *Large Classes*. As indicated in the chapter, this discusses many practical issues to do with large classes, referring particularly to communicative methodology.
2   Wright, T. (1987): *Roles of Teachers and Learners*. Explores the different possibilities for teacher and learner roles in the classroom, relating them to the wider context. This can usefully be read alongside Malamah-Thomas, *Classroom Interaction* (1987).
3   Haines, S. (1995): For and against, has a practical discussion of the pros and cons of pairwork.
4   Harmer, J. (2001b: ch. 8): *The Practice of English Language Teaching*, discusses many practical aspects of groups and pairs within some overall principles.

12
Individualization, Self-access and Learner Training

12.1 Introduction

In the last chapter we considered some of the different possibilities of structuring the classroom with groups and pairs of learners in mind. In this chapter we shall be looking at the concept of individualization in language learning and the extent to which this can be implemented both inside and outside the classroom. We shall begin by thinking about why we may wish to individualize the classroom. Then we shall examine some possible definitions of individualization, self-directed learning and self-access and try to relate them to actual learning situations. We shall then consider how recent developments in educational technology have provided further possibilities for individualizing language learning. Finally, we consider the emerging area of learner training in relation to individualizing the classroom.

Growth in the phenomenon of individualization began about 30 years ago and was nourished by the Threshold proposals of the Council of Europe (Richterich and Chancerel, 1980) and the notion of 'Permanent Education', or Education for Life, with respect to which pioneering work was undertaken at CRAPEL (Centre de recherches et d'applications pedagogiques en langues), a language teaching and research centre at the University of Nancy, France. Individualization in language learning is also symptomatic of the development of interest shown in the learner and the learners' needs, particularly, but not exclusively, in the realm of Languages for Specific Purposes, which has grown apace over the last three decades. Skehan shows how these developments represent a significant move away from the behaviourist, psychological approaches to language learning in the 1960s to a renewed interest in cognitive approaches to learning that emphasize 'the active, hypothesis forming nature of the learning process' (1980: 28). The phenomenon has grown to such an extent that entire conferences are now devoted to it. (See, for example, Brookes and Grundy (eds), ELT Documents 131, *Individualization and Autonomy in Language Learning* (1988), and C. Cecioni (ed.), *Autonomy in Language Learning* (1989).)

Why individualize the classroom? Before reading further, think of some reasons why classroom teachers may wish to individualize language learning.

First of all, it is clear that language learning normally takes place in groups and, as Bowers suggests, 'a major question therefore becomes that of ensuring that the place of the individual in planning and participating in the learning process is not suppressed by the built-in constraints of the group context' (1980: 72). Every class is composed of individuals, each of whom will have different capabilities and work rates; and among these heterogeneous groups it can obviously be a problem for the teacher to allow for the variety of pacing necessary if all students are to learn effectively. We sometimes speak of 'teaching up' to some students or, conversely, 'teaching down' to others. It is quite common to hear other teachers speaking about 'teaching to the middle range of the group' hoping that this will best satisfy students' needs. In this context individualization can help to break the lockstep of the classroom (the teacher mistakenly assumes that all learners have assimilated the same amount of material by the end of a class.) Individualization is not just limited to language learning either. 'Open learning' centres are sometimes used in industry as part of an in-service or professional development programme for workers, which may be tailored to their own individual needs and to the pace at which they prefer to learn.

Many practitioners believe that all learners can make satisfactory progress in learning a foreign language if given sufficient time plus the possibility of developing their preferred learning styles and habits. It is clear that some learners work better in groups, whereas others prefer to work alone. Some learners have a preference for a particular time of the day, and for many the place of study can be very important, be it in class, in the language laboratory or at home. In some learning contexts it can be difficult for learners to attend classes regularly, perhaps because of other commitments, and in these situations an individualized programme may prove to be an effective mode of learning. As Dickinson suggests (1989: 35) even though these practical reasons are important, individualization is also important for educational reasons:

> firstly, at its broadest, to help people to develop into independent individuals, able to think for themselves, and secondly, more narrowly, to prepare people to learn. That is, helping people learn how to learn. Thus, at the end of a successful educational process, the student should be capable of designing and managing his or her own learning projects.

In sum, individualization as a concept in language teaching and learning aims at providing as many permutations as possible to the learner in order to break the traditional lockstep of the classroom.

How do you cater for individual learner needs in your classroom at present?

12.2 Individualization: possible definitions

To some practitioners, individualization is a term used to cover all topics that focus on the learner as an individual. Geddes and Sturtridge (1982) start from this viewpoint. Brookes and Grundy (1988) also see it as a widely applicable concept, which has learners at its centre irrespective of whether they work with or without the help of a teacher. Chaix and O'Neil (1978) comment on how individualization involves the adaptation of criteria such as goals for learning, content, methodology and pacing to a particular individual, although whether this is determined from the perspective of the teacher or of the learner would need to be ascertained.

Brumfit and Roberts (1983: 193) argue that individualization involves 'the organization of learning and teaching in such a way as to allow the abilities, interests and needs of the individual learner to be enhanced as effectively as possible; with the consequence that the traditional notion of the "average student" and "aiming for the middle" in teaching is abandoned'.

The mention of the *organization* of teaching and learning above leads us to consider the notions of autonomy and self-directed learning in relation to individualization. Autonomy and self-directed learning entail individualization but, as Trim (1976: 1) has shown, 'it is possible to pursue individualization within a highly authoritarian framework. The teacher looks at the individual's problems, but decides herself how different types of individual should be treated.' If we consider the implications of Trim's statement, then an individualized programme in this sense would be the very antithesis of self-direction and autonomy. There is consequently an issue between freedom and control, between autonomous, self-directed learning and externally (teacher) directed learning. It may therefore be useful to see the totally externally directed mode and the totally self-directed mode as two polarities in individualizing language teaching, with the majority of programmes occurring somewhere between the two extremes (see figure 12.1). It is probably fair to state, therefore, that total autonomy is only pertinent if it results in an efficient and satisfying mode of learning for that particular individual.

Individualization is also a partial response to the belief that direct teaching in the classroom does not always result in learning taking place. Teaching can take place without learning, whereas learning can often occur without any formal teaching. As Riley (1982) points out, learning cannot be done *to* or *for* learners;

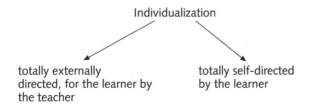

Figure 12.1 An overview of individualization.

it can only be done by them, and this is one of the basic principles in the definitions of individualization: that learners will assume some responsibility for their own learning at some stage in the process.

Individualization does not necessarily mean that the students will be working on their own either. In some cases individualization can take place in small groups or pairs where students work on a similar task. At other times the learner may work with a teacher or in a solitary mode.

It is useful to see individualization not as a method *per se*, but as a possibility of reorganizing the resources and management of the classroom environment, which has many implications for the teacher. Sheerin (1989: 3) quotes Strevens, who suggests that 'it takes better teachers to focus on the learner', and individualization may involve some teachers in hitherto unknown roles such as 'guide', 'helper', 'facilitator'. How we get learners to work in an individualized mode may depend on how much structure we wish to give them. All language learners need to have some purpose to be successful in their learning, and to help in the achievement of this Dickinson (1989) suggests analysing the language needs of the learners and then establishing a 'contract' with each of them. Points in each contract may include agreement between teacher and learner on learning object-ives in relation to different language skills, the level of improvement aimed at, and how and when this may be achieved. After this, it is up to the teacher and learner to decide exactly how to proceed from here. They may decide to allow the learner more or less total autonomy in trying to attain the objectives set, as a teacher from Italy reported to us:

> Ideally I wouldn't interfere with what the students select at all, but during the explanation of the materials I would suggest to students that they choose material in areas where they feel they have problems or which are their weakest areas. But after that, I wouldn't interfere at all. . . . they can select what they want and proceed with it themselves. . . . they know where their weak areas are. Generally students select the material that's most appropriate to their problems.

12.3 Implementation inside and outside the classroom

It is quite common to hear teachers complain about the many reasons why they feel that they cannot individualize their classrooms. These arguments sometimes relate to the fact that they are non-native speakers; that they are under-resourced in general; that the syllabus is strictly controlled; that class size is too large (perhaps even more reason for needing to individualize); that materials are 'fixed'; furniture is screwed to the floor, thereby restricting movement of learners; that they work in a school and not a university. In other words, all the vari-ables and constraints that we mentioned in chapter 1.

In this next section we hope to show that the provision of a measure of indi-vidual choice need not entail a full-scale reorganization of the classroom and resources and that individualization may be started in a relatively modest way.

One way of attempting to provide a measure of individual choice in the classroom is to use self-access activities where learners choose the tasks and activities that they wish to pursue with or without the help of a teacher. For example, learner X might have problems with reading skills and might opt to do extra work in this area, while learner Y might have a need to do some extra listening work. Of course self-access does not have to be remedial (implying that one is asking the learners to begin from a linguistic lack): some learners want to work in areas they enjoy and where they wish to enhance their performance. Some teachers programme self-access work into their weekly timetable – perhaps for two sessions a week to begin with – and build up from there. Self-access might be offered as integral to a particular course, or in a supplementary mode in a resource or self-access centre (see later in this chapter).

Something to note at this stage is that a self-access operation does not have to be a full-scale one to begin with. Where resources are limited, it is possible to set up the classroom as a mini self-access centre with different parts of the room being used for different activities – perhaps reading in one corner, listening with cassettes and headphones in another, and some computer assisted language learning (CALL) in another. As materials and hardware can perhaps be stored easily and transported on a trolley, a small-scale beginning may enable teachers working within administrative constraints or working with sceptical colleagues to start a self-access operation with the hope of extending it later. As teachers we all have to prepare materials for lessons and provide feedback to our learners anyway – either in class or through marked homework assignments (homework is in any case often set and marked on the lockstep principle outlined above). One suggestion, therefore, might be for two colleagues to collaborate over a mini self-access project by building up a small 'bank' of self-access materials.

> Consider your own teaching situation. What kind of self-access activities would be appropriate for your learners and, if they do not exist already, how could they be set up within your institution?

Reading is one area that provides ample scope for developing self-access work. Teachers can either design their own self-access boxes, perhaps working with other colleagues, as we suggested above, by dividing materials into different levels according to topic and level, or can use and adapt commercially available materials, depending on the types of students in the group, their proficiency level, the purpose of the course and so on. The British Council (1983) reports on how colleagues at a British Council teaching centre in Mexico worked together designing boxes of authentic materials for their learners; the Centre for British Teachers (CBT) has produced a well-utilized reading laboratory for use in German secondary schools. (For teachers interested in this idea, *Reading Choices* by Jolly (1982) provides many suggestions for reading activities.) Developing a reading laboratory for individualized classroom work is another possibility for teachers who may be working with limited resources. Stoller (1984) outlines the features that such a laboratory might usefully contain. Ideally it should

- accommodate a wide variety of student reading levels
- have a large variety of reading selections at each reading level
- have a selection of high-interest topics appropriate to the learners
- allow for systematic progression from one level to another
- permit students to progress at their own pace
- include a self-correction system
- include charts and graphs for easy record keeping
- include a placement test for accurate level assignment
- include exercises that require students to practise a variety of reading skills and strategies

Let us examine how this might work in practice. During the self-access class learner X decides to read a passage on ecology more or less at 'intermediate' level, which could be level 3 (level 5 being the highest). She goes to the reading laboratory at the front of the classroom, looks through the level 3 materials, selects the appropriate passage from the alphabetical index and takes the passage away to read. She might make notes on vocabulary and expressions, and has the option of answering the questions provided with the passage and checking them with a self-correcting key.

She notes down what she has completed in her contract or record book, and might enlist the teacher's help, depending on individual circumstances.

After working at this level (say level 3) the learner herself might decide to progress to the fourth level in the next class. In other words, the learner is exercising a good deal of individual choice and responsibility in what materials she selects and how she chooses to deal with them.

> Look at the self-access material in the extract on p. 213, which appears in Sheerin (1989). Think about how it could be set up and used with your learners. Would any adaptations be necessary, and if so, what would they be?

Walker (1987) gives an account of how she individualized a reading programme by getting the students themselves to bring along self-selected reading materials and making use of a 'standard reading exercise', which she adapted from elsewhere. In order to become part of an individualized language learning programme, self-access materials should enable the learners to decide what work they want to do; find the material and work through it; correct/assess answers where necessary; have work evaluated when desired. For many learners in educational contexts where the teacher alone is perhaps expected to dispense all knowledge, it is advisable to lead students in gradually, making sure they are satisfied with working in this particular mode, and that they understand the

3.3 Introducing Sherlock Holmes

CLASSIFICATION	R.CO/1 = Reading. Comprehension activity/1
LEVEL	Lower intermediate
AGE	Adolescent/young adult
ACTIVITY TYPE	Comprehension activity
AIM	To read and look closely at the most important parts of the text and to check comprehension.
PREPARATION	Look up the following words in a dictionary if you don't know them: *a wound, to heal, a client.*
INSTRUCTIONS	Read the text below and say whether the sentences which follow are true or false.

TASK SHEET

For many years, I shared an apartment in London with my friend, Sherlock Holmes,

My name is Doctor Watson. I worked as a doctor in the British Army for several years. While I was in the army, I
5   travelled to many strange and interesting places. I had   5
many exciting adventures.

Then one day, in Afghanistan, I was shot in the shoulder. My wound was deep and took many months to heal. I nearly died from pain and fever. At last I got better, but I
10 could not work in the army any more. I retired from the   10
army and came back to England.

That is why I was living in London with Sherlock Holmes. I had known my friend for many years. Our address was 221B, Baker Street, in the centre of the city.
15   I enjoyed sharing an apartment with Holmes. My friend   15
was a very clever man. He was the most famous private detective in London. He helped to solve crimes and catch criminals.

When people were in trouble or needed help, they came
20 to Holmes. Sometimes the police came to Holmes and   20
asked for help in catching a criminal.

Sherlock Holmes did not care if his clients were rich or poor. He enjoyed solving their interesting problems. He was very happy when he was working. It was the most
25 important thing in his life.   25

From *The Sign of Four* by Sir Arthur Conan Doyle, retold by Anne Collins.

True or false?

1 Sherlock Holmes and Doctor Watson lived in the same place.

2 Doctor Watson was a soldier in the army.

3 Doctor Watson came back to England because he was tired of the army.

4 When Doctor Watson came back to England, he got to know Sherlock Holmes.

5 Sherlock Holmes was a detective in the police force.

> 6 Sherlock Holmes helped people in trouble whether they could pay or not.
>
> 7 Sherlock Holmes liked using his mind.
>
> **KEY**
>
> 1 True (lines 1/2 and lines 13/14).
>
> 2 False. He was a doctor in the army (lines 3/4).
>
> 3 False. He 'retired from' (= 'left') the army and came back to England because he could not work. He could not work because he had been very ill (lines 7/11).
>
> 4 False. He knew Holmes before he went to Afghanistan (line 13).
>
> 5 False. Sherlock Holmes was a private detective. He sometimes helped the police but he did not work for them as an employee (lines 16/17 and 20/21).
>
> 6 True (lines 22/23).
>
> 7 True (lines 23/25).
>
> **FOLLOW-UP 1**
>
> If you got fewer than 4 answers right, try a comprehension exercise at elementary level.
>
> If you got between 4 and 6 answers right, try some more comprehension exercises at this level.
>
> If you got all the answers right, try a comprehension exercise at intermediate level.
>
> **FOLLOW-UP 2**
>
> If you are interested in Sherlock Holmes, read the rest of the story.
>
> **Comments to the teacher**
>
> 1 Students can gain more from such activities if the relevant line reference to the text is given after each answer.
>
> 2 Note that students can be advised to move to a lower or higher level depending on how many answers they got right. This technique can be used with many other activities.
>
> 3 Many published Readers contain examples of this kind of activity which it is possible to adapt for self-access.

Source: S. Sheerin, pp. 59–60 from *Resource Books for Teachers: Self-Access*. Oxford: Oxford University Press, 1989. © Oxford University Press, 1989.

rationale for the type of material they will be studying. Well-designed materials should make the learner secure enough to work alone. Aston (1993) also notes that by producing leaflets and reports for other users of the facilities learners may be encouraged to contribute to the learning resources of a self-access centre.

Earlier in the chapter we mentioned that self-access work can be done on a larger scale outside the classroom, and where this is the case, the self-access or resource centre should ideally contain the following software and hardware:

- resource room/s incorporating all materials
- consultation room/s for individual counselling
- listening (self-monitoring) section or laboratory
- computer assisted facilities with programmes on vocabulary, testing, reading and communication games
- video facilities

- wall charts analysing at a quick glance all materials available
- classified folders, drawers or boxes containing all the materials available in the centre
- answer sheets, or self-correcting keys where appropriate.

Sheerin (1989) gives a full account of how the centre can be equipped depending on the space available in the institution. Quiet activities such as reading, vocabulary work, grammar practice and general browsing for materials and cassettes should be located at one end of the centre, and 'noisier' activities such as self-access speaking, watching TV, video programmes, and doing CALL activities in pairs should be housed either in adjoining rooms or in side bays away from the main thoroughfare. The entrance and supervisor/librarian's desk should also be situated in a noisier part of the centre if at all possible away from the quieter more 'studious' activities. Miller (2000) gives details of how developing self-access language learning can begin in the classroom with a lesson plan that demonstrates how language and learning skills can be incorporated into class activities with secondary school pupils in Hong Kong in order to try to combat overdependency on the teacher.

It is common practice for an institution to offer a general orientation worksheet to a resource centre so that learners can quickly obtain an overview of the way the centre is organized, which permits them to explore 'routes' they may take in order to satisfy their needs. Below is an outline of a typical orientation worksheet, which can be handed out to learners so that they can familiarize themselves with the facilities available:

Self-Access-Centre
Orientation Worksheet

The questions on this sheet are designed to help you find your way around the materials and facilities available in the self-access centre. Please ask your teacher or the librarian if you run into any difficulties.

1   In which part of the centre would you find (a) English language magazines, (b) today's newspapers?
2   Where would you find the English dictionaries? Write down the reference number.
3   There are some materials you cannot borrow from the centre. What are they? Write down their reference numbers.
4   You would like to work on the microcomputer with a colleague. Which programs might be of interest to you?
5   What do you have to do in order to borrow a cassette tape?
6   When and where can you listen to the tape?
7   Write down the names of any tapes in your subject area that you would like to listen to.

8 You are interested in finding out more about the English language today. Which section would you look in?

9 Find the 'readers' section and note the titles of three books that you would like to read during the course of the term.

10 How many books can you borrow at any one time? How do you sign them out and how long may you keep them?

1 If you do not have the possibility of either setting up or using a self-access centre in your institution, think of ways open to you for reorganizing your resources in small ways to individualize your classroom more effectively.

2 If you do have a self-access facility, think about some of your learners and their individual characteristics, and devise a plan of activities for each learner who will visit the centre for up to six hours per week on three separate occasions.

Once students have found their way around the centre they can begin to devise an individualized plan that may, for example, include listening to general, social English, listening to lectures, some intensive reading (both general and perhaps subject specific), CALL practice and video listening with note-taking practice.

Many variables are involved in the setting up of a centre of these proportions, not least of which will be a range of staffing and budgetary issues. Materials will have to be prepared and written; the centre will have to be maintained and regularly added to, perhaps by learners themselves in some cases; the centre will have to be supervised and students will have to be advised/counselled.

We have attempted here to show the different proportions that self-access activities might take. As suggested earlier, it is possible for an institution, or even an individual teacher, to start off in a small way to begin with and to develop the facility when circumstances permit.

Advantages and shortcomings

Operating a self-access system will offer learners a wide choice of material and the possibility of becoming much more self-reliant and less teacher dependent. Learners should begin to understand more about their needs and how they prefer to learn. On the other hand, it has to be stressed that setting up a self-access system will involve a lot of time and work, usually on the part of the teaching staff, and that institutional constraints might mean that a full-scale centre will never become operational. However, if it is at all possible, the result is worthwhile.

From the materials point of view, there is a danger in providing too much that is related to classroom work: the materials become 'further practice' or 'follow-up activities' rather than allowing the students to explore and learn new things by themselves.

Individualization using the 'new technologies'

In recent years there has been a nascent interest shown in the learning of English, using the so-called 'new technologies', particularly the resources of the World Wide Web (WWW) and email communication. Many ELT practitioners now use these technologies as part of their teaching programme and the possibilities for individualizing language learning by using them are numerous, either within the classroom context or in a self-access and/or computing centre. The World Wide Web or Internet is essentially an international online database that allows participants to share linked multimedia documents. Eastment (1999) provides a clear account of how it works, including definitions, searching the Net, teaching and learning using the Internet and a section on the virtual school.

Some of the relatively common problems of distance discussed by Boyle (1994) can now be addressed by downloading data and using email communication. In fact many institutions of learning are now offering distance email writing courses where the writing can be 'tailored' to an individual student's needs. Refer to chapter 9 for a full discussion of this.

Let us now consider two possible class activities that utilize the Internet in two different educational contexts: the first is with a general EFL class, the second with a group of EAP students. Harmer (2001b) suggests an activity for a post-elementary group of learners that involves them searching for a suitable film by looking at the 'films' page of a national newspaper on their Website. The learners then have to check the films on offer in the town where they are studying, look at the rating and read the reviews of the films they would like to see. Finally, they select a film and justify their decision to the rest of the group.

In the context of the English for academic purposes classroom, using computers can enrich both IT (Information Technology) skills plus language skills simultaneously. Many learners in an academic context will have to begin to use computer facilities in their studies more or less immediately. The task sheet that follows is an example of one given to new EAP students on arrival at a UK university. The rationale behind this particular lesson was to allow learners

1   to work at their own speed
2   to familiarize themselves with the basics of computer equipment and to develop introductory IT skills
3   to begin to locate pertinent Websites and to work out how to send emails
4   to practise the language of comparing and contrasting information

EAP Programme, 2001/02
Tuesday 9 October

The aim of the session this afternoon is to introduce you to the computing facilities at Essex; to familiarize yourself with the equipment on offer and to access some useful Websites that will help you with the learning of English for academic purposes.

STEP 1   Log on. You are now on the computer labs home page. Try the following questions: the number of labs at Essex and their location; which one is for postgraduate use only?

STEP 2   Now go to the University of Essex home page (www.essex.ac.uk) and ˙find the department closest to your subject of study. Analyse the courses offered and then go to www.scit.wlv.ac.uk/ukinfo and find another university with a similar department. Compare and contrast the courses on offer.

STEP 3   You can get a virtual tour of a British campus by logging on to this British Council site: www.britishcouncil.org/eis/campus/htm. Note down some useful information from this site and try emailing it to a friend either at Essex or elsewhere.

STEP 4   The National Union of Students also has a site outlining information that will be useful to you while in the UK. Go to www.nus.org.uk. What does this site tell you about housing, health and finance?

Dudeney (2000) contains a range of Internet activities for different groups of learners. As for mainstream teaching materials, Tomlinson (2001) perceives a tendency for coursebooks to offer an increasing range of Web-search activities as an integrated part of the course in the near future and cites a coursebook from Singapore (*English for Life*, 2000), which includes this information.

A number of organizations now have their own Websites, which teachers and learners can explore for language learning purposes. For example, museums such as the British Museum in the UK (www.british-museum.ac.uk) have sites that may provide material of interest to certain learners. Newspapers, TV channels and medical societies can be another source of useful material. (For a list of suggested Websites see the appendix.)

As well as reading the material students can be encouraged to comment on findings with their peers by posting opinions and sending mail. One of the most famous Websites for teachers and learners of EFL/ESL is Dave Sperling's ESL cafe. This site (www.eslcafe.com) was specifically created by Sperling for teachers and learners, allowing participants to post questions, join discussions, get ideas for teaching and learning, or browse book lists.

Another example of the truly international flavour of the World Wide Web is provided by Vilmi (2000) in her account of setting up an international writing exchange that she managed from Helsinki, Finland. In this project participants from around the globe were able to contribute writing material via computer links and receive feedback on it. (See www.hut.fi/rvilmi/project.) Writing is also a major feature of some of the OWLS (online writing sites) where learners can contribute writing sometimes of a specialized nature such as a field of ESP and receive feedback on it. Purdue University in America is one of the most accessed sites offering this facility (www.owl.english.purdue.edu).

We have already examined in chapter 6 the use of dictionaries for vocabulary learning, but clearly they offer much scope for learning in an individualized context as well. One such example, which contains a wealth of information, is the Cambridge online dictionary (www.cup.cam.ac.uk/elt/dictionary).

At the time of writing it seems that the permutations of these new technologies for class and individualized learning are virtually endless. Certainly where teachers are informed about these new developments, and technology does not drive pedagogy, there is much to be gained. However, Slaouti (2002) offers a timely warning, suggesting that the explosion of this new technology is not a panacea for all ills, that the World Wide Web is basically unregulated and that teachers should not follow trends too slavishly without applying suitable critical judgement first.

12.4   *Focus on the learner through diary studies*

In recent years some EFL teachers have been exploring the advantages offered by learner diaries as yet another way of focusing on the learner as an individual with needs. There is now a growing awareness of how these diaries can establish an effective channel of communication between teacher and learners.

The process works as follows: the teacher enters into an individual 'contract' with each learner in the class whereby the learners keep a daily record of events that happen to them. The teacher will discuss contents of the diary in private with learners, who are free to develop the diary in whatever ways they wish. It may include observations of what they did on a particular day; observations and feelings about classes, teachers, peers, landladies; thoughts on how they feel they are learning with respect to a task, a class or the whole course. It is important for learners to understand the rationale behind the diary writing and the following example of guidelines developed for learners can be useful in establishing this:

LEARNER DIARY
The diary is a very important part of your studies here and will be of most help if you write it regularly. Your diary will enable you to express your opinions on all the classes that you take, and will help you to understand exactly what you need in your studies, as well as keeping a record of all the work you do. It will also give you valuable extended writing practice.

For the next few weeks we would like you to write each day about the lessons you have taken. There is no limit to the amount you can write, but we suggest that you spend at least 20 minutes a day on the diary. Your tutor will ask you to hand in the diary weekly; it will then be corrected, returned and discussed in tutorials.

It would be useful if your diary could include *some* of the following information:

date/lessons followed
how you think you performed
what difficulties you had
how you think that you might overcome these difficulties
what you found most enjoyable/least enjoyable
what you found most useful/least useful
what you feel about a specific lesson/the course/group/teacher/yourself
what you did in your spare time to practise your English
any other thoughts, feelings and experiences relevant to your personal progress
   on the course

Please look upon the diary as an exercise in writing fluently: your diaries will not be graded or strictly corrected, but frequent and important language errors will be pointed out to you. All diary entries will be treated confidentially.

Diary entries allow learners to report on a range of different observations according to the needs and wishes of each learner. Some learners may offer a simple account of what they have done during a particular day from a general point of view. Other learners, however, prefer to focus on particular classes that they have attended or a specific learning issue, such as how they feel they are progressing with vocabulary or with listening.

Diary writing can be very useful for learners. What sort of information for future work do you think the teacher might be able to get from reading the diaries?

As well as giving each student authentic written practice, these diaries can help the teacher with counselling the learner on specific learning problems that may not have surfaced in the classroom. They can sometimes offer a teacher a fresh insight into the study techniques of a particular learner, which, again, are not always apparent in the classroom, especially when the teacher may be dealing with large numbers. Nunan (1999: 167) provides samples of learner diary entries based on the learners' views of a writing class they had just taken. As a result of reading the diaries it may also be possible for teachers to adjust materials and methods and to rearrange group dynamics in subsequent classes. For teachers wanting to investigate particular issues within their own classroom, they offer numerous possibilities of looking at the ways that individuals approach tasks and how they conceptualize and categorize teaching and learning events. By adding other data as well, it may be possible for the teacher to do a longitudinal study of a particular learner or small group of learners over a period of time – perhaps four to six months – in order to see what sort of learning/study profiles emerge for these learners.

12.5   Learner training

We have examined individualization and some of its possible ramifications, such as using self-access activities both within and outside the classroom. We now start to look at other concrete possibilities for helping learners to learn more effectively by making them aware of their different language learning needs. As teachers, many of us have been involved in some aspects of learner training to a greater or lesser extent, by giving suggestions for organizing vocabulary books to using dictionaries more effectively, to how to exploit the environment outside the classroom for learning the target language wherever possible. As learner training can only really work effectively if we have some account of what a 'good' language learner actually *does*, let us briefly examine the background to some of this research. Attempts to develop systematic learner training can be traced back to research carried out in Canada in the 1970s by Naiman, Fröhlich and Stern into the strategies of 34 adults known to be 'good' language learners. (Readers are also referred to the work of Rubin and Thompson, 1982, for an account of the good language learner. See also chapter 3, which raised several of these issues.)

> Before reading further, what do you feel would be the characteristics of a 'good' language learner?

From Naiman et al. (1975) the following generalized strategies emerge as being of most importance. Good language learners

- are aware of their own attitudes and feelings towards language learning and to themselves as language learners
- realize that language works as an organized system and is a means of communication and interaction
- assess and monitor their progress regularly
- realize that language learning involves hard work and time and set themselves realistic short-term goals
- involve themselves in the L_2 and learn to take 'risks' in it
- are willing to experiment with different learning strategies and practise activities that suit them best
- organize time and materials in a personally suitable way and fully exploit all resources available

The research base for identifying issues dealing with language learning strategy training developed apace in the 1990s (see chapter 3 for a full discussion of strategies). Tudor (1996) provides a pertinent overview of recent trends in learner-centredness, including analysing the context, self-assessment, developing strategic learning awareness and fostering learner involvement. Materials that purport to help learners for independent learning and autonomy based on some of these findings have been developed for classroom use. Lowes and Target (1998) have some practical suggestions for achieving learner autonomy through a series of tasks designed to offer students choices about their learning, particularly in instances where students may come from educational backgrounds with very different cultural assumptions. The material is also designed to help teachers to reflect on the ways in which their teaching might help learners to make choices. The book also contains information on finding and using resources. However, even though many coursebooks now include an element of learner training in them (see Nunan (1995) for example) the main course in learner training is the book by Ellis and Sinclair (1989).

Taking these basic strategies as a starting point, Ellis and Sinclair developed what they called 'systematic' learner training during the 1980s; the final product was a published course in learner training entitled *Learning to Learn English*. Their systematic approach is designed to help learners to assume more responsibility for their own learning by providing tasks that include a focus on learning styles, self-assessment of needs, advice on how to use a self-access centre and strategies designed to improve each language skill. It is open to both teacher and learners to decide whether to integrate the course with the language learning materials that they are currently using, or to have distinct learner training periods during the course. The extract on pp. 223–4 aims at getting learners to analyse and prioritize their own needs.

Let us finish this section by looking at the following quotation from an EFL teacher being interviewed by Nunan (1991: 185), whose remark neatly encapsulates the feeling that a growing number of practitioners have with respect to the importance of learner training on their courses:

> As a teacher I see my role as being twofold. One is, yes, I am teaching the language, but I feel my other very important role is to assist the learners to take a growing responsibility for the management of their own learning. Within our programme, learners are with us for only a relatively – a short time, and we have to prepare them so that their learning can continue outside, erm, the length of their course.

On the whole, evidence tends to suggest that teachers are becoming increasingly aware of the various opportunities that individualizing the language classroom can offer to both learners and teachers alike.

> Consider the concept of learner training in your own teaching situation and the extent to which it would be feasible to incorporate it into your regular classes.

12.6   Conclusion

We began this chapter by looking at the concept of individualization in its broadest sense by examining some definitions of the term, and have suggested

1.3 Why do you need or want to learn English?

1 Analysing your needs

Before you start your course, it is a good idea to think carefully about what you need or want English for. You could analyse your needs like this.

a) Decide on your *main purpose* for learning English e.g. for work.
b) Make a list of the *specific situations* where you need to use English
   e.g. speaking on the telephone, answering enquiries, giving information, writing business letters.
c) Decide which *skills* you need for each situation: extending vocabulary, dealing with grammar, listening, speaking, reading or writing.

You should then have a better idea about which skills you need to work on and be able to establish your priorities.

Here is an example of how one learner analysed his needs. Stig is a Swedish Youth Hostel warden who needs English for his work. He filled in the following chart. You will find a blank chart on page 109 in the Appendix, which you could use to analyse your own needs.

Situations	Skills					
	Vocabulary (✓)	Grammar (✓)	Listening (✓)	Speaking (✓)	Reading (✓)	Writing (✓)
Youth Hostel Reception Desk						
– welcoming new guests	✓			✓		
– giving YH information	✓			✓		
– explaining regulations	✓	✓		✓		
– answering enquiries	✓		✓	✓		
– putting up notices	✓	✓				✓

1.3 Why do you need or want to learn English?

2 Prioritising your needs

How much do you know / can you do already?

Stig used an assessment scale from 1 to 5:
1 = this is the standard I would like to reach – my goal.
5 = I am a long way from my goal.
He considered each skill that he needed and circled the number that he felt represented his position on the scale, as follows:

Extending vocabulary	Dealing with grammar	Listening	Speaking	Reading	Writing
1	1	1	1	(1)	1
2	2	2	(2)	2	2
3	(3)	(3)	3	3	3
(4)	4	4	4	4	(4)
5	5	5	5	5	5

He was then able to see more clearly what he needed to improve most.
You will find a blank self-assessment scale in the Appendix (page 110) for your own use.

What are your priorities?

Stig then gave each skill a priority rating from 1 to 6:
1 = highest priority
6 = lowest priority

I thought I needed to improve my speaking, but now I realise that it is mainly vocabulary that is missing. My speaking is quite good, in fact. I also realise that I need to concentrate on my listening and writing. I can read English quite well – I don't need to do it much, anyway.

Stig, Sweden

Skill	Priority rating
Extending vocabulary	1
Dealing with grammar	4
Listening	2
Speaking	5
Reading	6
Writing	3

You could prioritise your own needs in the same way. If you do this, it will give you a clearer idea about which sections in Stage 2 of this book would be most useful for you. It will also give you a basis for negotiating the content of your course with the other members of your class and your teacher. You will find a blank record of priorities in the Appendix (page 110).

Source: B. Ellis and G. Sinclair, *Learning to Learn English*. Cambridge: Cambridge University Press, 1989. © Cambridge University Press, 1989.

various ways of implementing it both inside and outside the language classroom by incorporating combinations of self-access work, 'working with the new educational technologies', diary writing and learner training. We have tried to show that the most appropriate way of implementing individualization will depend, to some extent, on the *context* of the teaching operation that we work in. We have also attempted to illustrate that individualization is one way of reorganizing the management and resources of the classroom to try to maximize learning potential for as many people in the class as possible.

12.7 Further reading

1 Dickinson, L. (1987): *Self-instruction in Language Learning*, provides a helpful introduction to this topic.
2 Sheerin, S. (1989): *Self-access*, is a more practical account with useful suggestions on setting up individualized activities both inside and outside the classroom.
3 Dudeney, G. (2000): *The Internet and the Language Classroom*, offers plenty of ideas for teachers wanting to explore this area in more detail.
4 There is a useful survey of recent work on autonomy in language learning by Sinclair, B. (1999): Survey review.
5 The following Website contains useful information on learner autonomy and the Web:
http://www.insa.lyon.fr/Departments/CDRL/learner.html

13

Observing the Language Classroom

13.1 Introduction

In this chapter we shall be looking at language classrooms in order to analyse in some detail what occurs in them. We shall begin by considering why the classroom might be a useful place to observe. Then we shall move on to examine, as teachers in the classroom, some of the different issues we might want to look at to become better informed about our own practice, and thus to improve our own teaching. After this we shall look at some of the different methods that have been used by teachers/researchers to gather data from classrooms. Our final aim in the chapter is to make some suggestions for observation tasks that could be of use to teachers working in a wide variety of classrooms, and to apply these tasks to transcripts of actual classroom interaction. We hope this analysis will help teachers to become further informed about their own practice.

13.2 Why focus on the classroom?

Allwright and Bailey (1991) quote Gaies (1980), who comments that the classroom is essentially a crucible and when language learning occurs it is as a result of the combinations of the different elements of the teacher–learner, learner–learner relationships embodied in the numerous interactions in the classroom. We noted in the previous chapter that what we teach does not necessarily result in learning taking place, nor does the best prepared lesson plan result in that plan being followed absolutely in the classroom. As Allwright and Bailey (1991) suggest, this would be tantamount to a 'play reading' rather than a language lesson, and might impose a framework upon the class that some learners could find restricts rather than aids their learning. Because of this, what is often noticeable about classrooms is that they are not necessarily neat, organized places, while interaction patterns that occur in them can be highly erratic and variable: genuine interaction cannot be completely planned for and requires co-operative effort. Allwright and Bailey also suggest that the co-operation required in the classroom setting involves everyone (teacher and learners) in managing many things at the same time, including who gets the chance to speak, what they speak about, what each participant does with the different opportunities to speak, and what sort of classroom atmosphere is created by learners and the teacher. For us as teachers it is important to observe the interaction within the classroom because it can determine the learning opportunities that students get. We might also suggest that learners do not learn *directly* from a syllabus, but what they learn, or not, is the result of the manner in which this syllabus is 'translated' into the classroom environment, in the form of materials but also of their use by the teacher and learners in the class.

13.3   What to observe

Think about your own classroom situation. If you had the chance to observe your own or a colleague's class, what sorts of things would you want to look at?

Bailey (2001) sees traditional classroom observation as essentially covering four broad functions: first of all for pre-service teachers who are often observed by teacher educators who typically offer advice on the development of their teaching skills. Second, observers view a practising teacher's class for their own professional development. Third, practising teachers are observed by heads of schools / departments / inspectors for judgement purposes or to see the extent to which teachers adhere to the expectations of the institution. Lastly, data for classroom research are often gathered from observing classrooms.

Tsui (2001) notes how current trends in classroom research tend to be of a more ethnographic, naturalistic nature rather than being strictly experimental. Within ELT over the last decade several practitioners have attempted to focus on the language classroom within this perspective. Hopkins (1993) explains clearly the concept of 'action research', which involves teachers asking questions and researching their own classrooms from an angle often empathetic to learners' experiences in the classroom. Even though Hopkins's work was done within the field of general education, his ideas have been developed within ELT as whole. A collection of articles edited by Bailey and Nunan (1996) examines lesson plans, interviews and teachers' journals, and McDonough and McDonough (1997) provide a framework for teachers thinking of generating researchable issues in their own classrooms, including information on how to use diary studies, questionnaires and interviews and case studies. For further discussion of the teacher as researcher, see chapter 14.

As we mentioned in the previous section, the classroom is the basic focus of the teaching and learning process, and there are literally hundreds of different permutations of classroom processes that we may wish to focus on: some of them perhaps very 'macro' or wide-ranging, such as how a particular teacher/ group of learners use a textbook during a class; and some very 'micro', such as how a teacher elicits responses with a given class or how a particular learner or small group of individuals initiate turns in an oral skills class. We may wish to classify the information we get from observing the classroom into different areas such as information that focuses primarily on the teacher, the interaction patterns of learners in general, interaction of learners in pairs and/or groups, and the interaction of certain individuals with the teacher. If we wish to focus on the teacher the following criteria could be offered as factors for observation. We may wish to investigate each one in turn, or we may decide to focus on some or all of them during a particular lesson:

- the amount of teacher talking time (TTT) contrasted with student talking time (STT) during the course of a particular class
- the type of teacher talk that takes place in a given class and where it occurs in the lesson
- the teacher's questioning/elicitation techniques
- how the teacher gives feedback to learners
- how the teacher handles 'digressions' in the classroom
- the different roles a teacher takes on during the class ('manager', 'facilitator' etc.)
- the teacher's use of encouragement and praise with learners
- the technical aids and materials a teacher uses to create learning contexts, and how the teacher involves the learners in these activities
- how 'tightly' a particular teacher corrects the learners' work

There are many more possibilities, of course.

Think about other criteria that interest you as a teacher and add them to ours.

Nunan (1990) reports on a teachers' workshop where one of the groups participating in the workshop offered the following criteria as aspects of the class that they would like to look at. These were

wait time; repair techniques; 'fun'; questioning; materials; student–teacher interaction; scope of student response; amount of direction offered; class organization; lesson objectives; student and teacher talk time; control and initiative; who asks questions; context for language practice; how language is practised; methods used; digressions; variety of activities; interaction between students; lesson cohesion; teacher language; eliciting techniques; evaluation possibilities.

It is possible, of course, to extend these criteria, or combinations of them, to different classes in order to gain comparative data. For example, we may wish to compare the metalanguage (the language the teacher uses in the classroom to explain things) of the same teacher across a range of different classes – perhaps of different proficiency levels – in order to ascertain what similarities and differences exist across the various groups; or we may wish to observe how different teachers who teach the same class use the textbook or set of materials with that class. Some teachers feel that it would be useful to observe classes with a fundamentally different focus, such as a 'traditional', grammar-based class, in contrast to a more 'communicative' one, to see which could be deemed more successful from the learners' point of view. In a similar vein, we may wish to observe various things that occur in a given classroom with the learners themselves.

Kumaravadivelu (1990) writes how the teaching act has been the subject of much classroom observation, perhaps at the expense of the equally important tasks of observing the learning act and trying to understand learner perceptions of classroom events. It may be useful to observe the group dynamics of a particular class during a language lesson in order to observe the interaction patterns that occur as a result of the exercises/tasks that the teacher sets up and manages. We might observe how well the learners seem to work together as a whole group, in small groups, in pairs or, indeed, if some learners prefer to work individually. Allwright (1984, 1988) comments on the idiosyncratic nature of the language classroom and the fact that from the same lesson different learners will take away very different things. Analysing and perhaps contrasting two or more different learners in a class can help us as teachers to understand how these learners are using the classroom context to maximize their own learning potential, if at all.

To further illustrate the essentially puzzling nature of language learning in different classrooms, Allwright (1992) offers the following comments from teachers and learners, in different contexts, on what *they* found was particularly bewildering about language learning in their classrooms:

Teachers:

> Why do students feel that they have to know all the vocabulary in order to understand a text?
> Why do students use so little English in group work?
> Do students work better in small groups or pairs?
> What do students really want to learn from our lessons?

Learners:

> Nobody ever explains the purpose of the exercise.
> I don't understand why I don't understand English.
> We try to understand the words not the lessons.
> Teachers expect us to remember what we did in the last lesson but we don't operate like this.
> Why does a teacher only ask me a question when I don't know the answer?

Being armed with an awareness of these factors can make classroom observation highly fruitful in that we may be able to make corrective adjustments to classroom teaching and management as a result of analysing the data we collect.

13.4 *Different approaches to classroom observation*

We have already examined some recent trends in classroom observation at the beginning of this chapter and, having decided on the criteria we would like to observe in the classroom, we then have to decide which method we would like to use to gain access to the classroom for observation purposes. Allwright and Bailey (1991) list three main approaches classroom observers have typically used in classroom observation. The first of these is an experimental observation in which the teacher/researcher exercises a high degree of control over the classroom and purposefully becomes involved in the setting to try to discover the effects of the intervention. A control group would typically be set up. This 'scientific' approach to observation usually implies a one-way, (usually) top-down approach to classroom observation, since the teacher and class will be observed from the 'outside' by a linguistic 'expert' who will probably distinguish theoretical issues from actual classroom practice. The second main approach is called 'naturalistic enquiry' and may involve observers as participants either in their own or in someone else's class to 'see what happens'. The essential feature of this approach is to act as a fly on the wall and, where possible, not to influence normally occurring patterns of instruction and interaction.

Another way of implementing the approach is to video a class or to have one's own class videoed. However, sitting in on a class and/or videoing the experience are never neutral, because an unaccustomed presence in the class is bound to cause some disruption and alter the normal patterns of interaction. One advantage of this approach is that data from different classrooms can easily be seen and compared.

The third approach, already outlined earlier in this chapter, and an increasingly popular one, may be of more interest to practitioners as a whole as it is performed by teachers themselves from *within* the classroom. Wajnryb (1992) comments how classroom observation has often been perceived in judgemental terms of assessment, evaluation or experimentation. Assessment and evaluation through observing the classroom are still an integral part of many teacher training programmes across the world and are deemed useful, especially where it is thought that the trainee might benefit from the evaluation and feedback of a more experienced teacher or trainer. Today, however, there is a growth of emphasis on extending knowledge and understanding of what happens from *inside* the classroom (perhaps with some small-scale intervention). This is done by teachers themselves, perhaps collaborating with a colleague, either as part of a teacher development or classroom research project. (Classroom research by teachers is explored in the following chapter.) In this third approach, observation may include some naturalistic observation (perhaps of a colleague's class), but will typically involve teachers in the setting up of some small-scale intervention that will then be monitored by the teachers themselves over a period of time. Topics for this type of classroom research may be the development of oral competence of a learner/ learners, why the content of certain materials appears not to stimulate students, or, whether 'active' tasks actually improve the language learning.

Although the data for the observation may be gathered over a period of time, the teachers' observations are 'recycled' or fed back into the classroom process. Hence, within this framework, classroom observation does not occur from the outside, but instead the impetus comes from within the classroom in a 'bottom-up' fashion that allows the teachers themselves to decide which areas they wish to investigate. The observation involved in classroom research can be quite small-scale; it does not have to run to the dimensions of a large project.

Being observed at some stage during one's career as a teacher is usually mandatory. In the UK, for example, there is a (non-compulsory) national accreditation scheme for both public and private sector ELT, run by the British Council. Institutions are inspected according to several sets of criteria, one of which covers the expertise in the classroom of the teaching staff. Teachers working on the course are therefore observed during their lessons, inspectors paying attention to such factors as classroom rapport, teachers' knowledge of linguistic systems, involvement of learners in the lesson, monitoring of participation, error correction and so on. Many inspectors or assessors take notes on what they observe in the classroom and a possible 'observation of teaching' schedule is printed below.

Before reading this observation of teaching schedule, what areas would you want to look at if you were observing a teacher in a class? After reading, see how many similarities and differences you noted.

Observation of Teaching
(20–30 min. max.)

Group:

Class/Session:

A. Preparation of lesson

• specification of clear aims
• choice of appropriate material
• choice of appropriate teaching aids

B. Organization of lesson

• introduction
• progression of activities
• management of resources

C. Responsiveness to students' needs

- appropriate teaching techniques
- checking of students' understanding
- provision of helpful feedback
- involvement of students at all stages

D. Links between lesson and overall aims/syllabus
E. Evidence of professional expertise of teacher
F. Overall description of lesson and critical evaluation

> If you have been involved in any type of classroom observation, think about the approach you used. What were the advantages/disadvantages of this approach?

Using video recordings

If we are interested in understanding classrooms through observation in a co-operative way outside the realm of experiment/assessment (within a teacher development programme, for example), there are a number of advantages in using pre-recorded video tapes as a way of stimulating interest in the classroom for observation purposes. Sometimes various administrative constraints may make it impossible to work with colleagues or in a team, and in such cases videotaped classes can give teachers access to situations that they would not otherwise be able to observe. Videotaped lessons may also provide a spring-board for the teacher-initiated research outlined above, in that the issues raised on the tape may have relevance to the observer's own classroom and could help in the formulation of an action plan for that teacher.

There are several collections of videotaped lessons available in commercial packages for teacher education purposes. The British Council produced the much used *Teaching and learning in Focus* in 1983. A more recent one is *Looking at Language Classrooms* by Lubelska and Matthews (1997). This collection might also be useful to teachers as it links topics from Wajnryb's *Classroom Observation Tasks* (1992) to corresponding video material.

The topics include attending to the learner, the learner as doer, the teacher's metalanguage, the language of feedback to error, lesson planning, grammar as lesson content, eliciting and giving instructions (refer to Lubelska and Matthews 1997: 110 for more details).

Using video for classroom observation also has the advantage of being easy to set up – you do not have to disturb a class or organize one especially for the purpose, and you, the observer, have total control in that you may view, pause, replay and so on. Videotaped lessons are also useful to the extent that it is possible to focus on a single issue for one viewing, such as teacher talk, and then replay the tape to focus on a different issue, perhaps to observe how a pair of learners work together on an information-gap activity. It can be very motivating to see how other teachers work in the classroom without the threat of being evaluated oneself. When videos are viewed as a group activity with other teachers, any difference in perception and/or opinion that occurs can be usefully discussed. There is sometimes a danger, however, that we might see these lessons as offering a perfect model or, conversely, that we might be overcritical of what we consider to be the shortcomings of a particular teacher, rather than trying to get as balanced a perspective as possible.

As with all media, there are drawbacks to using video. We can rarely see the whole class performing as the camera can offer us only a partial view of the classroom. As lessons are usually edited, this also results in the observer getting an incomplete picture of the whole lesson. Nevertheless, given its versatility as a resource, videotaped material offers many possibilities for classroom observation.

13.5   *Devising classroom observation tasks*

Earlier in the chapter we suggested that we might wish to observe the 'macro' details of the classroom or to analyse a particular aspect in more depth – such as observing the teacher in as comprehensive a way as possible or looking at a subtopic, such as the amount of teacher talk in a given class. In this section we shall offer some suggestions for analysing different aspects of one area – that of teacher talk in the classroom – and then consider some criteria that we might wish to include in a general observation task sheet that could be used as an aid to provide an initial 'overview' of a classroom. Later we shall apply some of these details to the analysis of transcripts of EFL classes to see how they might operate on 'real' data in practice. Teacher talk in classrooms has been an area of interest to researchers for a long time. What often surprises teachers themselves, as Nunan (1991) points out, is the sheer amount of talking that they themselves do in the classroom, sometimes up to 80 per cent of the total class.

Depending on the aims of a particular lesson, the amount of teacher talk may vary; for example, a teacher may wish to focus on the explanation of a certain function or structure in one class that will entail a high degree of teacher talk, to be followed on by a range of student-centred tasks in the next class, which will include a higher amount of student talk. In the late seventies, in the heyday of the communicative approach in Britain, it was generally thought that teachers should strive for a high degree of student talking time (STT) and a low amount of teacher talking time (TTT) in the classroom (see the account by Gower and Walters, 1983). However, some practitioners feel teacher talking time is useful, not merely for organizing the classroom, but also because it can offer pertinent language practice, since the metalanguage used by the teacher can be considered as 'genuinely communicative' and may be of considerable benefit to the learners.

Consider your own teaching situation. Think carefully about how much time you spend talking in the classroom as a proportion of the total lesson. Does this surprise you?

We may wish to observe how the teacher talk relates to the specific function of the teacher in the class at that point in time. Stubbs and Delamont (1976) outline some of the functions of the teacher in the classroom, which include giving instructions, organizing seating arrangements, setting up and building up situations through questions, directing practice activities, giving cue-card prompts, using a student for demonstration practice in pairwork activities, correcting, setting written work, and developing 'rapport' / showing interest in the students.

Nunan (1991) adds a further dimension to Stubbs's and Delamont's perspective by outlining three factors that ought to be considered when assessing the appropriateness and quantity of teacher talk. These are the point at which the talking occurs; whether it is planned or spontaneous, and if spontaneous, whether the digression is helpful or not; and the value of the teacher talk as potentially useful input for acquisition purposes. What constitutes appropriacy and quality may be thought of as matters of judgement and may be subject to considerable variation. Evidence also tends to suggest that the questions a teacher asks in the classroom can be extremely important in helping learners to develop their competence in the language. It is useful to observe whether teachers put questions to learners systematically or randomly, how long they wait for a response, and the type of question asked, from that requiring a simple one-word reply to higher-order referential questions where learners can provide information the teacher does not know. Similarly, in the case of feedback and correcting learners, we can observe how and when the teacher does this, and whether all learners receive treatment systematically.

Thus far we have looked at some of the factors we might wish to observe pertaining to the teacher in the classroom. We could also, for example, turn our attention to one learner or to a pair of learners to compare how each of them tends to individualize whole-class instruction to their own benefit.

Let us now consider some of the general criteria we might find useful in order to observe as many facets of the language classroom as possible in the context of one language lesson. We have set these out in the form of a general observation task sheet (adapted from Thickett, 1986), which can be used as a prompt for making notes during an observation session:

1. *Focus on Learners*
Group Dynamics. How well do they work together as
a) a whole group
b) small groups
c) pairs. Do some prefer to work individually?
How well do they appear to relate and respond to the teacher?

2. *Focus on the Teacher*
a) What is the approximate amount of teacher talking time in the lesson. When does it occur? How much explanation/metalanguage is used? Is TTT all in the L_1, all in the L_2, or a mixture of both?
b) What are the different roles assumed by the teacher during the class?
c) How much encouragement is offered to the learners and how is it done?
d) If aids/materials are used what is their purpose in the lesson?

3. *Presentation and Practice*
a) How is a context for the lesson established?
b) Do all students get adequate practice? How does the teacher ensure this?

4. *Production Stage*
a) What activity/activities are the students asked to perform?
b) Do they seem to be pertinent/useful in realizing the objectives of the lesson?

5. *Classroom Management*
Are the activities smooth and effectively managed?
Do students seem to be clear about what they should be doing?

6. *Correction/Feedback*
a) How 'tightly' does the teacher correct students at various stages of the activities?
b) What type of feedback is offered to learners? Is it equally distributed?

7. *Motivation*
a) How would you characterize the atmosphere of this class? For example alert, hard-working, good humoured, keenly motivated etc.
b) Note down any particular motivating features of this lesson.

8. *Overall Comments/Observation*

> If you have the opportunity, try this observation schedule with a colleague by observing each other's classes and producing feedback to each other. Add any other factors you feel are important to you in your teaching situation.

13.6 Applying the tasks to classroom data

In this section we intend to look at the application to actual classroom practice of some of the observation tasks discussed above. We shall analyse materials and transcripts of different language classes in order to gain an

2B   Lesson planning

BEFORE VIEWING

Individual teachers vary in the amount of planning they do.
Look at the following diagram of lesson planning areas:

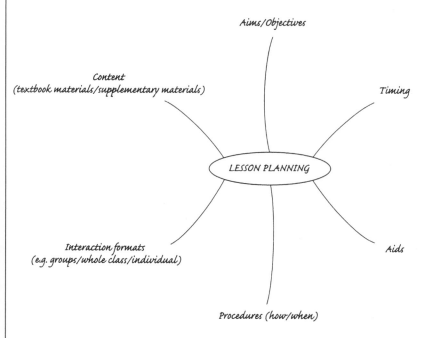

In pairs, rank these areas in order of importance, and discuss the reasons for your decision.
Discuss your ranking with the rest of the group, and add to the diagram any other points which
have come up in your discussion.

Sequence **2B Lesson planning**

WHILE VIEWING

1 You are going to watch part of a lesson based on the structures *used to* and *didn't use to*.
Here is an outline plan for the lesson. It contains details about the content, timing and aids, but
no information about interaction formats or procedures. As you watch the lesson, add details to
the outline plan about these two aspects. Then, after comparing your notes with a partner, watch
again to check them.
Note: Some parts of the lesson are not shown in the video extract.

```
                          Lesson plan

Aim:                By the end of the lesson, learners will be
                    able talk about past habits.
Target structures:  Used to / didn't use to
Aids:               Cassette recorder, cassette
Book material:      Blueprint Two, Unit 31.

1 Present language (5 mins).
   e.g.   I used to live in Cuba.
          I didn't use to be a teacher.
2 Listening and True/False statements (10 mins).
3 Asking and answering questions about past life (18 mins).
              • appearance
              • spare time
              • books
              • places
   e.g.   Did you use to have long hair?
          Yes I did.
          So did I. / I didn't.
4 Game - 'Call My Bluff' (7 mins).
   (Making statements about a partner's past life.)
```

---

2 Consider the way in which this lesson plan was written.
Would you write out your plan in this way? If not, how would you remind yourself what to do
during the lesson?
Discuss the presentation of plans with the rest of the group.

Sequence **2B**　**Lesson planning**

WHILE VIEWING (40 mins)

1 It will probably be necessary for participants to watch the video twice to do this task. Suggested annotations are as follows:

Lesson plan

Aim:　　　　　　　By the end of the lesson, learners will be able to talk about past habits.

Target structures: *Used to / didn't use to*

Aids:　　　　　　　Cassette recorder, cassette

Book material:　　*Blueprint Two*, Unit 31.

1 Present language (5 mins).
　e.g.　I used to live in Cuba.
　　　　I didn't use to be a teacher.

Write sample sentences on board and <u>leave there</u>.

2 Listening and True/False statements (10 mins).

Individual work: learners write down T or F.

3 Asking and answering questions about past life (18 mins).
　　　　　• appearance
　　　　　• spare time
　　　　　• books
　　　　　• places
　e.g.　Did you use to have long hair?
　　　　Yes I did.
　　　　So did I./ I didn't.

**Give an example of dialogue orally → Learners practise in pairs →
Some pairs present dialogue to class.**

4 Game – 'Call My Bluff' (7 mins).
　(Making statements about a partner's past life.)

**Learners prepare sentences about partner (true or false) → Two teams.
One learner keeps score on board.**

2B Lesson planning

School: Escuela Oficial de Idiomas, Las Arenas, Spain
Teacher: Ileana Reguera

Voiceover: At the start of the lesson, the teacher introduces the structure 'used to'.

Teacher: [writes on board] 'I didn't use to' pay attention to the negative. 'Use to', 'use to', hmm? Different from 'used to'. I didn't use to...work...as a teacher.

Tape: Woman 1: Exercise one. Dialogue.

Voiceover: The students then listen to the structure being used in a recorded dialogue, and answer some questions.

Tape: Man: There's the school I used to go to, when I was little.
Woman 2: It looks a bit old and depressing!
Man: I know! But it's all right inside. And you see that house over there?
Woman 2: What, the one with the white fence?
Man: Yes. I used to live there.

Teacher: Now, I would like you to work in pairs, with your partner, and, er...let's try to reproduce, sort of dialogue. [writes on board] You can talk about, er...your appearance...you can talk about, er...your spare time, or...the books...you read, or...the places...you went to...and so on. So thi...there are some cues, but of course you can speak about whatever you like. Er...the dialogue will consist of, er...A, for example, says, er...'What...', make a question...makes a question to B, for example, 'What did you use to look like when you were a little girl?' And B answers, 'Well, I used to have long, curly hair'. And A agrees, or disagrees. Hmm? If she agrees, 'Oh! So did I'. If she disagrees, 'Oh, I didn't'. And then B makes another question, to A; 'And what about you, did you use to wear glasses?' for example, and A answer 'Oh, yes, I did'. Right, so try to use short answers, 'yes I did', hmm? 'No, I didn't', or 'Nor did I'. Hmm? Is it clear? Just two minutes in pairs, and then you will speak aloud. Right? And you want to ask me any question, I will be ready to help you.

[Students work in pairs]

Student 1: What did you use to go, in the...
Student 2: I, er...used, er...to spend my holidays in Bilbao or Palencia because I used to live in Madrid.

[Fade out and in]

Teacher: OK? So, let's begin. Hmm? Let's break the ice. Estivaliz, can you play with, er...Rocio?
Student 3: Er...what did you use to look like as a child?
Student 4: Er...when I was a child...I used to be very fat, but now I don't eat too much, and I was thin.
Teacher: Yes, great! What about you, can you make...?
Student 3: No, I didn't. I was very thin, and...I used to have short, blonde hair.
Teacher: Really?
Student 4: And, what did use to...to do in your spare time?
Teacher: Good!
Student 3: I used to play with my sisters, at home.
Student 4: I...didn't.

Teacher: You didn't?
Student 4: No.
Teacher: Did you like...er...do you have any, I mean, have you got sisters or brothers to play with?
Student 4: Yes, er...I wa...well, *bueno* [=well], I am, er...one, er...sister, but I was, er...ten years, er...he was, er...one year.
Teacher: Oh, I see. So different ages. Good. What about you two, Elisa and, er...Rosa?
Student 5: Er...what did you use to look like as a child?
Student 6: I used to have short hair.
Student 5: Er...oh, I didn't, I used to have long hair.
Teacher: Did you? Long hair? What about now? What have you done with your long hair?
Student 5: Is more...I don't...*comódo* [=comfortable].
Teacher: Comfortable?
Student 5: Comfortable.
Teacher: Yes, good.
Student 6: Er...what did you use to do in your spare time?
Student 5: Er...I used to play tennis.
Student 6: Er...I didn't. I used to go with my friends.
Teacher: Did you? And what did you do with...what did you use to do with your friends? What did you use to play with, er...your friends? Or what did you use to go, or do?
Student 6: Mmm...we used to...to walk, er...
Teacher: Mm hmm. Along...
Student 6: Along, er...Las Arenas.
Teacher: Right. Mm hmm. Did you use to go and...for a picnic from time to time, with your friends?
Student 6: Yes. Some...sometimes, ermm...on Saturdays, for example.
Teacher: Mm hmm. Yes. Did you enjoy it? Yes?
Student 6: Yes.
Teacher: Right. What about you two?
Student 2: Er...what did you use, er...to...er...spend your holidays?
Student 1: I used to go...Europe...
Teacher: To Europe?
Student 1: French, and...and sometimes, *bueno* [=well]...when I have, er...a big time, I, er...I pass my...my holidays on, er...on climb mountains.
Teacher: Yes, you spend your holidays, ermm...practising exercise, you mean? Climbing up and down the mountains?
Student 1: Yeah.
Teacher: With your friends?
Student 1: Yeah.
Teacher: And you...and you?
Student 2: No, no I didn't.
Teacher: You didn't. You don't look like a...being a climber!
Student 2: No! I spend...I used to spend my holidays in Palencia. Or, er...I used to, ermm...go to know, er...the ous...the outskirts, the...Mad...of Madrid.

Teacher: Good.

Student 2: Er...the bor...bordering province.

Teacher: Yes. Good. So you...

Student 2: Such as Toledo, Segovia...

Teacher: Right. It's a very good thing, at least you know places. And, er...anybody can tell me...

[Fade out and in]

Teacher: Right, so...Umm...you are going to...for example, every pair of students, every pair of you, er...is going to think...or to say aloud three...well, three would be too much, two...two each, eh? Two each, four altogether. Two sentences talking about, er...past habits, eh? Past routines. But the more incredible the better, do you know why? Because then the other group, hmm?...has to tell if the sentences they said, hmm?...were true or false. Right?

[Fade out and in]

Student: True. And the second is false.

Teacher: Right, so. You have a...perfectly right. So, er...

Student: Two points.

Teacher: Two points, for group B. Two points. Right, er...Sonia and, er...Fagita. Come on.

Fagita: Er...Sonia w...when Sonia was ten, er...she used to live on a farm.

Teacher: On a farm? Good. Another one?

Fagita: Er...when Sonia was, er...five, er...she used to have bl...very blonde hair.

Teacher: [laughs] Good. What about you? Oh, I have forgotten about yours, Margerita. All right?

Sonia: Er...when Fagita was ten I used, er...to speak five language.

Teacher: She used to speak five languages. Or you? Fagita or you?

Sonia: Fagita.

Teacher: Fagita used to speak five languages. Good. And another one?

Sonia: Er...when she, er...he was, er...four I used to help, ermm...his mother.

Teacher: You used to help her mother.

Sonia: In the cooking.

Teacher: Cooking. Doing the cooking and so on? What's your opinion, er...[inaudible] on Fagita's sentences, true or false?

Student 7: I think, er...the last sentence in...is true, and, er...first is false.

Teacher: What's your opinion? Were you bluffing, or were you telling the truth? .

Fagita: I, er...wa...bluffing.

Teacher: You were bluffing? Number one? So?

Fagita: No.

Student: Yes!

Fagita: No, the two. The two sentences are, er...bluffing.

Teacher: So, how many points?

Student: One.

Teacher: Only one? OK. But I forgot about Margerita, so I have to for...forget about it. So only one person in each group, all right? What about you two? Come on!

Carmen: When did you...?

Teacher: [laughs] Don't be so impatient, Carmen!

Student 8: Er...no, er...Carmen, the last year, er...met, er...handsome man, er...and she is going to get married with...

Carmen: Yes! I am going to marry! This year!

Teacher: We are not using 'used to', but it's OK. And the second one? Try to use 'used to'.

Student 8: OK, er...er...she used to...to have, ermm...ermm...ermm...I don't...know...

Teacher: A small...? Cat, at home?

Student 8: No...in the...

Teacher: A what?

Student 8: A snake.

Teacher: A snake?

Student 8: Yes.

Teacher: My goodness! She used to have a snake at home. Right, remember them. What about you, Carmen? Tell me something incredible about you.

Carmen: I used to, ermm...working a nurse.

Teacher: As a nurse?

Carmen: As a nurse.

Teacher: Oh! Good. She used to work as a nurse. And, er...another one.

Carmen: Er...Santa Marina, er...

Teacher: No, another sentence. A new one. Another one, yes.

Carmen: Only one, now.

Teacher: [laughs] Just one sentence! And enough, for you. A lot of work. All right. Could you tell me if, ermm...just to finish, if, er...it is false?

Student 3: I think, er...your name?

Student 4: Arantxa.

Student 3: Arantxa is bluffing.

Teacher: Yes?

Student 3: In both.

Teacher: In both?

Student: In both.

Teacher: Were you bluffing?

Student: Yes, I was.

Teacher: So you are completely right. So...

Student: Two points. [pron: as French]

Teacher: Poi...no, two points [pron: correct]. Team B. OK, so we cannot go on, so we can say that...the winner is...group B!

[Fade out]

Talking about teaching

Teacher: Of course, I think, er...drills are very useful. But, er...in some ways, I mean, I prefer to present the new language first...I mean make them feel motivated with, er...the language, try...I...I try to make them, um...use the language, the new language, as their own. So, when I present a...a new passage, hmm?...first of all I...I make, er...questions about, ermm...their own life, their own feelings, their own, ermm...hobbies. Hmm? So I...I force them to use the new language, using them. And, er...well after...presenting the...the, umm...the new language of course, er...I...I made...I made them, er...work in pairs, hmm? So, this is something they like a lot. Because they...they don't feel on their own but, er...with a partner's help they...they

do it much better. And if I play some background
music [laughs]...even better! Because they feel more
relaxed and, er...they...they speak, er...more loudly
and so on.
Of course they commit, ermm...mistakes. But, today
was not the, ermm...the day to force them to speak
accurately. But just should get familiar with, er...the
new structure, the new language, and reproduce it,
and...getting it as their own.

Source: D. Lubeleska and M. Matthews, pp. 48, 50–1, 126–8 from *Looking at Language Classrooms*. Cambridge: Cambridge University Press, 1997. © Cambridge University Press, 1997.

overview of what is occurring in each of the classes. Clearly it would be useful to have access to the video material, but the transcripts also show a lot of detail.

In this first extract we are invited to consider the area of lesson planning. The first task is to 'brainstorm' the topic with a colleague wherever possible.

If you have access to the video, the 'while viewing' task is for teachers to add details of the interaction formats or procedures (the trainers' notes contain answers).

Finally, examine the transcript and reflect on the teacher's comments at the end.

When you have completed the above, read the transcript below, recorded from a third year Intermediate Class at the British Council Centre, Rabat, Morocco. The data are from a follow-up lesson on how to make and respond to polite request, based on Unit 6 of *Developing Strategies* by Abbs and Freebairn (1981).

Consider the following questions in relation to the transcript. Again work with a colleague if at all possible.

1 Analyse the four main activities that the teacher asks the learners to perform. Consider them in relation to the concept of integrated skills.
2 Observe what the learners appear to be doing during these activities. Analyse pair/group arrangements in relation to activity.
3 Do the activities seem useful in realizing the objectives of the lesson?
4 How much teacher talk is there in relation to student talk? What are the different functions of the teacher talk and when does it occur?
5 How much correction and feedback does the teacher provide? Does it seem to be equal for all learners?
6 Do you feel that this is a teacher- or a student-centred lesson? Why? Note what the teacher says himself.
7 Allwright and Bailey (1991) mention the 'atmosphere' created in the classroom co-production. How would you characterize the atmosphere of this particular class?

[16:00]   *   *   *   *   *   *

(Second Lesson)

T:	Let's imagine now then that you're talking to your wife Boujemaa. What, what do you say to your wife here?
BOUJEMAA:	Do you think – er – you could – er wa . . . er – no, wash the – the car for me please?
T:	And how – how would you answer Matgozata.
MATGOZATA:	If you want . . . (laughter) . . .
T:	She's a lovely wife isn't she. OK . . . that's charming that is. Can we have another one – um. You're having dinner Mrs Khadraoui and you're feeling very, very tired so what do you say to your husband?
GHITA:	I wonder if you'd mind washing up for me.
T:	OK, what I would like to do now, I'm going to give you a few of these cards each if you could work 2 or 3 people together and just practise asking each other for things. OK? But first of all decide who you are. Are you friends or are you acquaintances. OK. If you could work with René. And if you two could, could work together perhaps. And if you two wouldn't mind working together. Or perhaps you three could work together here. OK. Good.
MATGOZATA:	Oh thank you very much.
GHITA:	Here you are.
MATGOZATA:	Mine is broken.
GHITA:	OK.
GHITA:	Oh la have you got a screwdriver Matgozata?
MATGOZATA:	Yes I have one.
GHITA:	Could you – er – could you pass me yours. I . . . I . . . broked mine.
MATGOZATA:	Yes of course . . . it's no problem.
MATGOZATA:	. . . Oh . . . lovely . . . suitcase . . . can you . . .
RENÉ:	Would you mind phoning to my wife please.
T:	Would you mind phoning my wife please.
RENÉ:	My wife please – yes.
BOUJEMAA:	Certainly.
RENÉ:	Yes – um – yeh. Would you mind – er – washing the dishes please.
BOUJEMAA:	Um – that's difficult but – er – I going to do that.
T:	Can I ask a little question here. Who are you talking to here a friend or – or – an acquaintance?

BOUJEMAA:	Er . . . no . . . as . . . er . . .
RENÉ:	It's not a friend.
T:	Not a friend . . . somebody you know a little.
RENÉ:	Yeh.
T:	OK, excuse me, would you mind listening to me for the moment? OK – for homework last night I asked you to write some short dialogues for the pictures on – on page 47. If you remember, I hope you've done your homework have you? Done your homework Hilly?
HILLY:	No.
T:	Would you mind leaving the classroom. No I'm not serious. OK if you look at these 6 pictures now, for which some of you have prepared dialogues at home. Now could you just practise them with the person next, next to you first of all. OK and be very careful about who you are talking to again. OK. Just go through the 6 dialogues you've prepared for homework. But listen, just a second please, just a second. Before you start. Don't do all of them. If you could do the first two perhaps, and if you could practise the second two, and if you could practise the next two and if you could practise the first two again. OK. Carry on please.

[19:18]   *   *   *   *   *   *

s:	Do you think – er – you would made me – do you think.
s:	. . . er . . . open.
s:	Yes . . . oh . . . ah . . . you could help me to open the car . . . er . . . because I have a lot of to carry.
s:	Yes Mama of course.

[19:40]   *   *   *   *   *   *

T:	OK now then. I'd like to listen to some of this homework now. – like er – could you do number 1 for me – er – Boujemaa or René.
BOUJEMAA:	Yes, er . . . Do you think you could lift my suitcase down for me please?
RENÉ:	Of course.

T: Now then, we're going to do something a little different now, you will all need pen and paper, we're going to do a little bit of dictation, but not the usual kind of dictation. I don't want you to write what I say. I want you to write what the characters in my story say. OK. The first thing I'll do is introduce you to the characters. There they are. Mary and Jane. Now

Mary and Jane are two girls who live in the same street. They're very good friends and they're both typists and they work in a big office in the city centre. Now their boss is a man called Mr Smith, but we'll meet him later. Now I'm going to tell you the story and I want you to write what the people say. Whenever I want you to write I'll stop and give you time to write. All right? Before you write what a person says write the person's name as well. OK? So. One day Mary and Jane are working in the office and Mary asked Jane for a cigarette, so write what Mary says please.

[21:42] * * * * * *

T:	OK so we've got Mary, Jane and Mr Smith.
S:	The boss.
T:	OK the boss yes. Could you shut your books. Let's try it again without the books. OK carry on.
GHITA:	Have you got a cigarette Mary?
MATGOZATA:	Yes, of course, here you are.
GHITA:	Thank you.

DRISS:	Why are you smoking in the office? You know that, that I hate it. Er – now – er – Mary do you – er – would you mind opening – er – the window please.
GHITA:	Yes of course, I'm terribly sorry, sir.
T:	She looks sorry too doesn't she. Alright [sic] good. So I've got a text here, it's all about Sandra but what I've done is I've cut the text up into little pieces and I want you to rearrange the pieces in sequence, so that what you have is one long story.

[22:45] * * * * * *

S:	Do you agree.
T:	Let's see what Wafaa thinks . . . what do you think Wafaa?
WAFAA:	. . . I think . . . er . . . er . . . you put it . . . er . . . now.
S:	I think this is the . . .
S:	You think . . . me too . . . me too . . . I think it is my place here.
S:	I take another.
T:	Shall, shall I bring some boxing gloves?
S:	Yes.
T:	Some boxing gloves for you two.
S:	No . . . no problem.
T:	Try and work it out together then.
DRISS:	. . . . my boss. . . . by the way. . . . I thought my job was going to be really interesting . . . and – er.

GHITA:	Well I'm called a programme assistant but I'm really secretary, I type the letters and make tea for my boss.
MATGOZATA:	Yes, it, it's good and – er – and I, I've always wanted to work in the media but I'm a bit – er . . . now, my boyfriend, ah Mark also works there.
GHITA:	Ah yes . . . video technician . . . yes . . . ah . . . that's right . . . yes.

(*inaudible*)

T:	There it is yes thanks good. You carry on with what you're doing then. Good Driss, you're here, but I've got you as being absent yesterday too. Boujemma – Boujemma [*sic*] is not very good on the register is he.
DRISS:	He's not . . . er . . . a true friend.
T:	And Ghita you, you were absent as well yesterday . . . ah this is ridiculous. Good, and Mohamed – still away.
GHITA:	Yes he, he has a lot of work.
T:	Ah, very busy time.
GHITA:	Yes very busy yes.
T:	OK, and Matgozata.
MATGOZATA:	Yes.
T:	Good. You're here – how's – how's Farouk at the moment – how's Farouk – not well.
MATGOZATA:	He's not very very well.
T:	Is he working hard as well?
MATGOZATA:	Yes.
T:	OK. You carry on.

(*Group of 3 men*)

T: OK if you just stop for a second. Our time is almost finished, so we have to wind up here. If you want to see the correct sequence of the text, the text is on page 45 in your books. OK. Now we haven't got any time now but in the lesson tomorrow, well there's no lesson tomorrow [*sic*] it's the weekend isn't it? OK in the lesson on Monday I'll go over this text with you and we'll see if there – if there are any problems of understanding. OK, anyway thanks very much and I'll see you on Monday. Have a nice weekend all of you.

SS: Thank you . . . thank you very much.

T: They prefer the – um – the second kind of lesson, the lesson where they have control because the kind of English they're interested in is social English and they have very little opportunity for practising their English here in Morocco, so for them a – a large part of a lesson in fact is just to be in a situation and with people, so that they can speak English. In general I think a – a good teacher is one who can stimulate his class without dominating it and – er – create a relaxed atmosphere without turning it into – er – an afternoon tea party.

[26:00]   *   *   *   *   *   *

Source: The British Council, *Teaching and Learning in Focus*, Edited Lessons vol. 2, pp. 22–5 © The British Council, 1983.

13.7 Conclusion

In this chapter we have examined the reasons why classrooms are useful sources of information about teaching and learning and have considered some of the different criteria that we might want to observe in them. After this, we moved on to look at some of the different options open to us for observing the classroom. We then suggested that we might wish to concentrate in some detail on one aspect of the language classroom, such as teacher talk, or that we may wish to observe several criteria together, depending on our purpose. We then proposed a set of general observation criteria that we might find useful in order to get an overview of what is happening in a classroom. Finally, we examined transcribed data from different classrooms and applied focusing tasks to this data to try to gain further access to, and understanding of, what was occurring in these classrooms.

How might your approach to what you do in the classroom be affected as a result of reading this chapter?

13.8 Further reading

The following books give a useful overview of the area of classroom observation:

1   Allwright, R. L. and K. Bailey (1991): *Focus on the Language Classroom.*
2   Bailey, K. and D. Nunan (eds) (1996): *Voices from the Language Classroom.*

14

Views of the Teacher

14.1   Introduction

Chapters on 'the teacher' are often, even traditionally, to be found at the end of books concerned with aspects of language teaching methodology. While such a format might be criticized on the grounds of relegating teachers to last place on a scale of importance, with learners certainly, but also materials and methods, having primacy, in the present book this is emphatically not the intention, and the position of this chapter is deliberate. It has been chosen because the teacher arguably represents the most significant factor in any language teaching operation. The teacher is typically a 'constant' in the throughput of different students in the institution, and works in different ways at the interface of several systems – the classroom, the school, the educational environment – all of which affect a teacher's professional attitudes and behaviour. A principal aim of this chapter, then, is to offer a view of the teacher as a synthesizer of all the aspects we have covered, as a professional who has to make sense of the decisions, opinions and perceptions of many different people. Certainly teachers will often experience this as pressure and conflict, which may be difficult to resolve. Nevertheless, we wish to stress the importance of a positive and active professional self-image, rather than a more passive and reactive one.

The chapter is broadly divided into three sections. In the first of these we examine the concept of 'role' and explore its possible dimensions for English language teachers in general. We then go on to look particularly at the teacher's classroom role, focusing on the implications of innovation and change in materials and methods. These two sections, in other words, will be concerned first, with contextualizing 'role' and, secondly, with differences over time. Finally, a number of issues to do with the training and development of teachers will be raised, including a brief survey of the growing importance of teacher-research in ELT. We have included more activities and things to think about because of the nature of the topic and its reflective orientation, and the chapter finishes, quite intentionally, on an open-ended note.

14.2   The teacher's role

Make a few notes on what you actually do as a teacher in a regular working week. Keep the notes – we shall refer back to them later.

Our own list looks something like this:

Preparing timetables
Spending a certain number of contracted hours in class
Preparing materials and handouts
Seeing students individually
Attending staff meetings
Arranging out-of-class activities
Writing reports
Marking tests and examinations
Planning courses and their associated teaching activities
Liaison with outside bodies and other institutions.

There are two obvious points to be made here. The first concerns the fact that any job specification is part of a network of interacting and overlapping roles; secondly, and related to the first point, we do our job in the context of a whole 'environment'. This now takes us full circle, and we shall be referring back explicitly to the points first raised in chapter 1.

The concept of 'role'

Role theory is a very large topic on which a great deal has been written: it is, for example, a major research field in social psychology and related areas, including the investigation of behaviour in industrial and organizational settings. We can only touch on it here, and draw a few implications for the EFL teacher's work.

The list you have just made will show that you carry out a range of specified tasks within the social framework of an institutional structure. It is, then, self-evident that your work is not done in isolation, but that you need to interact, directly or indirectly, with a number of others – with students, obviously, with other teachers, with the head teacher (or head of department/principal), with non-teaching staff and so on. Both in your professional and in your private life you are a member of a *role set*, the group of people with whom you interact in any particular situation. Taking yourself as the 'focal person' (Handy, 1985), you might like to represent your own most important role sets in diagrammatic form as in figure 14.1. You could also do this with family and friends as the set, or alternatively for any leisure activity that you do regularly. Wright (1987) makes a further distinction between role set and *role network*, the latter signifying roles in some kind of hierarchical relationship to each other where each person accepts or at least understands the organizational chain of authority and accountability. One example of how this view works in practice can be found in

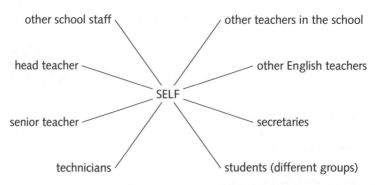

Figure 14.1 The role network.

the scheme organized by the British Council for inspecting and recognizing private language schools in the UK. As well as the obvious categories of 'teaching' and 'professional qualifications', the extent to which a school performs its central teaching function is also evaluated in terms of the overall management structures, in addition to resources and the physical environment of the institution. Thus a classroom teacher might be accountable to a senior teacher and through him to the principal, but also 'laterally', to colleagues with special areas of responsibility such as resource management.

A number of important points follow from these general features of the concept of 'role'. We shall take just three of them here.

1 We noted above the significant members of our own role set in any specific situation. The 'mirror image' of this, of course, is that *we* fulfil certain roles in the role sets and networks of other people: we are therefore at any one time colleagues, employees, perhaps authority figures in the classroom, somebody's superior, a casual acquaintance and so on. There will also be differences in what is accepted as appropriate institutional behaviour, and great variation in patterns of power and authority.

2 There is arguably a great deal of truth in the assertion that 'we are as others see us'. In other words, our image of ourselves as professionals will be an amalgam of a whole range of perceptions and expectations, and this takes us beyond the idea of a role as simply a list of tasks to be carried out, or an officially issued job description. Bush (1984), for example, refers to the theatrical image used by several writers in which the actor plays out a role in accordance with the expectations of an audience. This implies, however, that the actor is rather a passive figure: Bush goes on to remind us that a role is not tidy and objective, but that 'in practice the role-occupant brings to the position his or her values, perceptions and experience and these will interact with other expectations to determine the way the part is played' (76). Moreover the notion of a 'network' indicates that different people's expectations will carry different degrees of importance: for instance, an

organization with a powerful authority figure at the head may lead to a reduction in the weight attached to student views and needs.

3   Most writing in the field of role theory recognizes – as indeed the previous points imply – that people inevitably perceive their own role as multiple and complex. A number of secondary notions have therefore evolved that reflect this. Handy's (1985, ch. 3) list is comprehensive, and makes rather negative but probably realistic reading. He points out that a role occupant can experience one or more of the following, which are interrelated:

* *Role conflict* – for example, our role as a classroom teacher and as an institutional examiner may not be fully compatible.
* *Role ambiguity* – defined by uncertainty as to what is expected at any particular time.
* *Role overload* – not the same as work overload – where the focal person is not able to integrate roles that are too many and too varied. Many teachers who are required to take on increased administrative or external duties may experience this as a problem.
* *Role stress* – which Handy divides into role pressure (positive, where synthesis of roles and expectations remains possible), and its opposite, role strain.

Earlier in this section you drew up a simple 'role set' diagram with yourself as the focal person.
Consider now the range of roles that you play in your own institution. To whom are you responsible, and who is responsible to you? Do any of Handy's points match your own experience, for example as a result of increasing role diversification? In particular, is your own perception of your role(s) fully in line with what you take to be the expectations of others?

As Wright (1987: 5) briefly remarks, 'there is more to a role than just doing a job'.

The wider environment

Up to now, we have been thinking of teachers in the setting of their own institutions. However, crucial as that is, the concept of 'role' cannot be restricted to the institution in which we work, and in a sense, our workplace is a microcosm of the wider environment. In the first chapter of this book we proposed a framework for thinking about materials and methods in which a number of contextual variables – management decisions, resource factors, types of learners, and many more – were considered. Here we re-examine them from the perspective of the teacher as a 'focal person', and taking into account such factors as the teacher's potentially multiple roles, the expectations of others, and the inherent possibilities for conflict, pressure and so on. We might represent

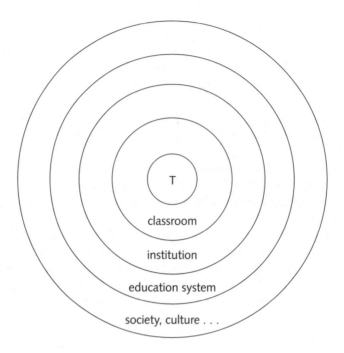

Figure 14.2   The teaching environment.

the situation as in figure 14.2 to show both the importance of the teacher as well as the direct and indirect effects of all these different 'layers' on the teacher's role.

> Beyond the immediate environment of your own institution/school, try to enumerate from the outer layers in particular (a) the people (the other 'actors') and (b) the variables that you think have most influenced your understanding of your own role.

You may have listed your family and friends, or your own tutors; your students' peer groups and parents; external inspectors or advisers; the authorities who draw up your contract and decide on your salary and conditions; the writers of commercially published materials; agencies and organizations sponsoring students to take your programmes. For example, low pay sometimes indicates low social esteem of the profession and even low self-esteem, and may in turn mean there is a need to take on extra work, leaving no time for any more than routine preparation of classes, certainly not professional development. Conversely, the combination of a consultative environment that considers the views of everyone involved both within and outside the institution, and a recognition that teachers may be more active and productive if they are given time to develop resources, for example, will clearly lead to a more positive working atmosphere.

A useful way of looking at these issues from the teacher's point of view was set out some time ago by Strevens (1979) in terms of the concept of 'control'. Apart from variables to do with the learner, which it is not necessary to list again here (except to note that our learners can exercise control, often legitimately, in a variety of ways), Strevens offers the two broad headings of *community-controlled* variables and *teacher-controlled* variables. A few representative examples are given here. Community-controlled variables include

- cultural norms and restrictions, for instance on materials or teaching styles
- standards of teacher training
- status of teachers in society
- attitudes to target language

Under this heading he also includes institutional factors, such as class size, resources, time available and so on. Sometimes, of course, these may be directly within an institution's control; often they are not. Teacher-controlled variables include

- approaches to syllabus design
- materials evaluation (and production)
- choice of methodology, techniques, classroom organization (see next section for a fuller discussion)

You may of course disagree with some of the details of where exactly the responsibility lies, but the 'control' notion is helpful in describing the many different facets of a teacher's role.

14.3   *Teachers in the classroom: change and innovation*

The chameleon

The full title of the article that we have just referred to is 'Differences in teaching for different circumstances or the teacher as chameleon' (Strevens, 1979). This is a striking image, and your dictionary will tell you that a chameleon is a type of lizard whose most significant characteristic is 'its ability to change its skin colour to match its surroundings' (*Longmans English Larousse*). While we certainly do not wish to suggest that teachers merely change to conform as a reaction to their working environment, this capacity to adapt to new circumstances, particularly over time, is a vital one. Strevens reinforces the point that we have made before, that no teaching/learning situation is really static. Political and educational circumstances change, as do resources available for teacher training; views of methodology change, as does the language itself; research is gradually disseminated; teachers develop; learners' expectations change; and there is a great increase in international travel. (The extent to which the elements of change can be considered positive is a separate issue, and is too context-specific to be examined in detail here.) Most of our discussion in this section will focus on the teacher's *classroom* role, picking up the key implications for teachers of the materials and methods examined in this book.

> We would like you at this point to try to set out the most important changes in your own job, and role, over the last few years (5–10 years might be a useful period if you have been teaching that long). For example, do you have new areas of responsibility, either administrative or pedagogic? Have there been many innovations in the types of materials used? Have your students' attitudes to learning English changed in any discernible way? Are there any techniques you have adopted in the classroom that you did not use a few years ago, or conversely, have you abandoned any? Some of the changes you identify will be concerned with your role within the classroom, some with your role outside. In so far as they are separable, please take more time to think about the *classroom* context – learners, materials, methods.

Teachers will all have their own version of changing circumstances. The present writers, who teach English at most proficiency levels to adults coming to Britain for a variety of purposes, noted these general trends:

- Students will often have spent time in an English-speaking country already.
- Classes have become increasingly participatory.
- More detailed attention to needs and expectations is required of us, and for an ESP teacher this often includes some familiarity with learners' jobs or subject specialisms.
- There is a great amount of published material now available, appropriate in varying degrees.
- We spend more time engaged in various forms of individualized instruction.

In sum, we think it likely that your role will have become more diversified on many fronts.

Before going on to identify some of the more specific aspects of classroom-based change, it is worth reflecting for a moment on the sources of innovation in language teaching. Prabhu (1987: 105) makes a valuable distinction between 'voluntary' change on the one hand, and 'statutory' or imposed change on the other. He writes:

> A new perception in pedagogy, implying a different pattern of classroom activity, is an intruder into teachers' mental frames – an unsettling one, because there is . . . a threat to prevailing routines and to the sense of security dependent on them. If, however, there is no compulsion to adopt new routines . . . the sense of security is largely protected and teachers' existing perceptions may then begin to interact with the new one and be influenced by it (an influence likely to be beneficial). Statutory

implementation of an innovation, by contrast, is likely to distort all these processes and aggravate the tensions in teachers' mental frames resulting in either
outright rejection, or at least rejection of the rationale behind the innovation.

In other words, the argument here is that statutory imposition may lead to
conformity and routine efficiency, but will be less likely to become part of a
teacher's own repertoire and to form the basis for personal development. Gaies
and Bowers (1990: 170) suggest the following as examples of 'statutory' decisions:

- the adoption of new textbooks
- the introduction of pedagogical/methodological 'reforms' that teachers have
  not been trained to implement
- the establishment of new goals for a language teaching programme
- the prescription of new teacher–learner role relationships (as when a central
  authority specifies less 'teacher-fronted' and more 'learner-centred' work).

It will be useful, then, to regard Prabhu's distinction as implicit throughout this
section.

Change, materials and methods

The main purpose of this book has been to survey current trends in materials
and methods for English language teaching, to trace the sources and development of those trends, and to link our everyday practice as teachers with the
principles on which that practice is based. Let us now briefly review some of the
themes that have recurred with reference to the classroom context.

1 There has been a significant shift towards more 'communicative' views of
   both language and behaviour, which in turn has led to, on the one hand,
2 an analysis of language that includes, but also goes beyond, sentence grammar
   to the level of 'discourse' – of paragraph structure and longer texts – and the
   incorporation of such an analytic framework into teaching materials. And
   on the other hand,
3 the acceptance and adoption of a variety of classroom 'management' techniques designed to allow for more realistic practice of language in use;
4 syllabuses and materials are often based not only on one or two, but on
   several organizing principles linked together in quite complex ways: the
   'multi-syllabus' idea tries to capture this complexity;
5 research into the characteristics of language skills has contributed to gradual
   changes in the materials we use for teaching reading and listening comprehension, as well as the productive skills of writing and speaking. For
   instance, the range of possible activities has been extended a long way beyond
   the traditional procedures of reading/listening, followed by a test of understanding through comprehension questions. In other words, we can now
   work with a notion of language-as-process, as well as language-as-product;

6   our methodology has also been affected by increased understanding of dif-
    ferences in learning styles and strategies, justifying the distinction between
    whole-class and smaller group work, and also allowing, where feasible, for
    the individualization of instruction in various formats.

Not all of these developments have taken place simultaneously, of course: the
various aspects of change have had differential impact and usefulness, and have
naturally occurred at different times in different contexts, as you will be well aware
from your own teaching situation. Note, too, that sometimes an innovation has
direct implications for what a teacher in some sense needs to know (knowledge
about text structure, for example, or the psychology of comprehension). At
other times it influences attitudes and perceptions about appropriate roles and
behaviour as well (such as restructuring the classroom arrangement or introducing self-access material). We can now reflect on how these perspectives
have contributed to the diversification of the teacher's role that we referred to
earlier.

1   Consider this general point of Littlewood's (1981: 92): 'The concept of the
    teacher as "instructor" is . . . inadequate to describe his overall function.'
2   Do you agree with this statement? If so, what other concepts might be
    useful in contributing to a fuller picture of the teacher's overall role?

A number of writers on methodology and teacher training have proposed
various ways of labelling the language teacher's potential roles. Harmer (2001b:
58ff.) offers these:

1   The teacher as *controller* of everything that goes on in the classroom.
2   The teacher as *organizer* (classroom manager) of a range of activities.
3   The teacher as *assessor*. Obviously the 'examiner' role is one of our tradi-
    tional functions, but Harmer extends it to include the importance of giving
    regular feedback, as well as just correction and grading.
4   The teacher as *prompter*, encouraging students by 'nudging' them forwards.
5   The teacher as *participant* (co-communicator) in an organized activity such
    as debate or role play.
6   The teacher as *resource* (consultant, adviser), most obviously as a language
    informant.
7   The teacher as *tutor*, particularly useful with small groups and individuals
    working on longer pieces of work.
8   The teacher as *observer*, both to give feedback but also to evaluate materials
    and methods.

Littlewood points out that these various roles can be put together under the
'umbrella' idea of the teacher as *facilitator* of learning. (He has a comparable
list to Harmer, and his own terms are included above in brackets.)

To give just two more examples. Bartram and Walton (1991: 104) see the teacher as

- social organizer
- encourager
- timekeeper
- counsellor
- educator
- language arbiter

Finally, Tudor (1993) discusses teacher roles with specific reference to the notion of the 'learner-centred classroom', arguing that this shift of focus will have obvious implications for that role. Far from the traditional conception, then, of 'knower' and 'activity organizer', the teacher will need to

- prepare learners (for awareness of goals, language and so on);
- analyse learner needs;
- select materials;
- transfer responsibility;
- involve learners;

which are challenging roles for many of us.

1 Look back over the list of teacher functions that you made earlier: to what extent does it overlap with/differ from the (fairly representative) list that we have just set out?
2 Now try to put the individual points in order of importance for your own teaching circumstances. For instance, are you primarily an instructor/assessor and only secondarily a 'resource' for your students?
3 If you are studying/working with other teachers, it will be interesting to compare your order of priority with theirs. Do colleagues working in the same situation necessarily have identical perceptions? And do teachers from different contexts see things differently from you?

As a short commentary on this activity, and to conclude this section, two observations can be restated. First of all, the roles and tasks that we perform result from a complex network of factors, and an objective definition, however necessary, will not be sufficient. They derive from our own perceptions, from the attitudes and expectations of many others, and not least from the language teaching materials that we are expected (or choose) to work with. Secondly, and finally, it should be remembered that this whole discussion has been based on the assumption that change and innovation are an inevitable part of our professional lives, and therefore no individual role description can be regarded as frozen in time.

14.4 Preparing the teachers

The 'good language teacher'

The idea that it is possible to characterize the 'good language learner' is, as we saw in chapters 3 and 12, now quite well established, and several researchers have investigated the types of learning strategies that successful learners appear to use. It would be logical to hope that teachers could eventually be described in a similar way, but the sheer number of variables involved in teaching will probably mean that this remains an impossible task. Even if we were to take the very straightforward criterion that a 'successful' teacher is one whose learners achieve good examination results, this in fact tells us rather little: we do not learn much about the relative importance of the teacher's preferred style and method, nor about the role of materials, and certainly nothing specific about the part played by different elements in an individual learner's success. Indeed this may have more to do with motivation, attitude, interest and so on, than with anything the teacher has to offer directly. Nevertheless, and despite the impossibility of precise measurement, most of us will have an opinion as to what constitutes a 'good language teacher'.

> Assume that you have some responsibility for the selection of English language teachers for the specific context in which you work. Make a list of the qualities you would be looking for in that selection process.

Your suggested list may contain some of the following, and you may have others that we have not thought of:

Knowledge of the language system
Good pronunciation
Experience of living in an English-speaking country
Qualifications (perhaps further training taken, or in-service development)
Classroom performance
Evidence of being a good colleague
Length of time as a teacher
Ability to write teaching materials
Careful planning of lessons
Same L_1 as students, or a sound knowledge of it
Experience of a variety of teaching situations
Personal qualities (outgoing, interested in learners and so on)
Publications
Knowledge of learning theories
Wide vocabulary
Ability to manage a team of teachers

We should note here that this list includes factors of different kinds: some are specific to (English) language teaching, while others are more to do with the general qualities that might be expected of all teachers. Day (1990) formalizes this by referring to the distinction between *subject matter* knowledge and *action-system* knowledge. In his words, the former 'refers to the specific information needed by teachers to teach content' (the language system, for example), and the latter to 'information dealing with teaching and learning in general, regardless of the subject matter. Included in action-system knowledge are such issues as classroom management and teacher expectations' (43). Although it is difficult to categorize our list of teacher qualities under one heading or the other in any precise way, Day's basic distinction is quite helpful when considering the 'training' of teachers, to which we now turn.

Teacher training, teacher education

Opinions as to the necessary and desirable qualities of a teacher form the basis for the specification (whether by education authorities, training bodies, colleges and so on) of the goals of teacher training and teacher education programmes. Detailed design of such programmes will in turn derive from this setting of aims and objectives.

There is a large literature on the issue of 'training' versus 'education', and on the more concrete design specifications for a variety of training programmes for different levels of experience, different contexts, differing in duration and with varying degrees of generalizability. A few references are given in the further reading section at the end of this chapter. It has not been the purpose of this book to conclude with a detailed proposal for a particular kind of teacher preparation programme, a topic well covered elsewhere, but rather to trace developments and trends in materials and methods in our field and then to ask, in this final chapter, what might be the most appropriate perspectives on the role and training of teachers. With this in mind we look, first, at the relevance of the training/education debate, and secondly, invite you to formulate your own ideas for the in-service preparation of teachers.

Sometimes the notion of 'training' is used to refer to pre-service programmes for new teachers, with 'education' the preferred term for in-service work with experienced professionals. The idea here is that the narrower concept of training is more applicable to people who need to acquire a knowledge of the basic 'tools' of the job, whereas education implies a broader range of knowledge and skills. More usually, it is argued that *both* beginning *and* experienced teachers need elements of each, albeit with differing emphasis and depth. If we glance back at the list of possible teacher qualities, it is quite difficult to claim that some are relevant in pre- or, conversely, in-service situations. Pennington (1990: 134) relates the issue to the concept of professionalism, and argues that teachers require both 'a repertoire of skills' and 'judgement to apply these skills'. Richards (1990) puts forward a similar distinction with the terms 'macro' and 'micro' as approaches to teacher preparation. By 'micro' he means techniques – what teachers actually do that is directly observable and quantifiable (amount of teacher talk, questioning techniques, types of classroom tasks and the like). By 'macro' he means a 'holistic' approach that focuses on 'the total context of classroom teaching and learning in an attempt to understand how the interactions between and among teachers, learners and classroom tasks affect learning' (9). In other words, a macro approach is concerned with a teacher's ability to make judgements and inferences, to explore the relationship between different types of activity and their effect on learning, and to raise questions about one's own practice. It is both exploratory and generative. Clearly a teacher needs to be familiar with both kinds of approach.

1   We would like to ask you now to consider the design of a possible teacher preparation programme. In order to keep the task within manageable proportions, we suggest a number of guidelines.
2   Assume you have responsibility for planning an *in*-service course for teachers. Think in terms of a short programme of one or two weeks' duration, and relate your planning to a teaching context with which you are familiar.

   • What components would you wish to include?
   • Approximately what proportion of time would you devote to each one?
   • What would be your preferred methodology – lectures, workshops, discussion, observation of teaching?
   • To what extent, if at all, would you give consideration to participants' personal proficiency?
   • If possible, try also to decide whether you are more concerned with 'macro' or 'micro' approaches, and with 'subject matter' or 'action-system' knowledge, as we defined them earlier in this section.

We have worked with a number of different groups of teachers from many different countries, and have also asked them to design a teacher programme along these kinds of lines. Some groups have chosen to work on a specific area or theme only. Examples would be 'Approaches to Skills Teaching and Learning', 'The Development of Self-access Materials' or 'Communicative Methodology'. More often, these teachers have designed a broader-based programme, and the following content headings are typical (the points are not given in any particular order and are illustrative, not rules):

Errors: analysis and treatment
Syllabus design and lesson planning
Materials evaluation
Principles of learning
Audio-visual aids

Observation of teaching (using video if possible)
Preparing supplementary materials
Using English outside the class
Sharing problems
Test design
Sound system of English

Suggested methodology of presentation is a mixture of lecture input and workshop-discussion, depending on the area under consideration. Our groups have placed particular emphasis on the importance of working out in advance the needs and interests of teachers on such an in-service course, and on the principle that a starting point of enquiry in everyday practice will usually be more fruitful than a rundown of theory for its own sake, however stimulating.

14.5 Teacher development and teacher research

At several points in the preceding section we indicated the importance of seeing language teachers not only as carriers of knowledge about language and techniques, but as active and questioning professionals who are able to make generalizations and inferences from the basis of their own practice. Ramani (1987) refers to this as 'theorizing from the classroom': she proposes a teacher training procedure the starting point for which is the sharing of subjective responses to various kinds of classroom data (see chapter 13 of this book for a number of examples). Just as 'training' is embedded in 'education', so this more exploratory perspective extends education itself into the idea of teacher *development*. These three overlapping but distinct views of teacher preparation – training, education, development – are seen by Wallace (1991) as three models, which he terms (a) the 'craft' model, where a range of practical techniques is learned from an experienced person; (b) the 'applied science' model, implying a one-way application, and often therefore separation, of theoretical research to practice; and (c) the 'reflective' model, with the teacher as a 'reflective practitioner'.

The notion of *critical reflection* is a rapidly growing area of attention because it is seen as the first step for teachers to become investigators of pedagogical issues, that is, classroom researchers. There is a long tradition in general education of encouraging classroom teachers to be *initiators* of research and development, as well as *recipients* of external investigation and results (for example by professional researchers or educational administrators). Research, in other words, is done 'by', not only 'on' or 'to' teachers, and is thus much more readily integrated into questions of practice. Hopkins (1993) offers a clear overview of 'the teacher as researcher', and also introduces the closely related concept of 'Action Research'. The key point, in Hopkins's words (1993: 7) is 'the teacher's ability . . . to think systematically and critically about what he or she is doing and to collaborate with other teachers. Central to this activity is the systematic reflection on one's own classroom experience to understand it and to create meaning out of that understanding.' Freeman (1996) puts it at its most basic: 'You have to know the story to tell the story'.

In ELT there is a growing literature on ways in which a 'reflective' approach – put simply, an attitude of curiosity – can lead to teacher-generated investigations. Burns, although referring to 'action research', makes the following point that is relevant to any kind of teacher-generated research: 'The major focus of action research is on concrete and practical issues ... It is conducted in naturally occurring settings ... Its approaches are essentially "participatory" in that they are conducted by and with members of the actual community under study' (1999: 24). She lists a wide range of areas nominated by teachers as starting points for such research, including affective factors, course design, materials and resources, learning strategies, classroom dynamics, the teaching of specific skills, and assessment (56–8). A similar perspective is put forward by Richards and Lockhart (1994), who discuss the following 'dimensions', each of which can of course be subdivided, as suitable for reflection and practical investigation:

- Exploring teachers' beliefs.
- Focus on the learner.
- Teacher decision-making.
- The role of the teacher.
- The structure of a language lesson.
- Interaction in the second-language classroom.
- The nature of language learning activities.
- Language use in the classroom.

There is no space here to discuss methods in detail. Briefly, however, all the following methods are possible even within modest and small-scale teacher research projects. In no particular order:

1 Classroom observation (systematic, open, descriptive).
2 Teaching and learning diaries and logs.
3 Introspection and verbal reports (such as think-aloud).
4 Questionnaires and surveys.
5 Interviews (structured, semi-structured, ethnographic).
6 Experiments and quasi-experiments.
7 Case study (not strictly a 'method'; normally uses a mix, to study individuals, groups, or specific contexts).

For details of available research methods, and for discussion of both quantitative and qualitative approaches, readers are referred to the references at the end of the chapter.

Finally, teacher development can also be equated with personal development. There are many activities that teachers can in principle engage in if they wish to extend their understanding of their role. They may, for instance, put themselves in the position of their students by learning another language (Gower, 1999; J. McDonough, 2002). They may choose to attend courses or workshops, join a local teachers' network, go to conferences, write a regular teaching diary, learn something about educational management or counselling. Obviously each individual's working environment will determine to what extent these courses of action are realistic. This whole area has been incorporated into various teachers' organizations, including TESOL (Teaching English to Speakers of Other Languages) and IATEFL (International Association of Teachers of English as a Foreign Language). IATEFL, for example, has associate organizations in a number of countries, and also runs several Special Interest Groups (SIGs), one of which in fact is concerned with Teacher Development.

Wallace's conclusion (1991: 166) offers an appropriate ending to this book too, which has throughout attempted to encourage teachers to think critically about the major aspects of their own everyday professional reality. Wallace writes:

> An important aim of the reflective approach to teacher education is to empower teachers to manage their own professional development. Surely few things could be more conducive to raising the standards of teaching than a cadre of teachers who have the skills, ability and motivation to develop their practice ... A second aim of this approach is to enable teachers to be more effective partners in innovation. In many situations teachers themselves are not recognized as possible agents of change ... innovation is always a top-down affair ... If foundations have been laid where, during their training period, at least some teachers have had an opportunity to be reflective and collaborative, then it might be possible for their professional expertise to be harnessed to implement innovation more effectively.

We would like you to consider two final questions here relating to your own development as a teacher:

1   What kinds of activities have you done – or would you like to do – outside the daily classroom context that are of professional interest to you? A little earlier we gave just a few examples, which you might like to refer back to.
2   What are some of the issues that concern you as a teacher? For instance, would you like to have a clearer picture of the contribution of group work techniques to learning? Are you interested in the 'acceptability' to different people of the errors that your learners make? Would you like to compare your experiences of a particular class with those of a colleague? How useful are bilingual dictionaries, and do they affect a student's memory for vocabulary? Would it be useful to carry out a longitudinal 'case study' of an individual learner? How can we match more closely the statutory teaching materials to learners' needs and interests?

But these only represent a few of *our* questions, and we leave you now to generate some of your own.

14.6 Further reading

1 Hopkins, D. (1993): *A Teachers Guide to Classroom Research*. This book was written in the context of mainstream education. The title is self-explanatory, as a way into issues of professional development.
2 The following texts offer an overview for language teacher preparation:
Harmer, J. (2001b): *The Practice of English Language Teaching*.
Richards, J. C. and D. Nunan (eds) (1990): *Second Language Teacher Education*.
Wallace, M. J. (1991): *Training Foreign Language Teachers*.
3 For practical discussion of teacher reflection and research in ELT, see Burns, A. (1999): *Collaborative Action Research for English Language Teachers*. Richards, J. C. and C. Lockhart (1994): *Reflective Teaching in Second Language Education*.
4 For a comprehensive overview of methods in the broader context of the theory and principles of research, see McDonough, J. and S. H. (1997): *Research Methods for English Language Teachers*.

Appendix:
Websites for ELT

Websites for teachers and learners can only be very selective. Many of the sites listed here also have extensive links to pages to other sites. These include TESOL, IATEFL and the British Council. Some newsletters, for example the *EL Gazette*, *IATEFL Newsletter* and so on also have regular columns. Some of the references cited (Eastment (1999), for example), have lists of sites.

1. Sites for learners

Dave's ESL Cafe (created for EFL/ESL students around the world, but also of use to teachers):
http://www.eslcafe.com

Focus on words (a vocabulary development page):
http://www.wordfocus.com/index.html

2. Sites of interest primarily for teachers

Organizations

IATEFL	http://www.iatefl.org
TESOL	http://www.tesol.edu
BALEAP	http://www.baleap.org.uk
British Council	http://www.britcoun.org/english/index.htm
JALT	http://www.jalt.org

Journals

ELTJ Journal	http://www3.oup.co.uk/eltj
System	http://www.elsevier.com/locate/system
Language Teaching Research	http://www.arnoldpublishers.com/journals/ pages/lan_tea/13621688.htm
TESOL Quarterly	http://www.tesol.org/pubs/magz/tq.html

Miscellaneous

Online writing: http://www.owl.english.purdue.edu
Learner training: http://www.insa.lyon.fr/Departments/CDRL/learner.html
Younger learners: http://www.linguistic-funland.com
ESP: http://unav.es/espsig/esponweb.html
Testing and exam bodies: http://www.surrey.ac.uk/ELI/ltr.html
University of Reading site: http://www.reading.ac.uk/Acadepts/cl/slals/links.htm
TEFLnet (handouts etc. fro teachers) http://www.tefl.net

3. *General interest sites for learners and teachers*

A useful general site is
http://www.comenius.com

Newspapers and news services

The Guardian	http://www/guardian.co.uk
The BBC	http://www.news.bbc.co.uk
Financial Times	http://www.ft.com
The Independent	http://www.independent.co.uk
CNN	http://www.cnn.co.uk
USA Today	http://www.usatoday.com

Online dictionaries

Cambridge dictionaries online: http://www.dictionary.camb.org
Longman dictionaries: http://www.longman-elt.com/dictionaries
Slang dictionary: http://www.peevish.co.uk/slang/frames.htm

British Museum

http://www.british-museum.ac.uk

The BBC

(Links to many topics of interest) http://www.bbc.co.uk

Examination information

IELTS   http://www.english-net.com/ielts/index.htm
TOEFL   http://www.toefl.org
UCLES   http://www.cambridge-efl.org.uk/exam

Materials

Abbs, B. and I. Freebairn (1977): *Starting Strategies*. Harlow: Longman.

Abbs, B. and I. Freebairn (1981): *Developing Strategies*. Harlow: Longman.

Aston, G. (1982): *Interact: An Interaction Workbook*. Loughborough: Modern English Publications.

Bell, J. (1990): *Integrated Skills: Upper Intermediate*. Oxford: Heinemann.

Brewster, S. (1991): *Intermediate Listening*. Walton-on-Thames: Nelson.

Cooper, J. (1979): *Think and Link*. London: Edward Arnold.

Cunningham, S. and P. Moor (1999): *Cutting Edge: Intermediate*. Harlow: Longman.

Dellar, H. and D. Hocking (2000): *Innovations*. Hove: Language Teaching Publications.

Digby, C. and J. Myers (1993): *Making Sense of Spelling and Pronunciation*. New York: Prentice-Hall.

Doff, A. and C. Becket (1991): *Listening 2*. Cambridge: Cambridge University Press.

Floyd, J. (1984): *Study Skills for Higher Education*. Harlow: Longman.

Forman, D., F. Donoghue, S. Abbey, B. Kruden and I. Kidd (1990): *Campus English*. London: Macmillan.

Gairns, R. and S. Redman (1998): *True to Life*. Cambridge: Cambridge University Press.

Geddes, M. and G. Sturtridge (1980): *Listening Links*. London: Heinemann.

Geddes, M. and G. Sturtridge (1982): *Reading Links*. London: Heinemann.

Glendinning, E. H. and B. Holmstrom (1992): *Study Reading: Reading Skills for Academic Purposes*. Cambridge: Cambridge University Press.

Goodale, M. (1987): *Meetings: Ten Simulations on International Topics*. Hove: Language Teaching Publications.

Hall, D. and M. Foley (1988): *Speaking Out*. Walton-on-Thames: Nelson.

Heaton. B. and D. Dunmore (1992): *Learning to Study in English*. London: Macmillan.

Hedge, T. (1983a): *Freestyle*. Walton-on-Thames: Nelson.

Hedge, T. (1983b): *Pen to Paper*. Walton-on-Thames: Nelson.

Herbert, D. and G. Sturtridge (1979): *Simulations*. London: NFER.

Hewings, M. (1993): *Pronunciation Tasks*. Cambridge: Cambridge University Press.

Hopkins, A. (1989): *Perspectives*. Harlow: Longman.

Imhoof, M. and H. Hudson (1975): *From Paragraph to Essay*. London: Longman.

James, K. (1979): *Listening Comprehension and Note-Taking Course*. London: Collins.

Johnson, K. (1981): *Communicate in Writing*. Cambridge: Cambridge University Press.

Johnson, K. and K. Morrow (1978): *Communicate*. Cambridge: Cambridge University Press.

Jolly, D. (1982): *Reading Choices*. Cambridge: Cambridge University Press.

Jones, L. (1981): *Functions of English*. Cambridge: Cambridge University Press.

Jones, L. (1983): *Eight Simulations*. Cambridge: Cambridge University Press.

Jordan, R. R. (1982): *Figures in Language: Describe and Draw*. Glasgow: Collins.

Jupp, T. C. and J. Milne (1969): *Guided Course in English Composition*. London: Heinemann.

Jupp, T. C. and J. Milne (1972): *Guided Paragraph Writing*. London: Heinemann.

Keller, E. and S. Warner (1988): *Conversation Gambits*. Hove: Language Teaching Publications.

Lawrence, M. (1972): *Writing as a Thinking Process*. Ann Arbor: University of Michigan Press.

Lynch, M. (1977): *It's your Choice: Six Role Playing Exercises*. London: Edward Arnold.

Lynch, T. and K. Anderson (1992): *Study Speaking*. Cambridge: Cambridge University Press.

Mackin, R., J. Webb and R. L. Scott-Buccleuch (1970): *OPEAC Oral Drills Workbook*. London: Oxford University Press.

Maley, A. and R. S. Newberry (1974): *Between You and Me: Guided Dialogues for Conversation Practice*. Sunbury-on-Thames: Nelson.

Martinez, R. (1997): *Conversation Lessons: The Natural Language of Conversations. An Intermediate Course*. Hove: Language Teaching Publications.

Milne, B. (1991): *Integrated Skills: Intermediate*. Oxford: Heinemann.

Moody, K. W. (1974): *Frames for Written English*. London: Oxford University Press.

Morrow, K. and K. Johnson (1980): *Communicate 2*. Cambridge: Cambridge University Press.

Nunan, D. (1995): *ATLAS: Learning-Centred Communication 1–4*, Boston, Mass.: Heinle and Heinle.

O'Connor, J. D. and C. Fletcher (1989): *Sounds English*. Harlow: Longman.

O'Neill, R., R. Kingsbury and A. Yeadon (1971): *Kernel Lessons Intermediate*. London: Longman.

O'Neill, R. with P. Mugglestone (1989): *The Third Dimension/The Fourth Dimension*. Harlow: Longman.

Phillips, D. and S. Sheerin (1990): *Signature*. Walton-on-Thames: Nelson.

Porter-Ladousse, G. (1983): *Speaking Personally*. Cambridge: Cambridge University Press.

Rogerson, P. and J. P. Gilbert (1990): *Speaking Clearly*. Cambridge: Cambridge University Press.

Soars, L. and J. (1996): *New Headway English Course (Intermediate)*. Oxford: Oxford University Press.

Spencer, D. H. (1967): *Guided Composition Exercises*. London: Longman.

Stephens, M. (1996): *Practice Writing*. Harlow: Eurocentres/Longman.

Swan, M. and C. Walter (1990): *New Cambridge English Course*. Cambridge: Cambridge University Press.

Tribble, C. (1989): *Word for Word*. Harlow: Longman.

Underwood, M. and P. Barr (1980): *Listeners*. Oxford: Oxford University Press.

Ur, P. (1981): *Discussions That Work*. Cambridge: Cambridge University Press.

Watcyn-Jones, P. (1979): *Impact*. Harmondsworth: Penguin.

Watcyn-Jones, P. (1981): *Pairwork*. Harmondsworth: Penguin.

Waters, M. and A. Waters (1995): *Study Tasks in English*. Cambridge: Cambridge
    University Press.
Williams, R. (1982): *Panorama: An Advanced Course of English for Study and Examina-
    tions*. Harlow: Longman.
Willis, J. and D. (1989): *COBUILD English Course*. London: Collins.

Bibliography

Allwright, R. L. (1984): Why don't learners learn what teachers teach? The interaction hypothesis. In D. M. Singleton and D. G. Little (eds): *Language Teaching in Formal and Informal Contexts*. Dublin: IRAAL, 3–18.

Allwright, R. L. (1988): Autonomy and individualisation in whole class instruction. In A. Brookes and P. Grundy, 35–44.

Allwright, R. L. (1992): Understanding classroom language learning: an argument for exploratory teaching. Talk given at Essex University, February 1992.

Allwright, R. L. and K. Bailey (1991): *Focus on the Language Classroom*. Cambridge: Cambridge University Press.

Anderson, A. and T. Lynch (1988): *Listening*. Oxford: Oxford University Press.

Aston, G. (1993): The learner's contribution to the self-access centre. *ELT Journal* 47/3, 219–27.

Bailey, K. (2001): Observation. In Carter and Nunan, 114–19.

Bailey, K. and D. Nunan (eds) (1996): *Voices from the Language Classroom*. Cambridge: Cambridge University Press.

Ballard, B. (1984): Improving student writing: an integrated approach to cultural adjustment. In R. Williams, J. Swales and J. Kirkman (eds): *Common Ground: Shared Interests in ESP and Communication Studies*. ELT Documents 118. London: Pergamon/ The British Council, 43–54.

Bartlett, F. C. (1932): *Remembering: A Study in Experimental and Social Psychology*. Cambridge: Cambridge University Press.

Bartram, M. and R. Walton (1991): *Correction: Mistake Management: A Positive Approach for Language Teachers*. Hove: Language Teaching Publications.

Beaumont, M. (1983): Take it from the text: an approach to the teaching of reading. In R. R. Jordan (ed): *Case Studies in ELT*. London: Collins, 26–34.

Bowers, R. (1980): The individual learner in the general class. In H. Altman and C. James (eds): *Foreign Language Teaching: Meeting Individual Needs*. Oxford: Pergamon, 66–80.

Boyle, R. (1994): ESP and distance learning. *English for Specific Purposes* 13/2, 115–28.

Breen, M. (1987): Contemporary paradigms in syllabus design. *Language Teaching* 20/ 2, 81–92; 20/3, 157–74.

Breen, M. and C. Candlin (1987): Which materials? A consumer's and designer's guide. In L. E. Sheldon (ed): *ELT Textbooks and Materials: Problems in Evaluation and Development*. ELT Documents 126. London: Modern English Publications/The British Council, 13–28.

British Council (1983): *Teaching and Learning in Focus*. London.

Brookes, A. and P. Grundy (eds) (1988): *Individualisation and Autonomy in Language Learning*. ELT Documents 131. London: Modern English Publications/The British Council.

Brown, G. and G. Yule (1983a): *Teaching the Spoken Language*. Cambridge: Cambridge University Press.

Brown, G. and G. Yule (1983b): *Discourse Analysis*. Cambridge: Cambridge University Press.

Brumfit, C. J. (1980): Seven last slogans. *Modern English Teacher* 7/1, 30–1.

Brumfit, C. J. (1984): *Communicative Methodology in Language Teaching: The Roles of Fluency and Accuracy*. Cambridge: Cambridge University Press.

Brumfit, C. J. and J. T. Roberts (1983): *A Short Introduction to Language and Language Teaching*. London: Batsford.

Burns, A. (1999): *Collaborative Action Research for English Language Teachers*. Cambridge: Cambridge University Press.

Bush, T. (1984): Key roles in post-school management. In *Management in Post-Compulsory Education*. Block 3 Course Materials, Course E324. Milton Keynes: The Open University.

Bygate, M. (1987): *Speaking*. Oxford: Oxford University Press.

Byrne, D. (1981): Integrating skills. In Johnson and Morrow, 108–14.

Byrne, D. (1988): *Teaching Writing Skills*. London: Longman, new edition.

Canale, M. (1983): From communicative competence to communicative language pedagogy. In J. C. Richards and R. W. Schmidt (eds): *Language and Communication*. London: Longman, 2–27.

Carrell, F., J. Devine and D. Eskey (eds) (1988): *Interactive Approaches to Second Language Reading*. Cambridge: Cambridge University Press.

Carter, R. (1998): *Vocabulary: Applied Linguistic Perspectives*. London: Routledge.

Carter, R. (2001): Vocabulary. In Carter and Nunan, 42–7.

Carter, R. and D. Nunan (eds) (2001): *The Cambridge Guide to Teaching English to Speakers of Other Languages*. Cambridge: Cambridge University Press.

Cecioni, C. (ed) (1989): *Autonomy in Language Learning*. Florence: Language Centre, University of Florence.

Celce-Murcia, M. and E. Olshtain (2000): *Discourse and Context in Language Teaching*. Cambridge: Cambridge University Press.

Chaix, P. and C. O'Neil (1978): *A Critical Analysis of Forms of Autonomous Learning (Autodidaxy and Semi-Autonomy) in the Field of Foreign Language Learning*. Final Report, UNESCO Doc Ed 78/WS/58.

Chambers, F. (1997): Seeking consensus in coursebook evaluation. *ELT Journal* 51/1, 29–35.

Clarke, D. F. (1989): Communicative theory and its influence on materials production. *Language Teaching* 22/2, 73–86.

Cohen, A. D. (1998): *Strategies in Learning and Using a Second Language*. Harlow: Longman.

Collins (2001): *COBUILD English Language Dictionary*. London: Collins, new edition.

Connor, U. (1996): *Contrastive Rhetoric: Cross-Cultural Aspects of Second Language Writing*. Cambridge: Cambridge University Press.

Cook, G. (1989): *Discourse Analysis*. Oxford: Oxford University Press.

Cook, G. (1997): Key concepts in ELT: schemata. *ELT Journal* 51/1, 86.

Cook, V. J. (2001): *Second Language Learning and Language Teaching*. London: Arnold, 3rd edition.

Cunningsworth, A. (1984): *Evaluating and Selecting ELT Materials*. Oxford: Heinemann.

Cunningsworth, A. (1995): *Choosing Your Coursebook*. London: Longman.

Dalton, C. and B. Seidlhofer (1994): *Pronunciation*. Oxford: Oxford University Press.

Davies, F. (1995): *Introducing Reading*. London: Penguin.

Day, R. R. (1990): Teacher observation in second language teacher education. In Richards and Nunan, 43–61.

Dickinson, L. (1987): *Self-instruction in Language Learning*. Cambridge: Cambridge University Press.

Dickinson, L. (1989): Learning purpose, learning structure and the training of learners for autonomy. In C. Cecioni (ed): *Proceedings of the Symposium on Autonomy in Foreign Language Learning*. Florence: Language Centre, University of Florence, 30–42.

Dubin, F. and E. Olshtain (1986): *Course Design*. Cambridge: Cambridge University Press.

Dudeney, G. (2000): *The Internet and the Language Classroom: A Practical Guide for Teachers*. Cambridge: Cambridge University Press.

Eastment, D. (1999): *The Internet and ELT*. Oxford: Summertown.

Ellis, B. and G. Sinclair (1989): *Learning to Learn English*. Cambridge: Cambridge University Press.

Ellis, G. (1996): How culturally appropriate is the communicative approach? *ELT Journal* 50/3, 213–18.

Ellis, R. (1997): The empirical evaluation of language teaching materials. *ELT Journal* 51/1, 36–42.

Freeman, D. (1996): Redefining the relationship between research and what teachers know. In Bailey and Nunan, 88–118.

Gaies, S. (1980): Classroom-centered research: some consumer guidelines. Paper presented at second annual TESOL summer meeting, Albuquerque, NM.

Gaies, S. and R. Bowers (1990): Clinical supervision of language teaching: the supervisor as trainer and educator. In Richards and Nunan, 167–81.

Gower, R. (1999): Doing as we would be done by. *Modern English Teacher* 8/4, 7–15.

Gower, R. and S. Walters (1983): *Teaching Practice Handbook*. London: Heinemann.

Grabe, W. and R. Kaplan (1996): *Theory and Practice of Writing*. London: Longman.

Grant, N. (1987): *Making the Most of Your Textbook*. London: Longman.

Grellet, F. (1981): *Developing Reading Skills*. Cambridge: Cambridge University Press.

Haines, S. (1995): For and against: pairwork. *Modern English Teacher* 4/1.

Halliday, M. A. K. and R. Hasan (1976): *Cohesion in English*. London: Longman.

Handy, C. B. (1985): *Understanding Organisations*. London: Penguin, 3rd edition.

Harmer, J. (1998): *How to Teach English*. Longman: Harlow.

Harmer, J. (2001a): Coursebooks – a human, cultural and linguistic disaster? *Modern English Teacher* 10/3, 5–10.

Harmer, J. (2001b): *The Practice of English Language Teaching*. London: Longman, 3rd edition.

Hayes, J. R. and L. S. Flower (1983): Uncovering cognitive processes in writing: an introduction to protocol analysis. In P. Mosenthal, L. Tamor and S. Walmsley (eds): *Research on Writing: Principles and Methods*. New York: Longman, 207–20.

Hedge, T. (1988): *Writing*. Oxford: Oxford University Press.

Hedge, T. (2000): *Teaching and Learning in the Language Classroom*. Oxford: Oxford University Press.

Holliday, A. (1994): *Appropriate Methodology and Social Context*. Cambridge: Cambridge University Press.

Hopkins, D. (1993): *A Teacher's Guide to Classroom Research*. Buckingham: Open University Press, 2nd edition.

Howarth, P. and R. Hetherington (eds) (2000): *EAP Learning Technologies*. Leeds: Leeds University Press.

Hymes, D. (1972): On communicative competence. In J. B. Pride and J. Holmes (eds): *Sociolinguistics*. Harmondsworth: Penguin, 263–93.

Jacobs, G. (1988): Co-operative goal structure: a way to improve group activities. *ELT Journal* 42/2, 97–101.

Johnson, K. (1981): Some background, some key terms and some definitions. In Johnson and Morrow, 1–12.

Johnson, K. (1982): *Communicative Syllabus Design and Methodology*. Oxford: Pergamon.

Johnson, K. (2001): *An Introduction to Foreign Language Learning and Teaching*. Harlow: Longman.

Johnson, K. and H. Johnson (eds) (1998): *Encyclopedic Dictionary of Applied Linguistics*. Oxford: Blackwell.

Johnson, K. and K. Morrow (eds) (1981): *Communication in the Classroom*. London: Longman.

Jordan, R. R. (1997): *English for Academic Purposes*. Cambridge: Cambridge University Press.

Kanan, J. and P. Towndrow (2002): On-line feedback. *Modern English Teacher* 11/1, 62–7.

Kennedy, C. (1983): Video in ESP. In *Video Applications in English Language Teaching*. ELT Documents 114. Oxford: Modern English Publications/The British Council, 95–102.

Kenworthy, J. (1987): *Teaching English Pronunciation*. London: Longman.

Kumaravadivelu, B. (1990): Classroom observation: a neglected situation. *TESOL Newsletter* 24/6, 5–32.

Lewis, M. (1993): *The Lexical Approach: The State of ELT and a Way Forward*. Hove: Language Teaching Publications.

Littlejohn, A. and S. Windeatt (1988): Beyond language learning: perspectives on materials design. In R. K. Johnson (ed): *The Second Language Curriculum*. Cambridge: Cambridge University Press.

Littlewood, W. T. (1981): *Communicative Language Teaching*. Cambridge: Cambridge University Press.

Littlewood, W. T. (1992): *Teaching Oral Communication*. Oxford: Blackwell.

Long, M. H. (1975): Group work and communicative competence in the ESOL classroom. In M. K. Burt and H. C. Dulay (eds): *On TESOL '75: New Directions in Second Language Learning, Teaching, and Bilingual Education*. Washington, DC: TESOL, 211–23.

Long, M. H. and P. A. Porter (1985): Group work, interlanguage talk and second language acquisition. *TESOL Quarterly* 19, 211–23.

Lowes, R. and F. Target (1998): *Helping Students to Learn: A Guide to Learner Autonomy*. London: Richmond Publishing.

Lubelska, D. and M. Matthews (1997): *Looking at Language Classrooms*. Cambridge: Cambridge University Press.

Madsen, K. S. and J. D. Bowen (1978): *Adaptation in Language Teaching*. Rowley, Mass.: Newbury House.

Malamah-Thomas, A. (1987): *Classroom Interaction*. Oxford: Oxford University Press.

McCarthy, M. and R. A. Carter (1994): *Language as Discourse: Perspectives for Language Teaching*. London: Longman.

McDonough, J. (2002): The teacher as language learner: worlds of difference? *ELT Journal* 56/4, 404–11.

McDonough, J. and S. H. (1997): *Research Methods for English Language Teachers*. London: Arnold.

McDonough, S. H. (1986): *Psychology in Foreign Language Teaching*. London: Allen and Unwin, 2nd edition.

McDonough, S. H. (1995): *Strategy and Skill in Learning a Foreign Language*. London: Arnold.

McDonough, S. H. (1999): Learner Strategies. *Language Teaching* 32, 1–18.

Miller, L. (2000): What have you just learnt? Preparing learners in the classroom for self-access language learning. *Modern English Teacher* 9/3, 7–13.

Morrow, K. (1981): Principles of communicative methodology. In Johnson and Morrow, 59–66.

Naiman, N., M. Fröhlich and H. H. Stern (1975): *The Good Language Learner*. Toronto: Modern Language Centre, Department of Curriculum, Ontario Institute for Studies in Education.

Nolasco, R. and L. Arthur (1986): Try doing it with a class of forty! *ELT Journal* 40/2, 100–6.

Nolasco, R. and L. Arthur (1988): *Large Classes*. London: Macmillan.

Nunan, D. (1988): *The Learner-Centred Curriculum*. Cambridge: Cambridge University Press.

Nunan, D. (1989): *Designing Tasks for the Communicative Classroom*. Cambridge: Cambridge University Press.

Nunan, D. (1990): Action Research in the Classroom. In Richards and Nunan, 62–81.

Nunan, D. (1991): *Language Teaching Methodology: A Textbook for Teachers*. Hemel Hempstead: Prentice-Hall International.

Nunan, D. (1999): *Second Language Teaching and Learning*. Boston, Mass.: Heinle and Heinle.

Nuttall, C. (1996): *Teaching Reading Skills in a Foreign Language*. London: Heinemann, new edition.

O'Neill, R. (1982): Why use textbooks? *ELT Journal* 36/2, 104–11.

Oxford, R. L. (1990): *Language Learning Strategies: What Every Teacher Should Know*. New York: Newbury House/Harper and Row.

Pattison, P. (1987): *Developing Communication Skills*. Cambridge: Cambridge University Press.

Pennington, M. C. (1990): A professional development focus for the language teaching practicum. In Richards and Nunan, 132–52.

Pica, T. and C. Doughty (1985): Input and interaction in the communicative classroom: a comparison of teacher-fronted and group activities. In S. M. Gass and C. G. Madden (eds): *Input in Second Language Acquisition*. Rowley, Mass.: Newbury House, 115–32.

Prabhu, N. (1987): *Second Language Pedagogy*. Oxford: Oxford University Press.

Pugh, A. K. (1978): *Silent Reading*. London: Heinemann.

Raimes, A. (1983): *Techniques in Teaching Writing*. New York: Oxford University Press.

Ramani, E. (1987): Theorising from the classroom. *ELT Journal* 41/1, 3–11.

Richards, J. C. (1985): *The Context of Language Teaching*. Cambridge: Cambridge University Press.

Richards, J. C. (1990): The dilemma of teacher education in second language teaching. In Richards and Nunan, 3–15.

Richards, J. C. and C. Lockhart (1994): *Reflective Teaching in Second Language Classrooms*. Cambridge: Cambridge University Press.

Richards, J. C. and D. Nunan (eds) (1990): *Second Language Teacher Education*. Cambridge: Cambridge University Press.

Richards, J. C., J. Platt and H. Weber (1985): *Longman Dictionary of Applied Linguistics*. London: Longman.

Richards, J. C. and T. S. Rodgers (2001): *Approaches and Methods in Language Teaching*. Cambridge: Cambridge University Press, 2nd edition.

Richterich, R. and J. L. Chancerel (1980): *Identifying the Needs of Adults Learning a Foreign Language*. Oxford: Pergamon.

Riley, P. (1982): Learners lib: an experimental autonomous learning scheme. In M. Geddes and G. Sturtridge (eds): *Individualisation*. Loughborough: Modern English Publications, 61–3.

Rivers, W. and M. Temperley (1978): *A Practical Guide to the Teaching of English as a Foreign or Second Language*. New York: Oxford University Press.

Rixon, S. (1986): *Developing Listening Skills*. London: Macmillan/Modern English Publications.

Rost, M. (1990): *Listening in Language Learning*. London: Longman.

Rost, M. (1994): *Introducing Listening*. Harmondsworth: Penguin.

Rubin, J. and I. Thompson (1982): *The Good Language Learner*. Boston, Mass.: Heinle and Heinle.

Seedhouse, P. (1997): Combining form and meaning. *ELT Journal* 51/4, 336–44.

Seedhouse, P. (1999): Task-based interaction. *ELT Journal* 53/3, 149–56.

Sheerin, S. (1989): *Self-access*. Oxford: Oxford University Press.

Sheldon, L. E. (1988): Evaluating ELT textbooks and materials. *ELT Journal* 42/4, 237–46.

Sheldon, L. E. (ed) (1987): *ELT Textbooks and Materials: Problems in Evaluation and Development*. ELT Documents 126. Oxford: Modern English Publications in Association with The British Council.

Sinclair, B. (1999): Survey review: recent publications on autonomy in language learning. *ELT Journal* 53/4, 309–29.

Skehan, P. (1980): Team-teaching and the role of the ESP teacher. In *Study Modes and Academic Development of Overseas Students*. ELT Documents 109. London: The British Council, 23–37.

Skehan, P. (1989): *Individual Differences in Second Language Learning*. London: Edward Arnold.

Slaouti, D. (2002): The world wide web for academic purposes: old study skills for new. *English for Specific Purposes* 21/2, 105–24.

Smith, F. (1978): *Reading*. Cambridge: Cambridge University Press.

Spratt, M. (1994): *English for the Teacher: a Language Development Course*. Harlow: Longman.

Spratt, M. (1999): How good are we at knowing what learners like? *System* 27/2, 141–55.

Stern, H. H. (1983): *Fundamental Concepts of Language Teaching*. Oxford: Oxford University Press.

Stevick, E. W. (1972): Evaluating and adapting language materials. In H. B. Allen and R. N. Campbell (eds): *Teaching English as a Second Language*. New York: McGraw-Hill, 102–20.

Stoller, F. (1984): Designing an effective reading lab. *TEAM*. Dharan: University of Dharan Language Centre, no. 49.

Storch, N. (2001): How collaborative is pairwork? ESL tertiary students composing in pairs. *Language Teaching Research* 5/1, 29–53.

Strevens, P. (1979): Differences in teaching for different circumstances or the teacher as chameleon. In C. A. Yorio, K. Perkins and J. Schachter (eds): *On TESOL '79: The Learner in Focus*. Washington, DC: TESOL, 2–11.

Stubbs, M. and S. Delamont (eds) (1976): *Explorations in Classroom Observation*. New York: John Wiley.

Swan, M. (1985): A critical look at the communicative approach. *ELT Journal* 39/1, 2–12; 39/2, 76–87.

Thickett, P. (1986): The use of TLF on an RSA preparatory certificate course. In *English Teaching Information Circular* (ETIC). London: The British Council.

Thompson, G. (1996): Some misconceptions about communicative language teaching. *ELT Journal* 50/1, 9–15.

Tomlinson, B. (1999): Developing criteria for evaluating L2 materials. *IATEFL Issues* 47, March.

Tomlinson, B. (2001): Materials development. In Carter and Nunan, 66–71.

Tomlinson, B., B. Dat, H. Masuhara and R. Rubdy (2001): Survey Review: ESL Courses for Adults. *ELT Journal* 55/1, 80–101.

Tribble, C. (1996): *Writing*. Oxford: Oxford University Press.

Trim, J. L. M. (1976): Some possibilities and limitations of learner autonomy. In E. Harding-Esch (ed): *Self-Directed Learning and Autonomy*. Cambridge: mimeo, 1–11.

Tsui, A. B. M. (1996): Reticence and anxiety in second language learning. In Bailey and Nunan, *Voices from the Language Classroom*, 145–67.

Tsui, A. B. M. (2001): Classroom interaction. In Carter and Nunan, 120–5.

Tudor, I. (1993): Teacher roles in the learner-centred classroom. *ELT Journal* 47/1, 22–31.

Tudor, I. (1996): *Learner-Centredness as Language Education*. Cambridge: Cambridge University Press.

Underwood, M. (1989): *Teaching Listening*. London: Longman.

Ur, P. (1987): *Teaching Listening Comprehension*. Cambridge: Cambridge University Press.

Ur, P. (1996): *A Course in Language Teaching*. Cambridge: Cambridge University Press.

Vandergrift, L. (1999): Facilitating second language listening comprehension: acquiring successful strategies. *ELT Journal* 53/3, 168–76.

Van Ek, J. A. (1977): *The Threshold Level for Modern Language Learning in Schools*. London: Longman.

Van Ek, J. A., L. G. Alexander and M. A. Fitzpatrick (1980): *Waystage English*. Oxford: Pergamon (on behalf of the Council of Europe).

Van Lier, L. (1988): *The Classroom and the Language Learner*. London: Longman.

Vilmi, R. (2000): Collaborative writing projects on the internet: more than half a decade of experimentation. In Howarth and Hetherington, 28–42.

Wajnryb, R. (1992): *Classroom Observation Tasks*. Cambridge: Cambridge University Press.

Walker, C. (1987): Individualising reading. *ELT Journal* 41/1, 46–50.

Wallace, M. J. (1991): *Training Foreign Language Teachers: A Reflective Approach* Cambridge: Cambridge University Press.

Wenden, A. and J. Rubin (1987): *Learner Strategies in Language Learning*. New York: Prentice-Hall International.

White, G. (1998): *Listening*. Oxford: Oxford University Press.

White, R. V. (1980): *Teaching Written English*. London: Allen and Unwin.

White, R. V. (1981): Reading. In Johnson and Morrow, 87–92.

White, R. V. (1982): *The English Teacher's Handbook*. Walton-on-Thames: Nelson.

Widdowson, H. G. (1978): *Teaching Language as Communication*. Oxford: Oxford University Press.

Widdowson, H. G. (1979): The simplification of use. In H. G. Widdowson: *Explorations in Applied Linguistics*. Oxford: Oxford University Press, 185–91.

Wilkins, D. A. (1976): *Notional Syllabuses*. Oxford: Oxford University Press.

Williams, E. (1984): *Reading in the Language Classroom*. London: Macmillan.

Willing, K. (1988): *Learning Styles in Adult Migrant Education*. Adelaide: National Curriculum Resource Centre, Adult Migrant Education Program.

Willis, D. (1990): *The Lexical Syllabus*. London: Collins.

Willis, J. (1996): *A Framework for Task-Based Learning*. Harlow: Longman.

Wright, T. (1987): *Roles of Teachers and Learners*. Oxford: Oxford University Press.

Yalden, J. (1983): *The Communicative Syllabus: Evolution, Design and Implementation*. Oxford: Pergamon.

Index